D0520299

ADOBE® MASTER CLASS
ADVANCED COMPOSITING
IN PHOTOSHOP

INSPIRING ARTWORK AND TUTORIALS BY BRET MALLEY

Adobe

ADOBE MASTER CLASS
Advanced Compositing in Photoshop
Bret Malley

This Adobe Press book is published by Peachpit.
For information on Adobe Press books and other products, contact:

Peachpit
www.peachpit.com

For the latest on Adobe Press books, go to www.adobepress.com
To report errors, please send a note to errata@peachpit.com
Peachpit is a division of Pearson Education.

Copyright © 2014 by Bret Malley

Project Editor: Valerie Witte
Senior Production Editor: Lisa Brazieal
Developmental and Copyeditor: Linda Laflamme
Proofreader: Bethany Stough
Composition: Kim Scott/Bumpy Design
Indexer: Rebecca Plunkett
Cover Design: Charlene Charles-Will
Interior Design: Charlene Charles-Will and Kim Scott/Bumpy Design
Cover Images: Bret Malley

Notice of Rights

All rights reserved. No part of this book may be reproduced or transmitted in any form by any means, electronic, mechanical, photocopying, recording, or otherwise, without the prior written permission of the publisher. For information on getting permission for reprints and excerpts, contact permissions@peachpit.com.

Notice of Liability

The information in this book is distributed on an "As Is" basis, without warranty. While every precaution has been taken in the preparation of the book, neither the author nor Peachpit shall have any liability to any person or entity with respect to any loss or damage caused or alleged to be caused directly or indirectly by the instructions contained in this book or by the computer software and hardware products described in it.

Any views or opinions presented in the interviews in this book are solely those of the author and interviewee and do not necessarily represent those of the companies included in this book.

Trademarks

Many of the designations used by manufacturers and sellers to distinguish their products are claimed as trademarks. Where those designations appear in this book, and Peachpit was aware of a trademark claim, the designations appear as requested by the owner of the trademark. All other product names and services identified throughout this book are used in editorial fashion only and for the benefit of such companies with no intention of infringement of the trademark. No such use, or the use of any trade name, is intended to convey endorsement or other affiliation with this book.

ISBN-13: 978-0-321-98630-6
ISBN–10:   0-321-98630-X

9 8 7 6 5 4 3 2 1
Printed and bound in the United States of America

*To Erin, who makes the impossible possible without the help
of Photoshop, every minute, every hour, every day.*

*To Kellen, who is my own personal super-hero and always will be.
May the world be yours to save.*

*To my mom, who knew when not to call, and send love instead—
and stale cookies through the mail. I ate every crumb.
They were really bad...I loved them still.*

CONTENTS

SECTION III: **INSPIRATION**

ACKNOWLEDGMENTS

Thank you first of all to Linda Laflamme for her keen editing mind, endless fortitude, spot-on advice, and for patiently walking (well, more like sprinting in truth) this first timer through the trials and tribulations of writing a book in five months. You are a true genius at what you do (and I'm fairly certain a genius in general), and I am so thankful to have had you on my team. It has been an honor. Thank you as well to Wayne Palmer who helped navigate some of my more outlandish technical declarations and for the thoughtful suggestions of alternative phrasing throughout. To Valerie Witte for taking care of everything that came up along the way, from moments of author panic (such as when I landed a new full-time teaching job at the height of writing) to working and leveraging all the background and inner workings of getting a book published: Thank you for your kindness in working with me and your consistent encouragement with each chapter submission! Thanks, as well, to Lisa Brazieal, Bethany Stough, Kim Scott, and the rest of the Peachpit team who worked behind the curtain to make the magic happen on this book, I wish I knew you all better! All I know is that you *rock* and that I am so grateful for your dedication and care. Thank you Victor Gavenda for your introduction to my amazing team and welcoming me to the Peachpit family. I will never forget how great you were to talk to during those first conversations and all the following emails in getting the process started; thank you! And thank you Ric Getter for the first idea and encouragement in sending out a book proposal! Your belief in me and solid advice began this entire process.

To my colleagues and students at Chemeketa Community College, thank you for your patience and understanding of my temporary insanity, consistently dazed look, and incoherent sentences from many sleepless months of working on this book! You have all been encouraging, supportive, and inspiring, so thank you!

Special thank you to lighting Jedi, Jayesunn Krump at www.JKrump.com and model Miranda Jaynes for your contributions and support. Thank you to the featured artists, Zev and Aliza Hoover, Erik Johansson, Christian Hecker, Holly Andres, Martín De Pasquale, Mario Sánchez Nevado, and Andrée Wallin. You are all *so* talented and inspiring, and I hope readers will follow you and keep a close eye on all your future work like I do! To the rest of my family, thank you (with copious amounts of love!) for your advice over the months, your patience, and just being there through it all! And again, thank you Kellen for the wonderful dream, Erin for making it possible, and Mom for telepathically crossing the finish line with me. I will always love you all.

ABOUT THE AUTHOR

Bret Malley is an award-winning digital artist and full-time college instructor living in Portland, Oregon, with his wife, Erin, and son, Kellen. He has an MFA in Computer Art from Syracuse University, a bachelors in digital media from University of California Santa Cruz, and teaches photography, multi-media, design, and Adobe Photoshop to university and college students of all levels and backgrounds. As a computer artist, he is crazy about digital tools and art-making of all kinds, and especially enjoys working in Photoshop, his ultimate favorite of all applications.

Bret is also an Irish bodhran drummer, hiker, juggler, snowboarder, filmmaker, traveler, didgeridoo player, and cat lover. Bret sometimes wonders why people always mention their pets in these kinds of third-person descriptions. He also likes to abide by some conventions from time to time.

Adobe Photoshop is the ideal hub for nearly limitless creativity. With it you can composite disparate images together to create a new reality—or a real mess. The goal of *Adobe Master Class: Advanced Compositing in Photoshop* is to excite your imagination and inspire you to do the first, while giving you the tools, techniques, and instruction to avoid the second. Whether you are endowing children with super-powers, envisioning endless vistas, bringing strange new creatures to life, or populating beautifully rendered dreamscapes, let this book be your guide and master class for nearly any style of Photoshop compositing, so that by its end you are able to not only composite your own highly imaginative works, but craft them like a pro.

Adobe Master Class: Advanced Compositing in Photoshop will lead your exploration into many fascinating aspects of Photoshop and the nature of compositing. After revealing some nifty techniques and features hidden behind the basic tools, layers, and adjustments, I will then move on into a whole world of editing methods for advanced image manipulation and compositing. Whether you are a quick-study Photoshop initiate or a seasoned wiz, there is always something more to learn about this brilliant application, and this book is going to help you master it!

What's in This Book?

Adobe Master Class: Advanced Compositing in Photoshop is composed of three sections:

- **Section I** provides a lively orientation to the repertoire of tools and concepts you'll need for the later tutorials, then outlines some photography basics and strategies for compositing. This first section of the book is especially good for those of you still picking up a few things or feeling fairly rusty with your Photoshop chops.

- **Section II** is filled with hands-on tutorials where you get to finally play with fire. (Think I'm kidding? Read Chapter 8.) In this section, theory turns into step-by-step instruction and practice—not to mention pure digital fun as you get to jump into a few of my worlds and build your own versions.

- **Section III** presents a wide range of inspirational project demonstrations explaining how I created different styles of composites. These are geared to get your own creative juices flowing and provide some insights and helpful tips I learned along the way.

Nested between the Section III chapters are some additional gems: the **"Masters Voices"** interviews with master digital artists who are brimming with creativity and genius knowledge of Photoshop and compositing. It is my hope that you will be as inspired as I am by these folks and will take their words of wisdom and personal insights to heart—and then create something brilliant of your own!

Downloading the Bonus Chapter and Tutorial Resources

To keep the book focused, I had to be pretty selective about what I put in each chapter. The problem is that there is a little more information that might come in handy after you've gone through all the chapters. So as an added value for you, I have written a bonus chapter called "Fly-Time: Sci-Fi Speed." The chapter covers speed painting (creating a project as quickly as possible), which can be a fun personal challenge or an essential skill when you're on a deadline. Either way it's a stellar exercise for bringing your work and craft to another level.

To work along with me through the tutorials in Section II, you'll need each chapter's accompanying resource files. To download them, log in or set up an account at peachit.com. Enter the book's ISBN or go directly to the book's product page to register.

Once on the book's page, click the Register Your Product link. The book will show up in your list of registered products along with a link to the book's bonus content (including Bonus Chapter 16, which is not in printed versions of the book). Click the link to access the resource files for each chapter. For example, all the files you need for Chapter 8 are contained within *Chapter8_Resources*. The files are waiting for you. Download them when you're ready to work, or log on and start downloading now so you can be ready to go once you get to Section II—just make sure you remember where you put them.

Is This Book for You?

So, the book description sounds nice and all, but how do you know for sure if the book is for you? Try this out. If you recognize yourself in the following list, then you'll benefit from the chapters to come:

- You want to learn about Photoshop and seamless editing, especially compositing.

- You like fantasy and sci-fi effects and imagery and want to try creating some yourself.

- You want to learn about blending modes and clever uses for getting stunning results.

- You want to make the most out of even the basic tools and discover their lesser known features.

- You want to learn how to paint with textures and other images from a custom photo palette.

- You want to master masking, Smart Objects, and other nondestructive workflow techniques and features.

- You are looking to learn how to shoot your own imagery and build a photo archive for any number of projects.

- You are interested in composition strategy and finishing effects for color, lighting, and other adjustments.

- You love Photoshop, but you fall asleep every time you crack open a technical book or manual about it.

In summary, this book should be for you, whoever you are and whatever your compositing goals. I sincerely hope you find it of good and entertaining use!

Dig into Photoshop

Mastering Photoshop is very much like mastering a language: Frequent repetition is the key. Practice every day if you can, and at least twice a week. Teaching Photoshop-intensive courses has shown me that *just* once a week practice is simply not enough for most of us.

While you practice, don't neglect the keyboard. My students often ask if keyboard shortcuts are really that useful. This is art, they say, not programming. Yes, the shortcuts are truly *that* useful. For the majority of people who want to use Photoshop with increased regularity and at a professional level, shortcuts help tremendously with efficiency. For a select few though, keyboard shortcuts are truly just too much. If

that group includes you, that's fine. I, myself, am dyslexic and understand when things just don't sense make. You can still accomplish just about everything without shortcuts, but definitely try to pick up a few as you go.

No matter what, get hands on as often as possible. Repetition is critical. Repetition enables you to take short term "that is neato!" memory and store it in the doing-without-thinking part of your brain. So pick something fun to work on each week and just do it! Repeatedly. You will be glad you did, eventually you'll work by using your Photoshop instincts alone. Masterful things may come of it! *Will* come of it!

I began my own computer art career as a little dude sitting on my dad's lap some 25 years ago, and I haven't really stopped using these machines to make art ever since. While my love for this medium has never changed, the creative tools available definitely have come a long-long way—and boy am I glad. Now with two degrees in the digital arts, I am still continually acquiring more tools for my craft.

Tools and techniques are nothing, however, without the passion and vision to create that we each bring to our work. My hope is that something—a tip, an idea, an image—within this book will ignite your imagination and help you bring it to life with Photoshop. As I tell all my students, anything is possible in Photoshop—now it's time to enjoy and learn how!

SECTION I
BASICS

CHAPTER 1

Get Oriented

Adobe Photoshop has so much packed into it, navigating can be a bit challenging at times. The best way to approach it is as you would a city: Get to know some of the main streets so you can get to the key spots, then learn the rest as you go. Reading the official Adobe Photoshop manual from end to end would have no substantive context without this basic map sense, and your brain needs context for making complex connections—at least mine does. The key is to have digital-courage! Photoshop is huge, but do not be afraid to click on something, try a new thing, or act on impulsive curiosity. You can always undo or go back a few steps in your history (unlike in real life; believe me, I've tried that one). So have courage, digital-courage!

Later chapters will explore plenty of tools in the context of projects, while this chapter concentrates on those mainstay features and ensures we're all oriented to the same layout of Adobe Photoshop.

▶ IMPOSSIBLE (2013)

Navigating the Workspace

In this book, I will mainly use Adobe Photoshop CC, but will occasionally contrast it with CS5 and CS6. Don't worry; whatever version you have, many things have stayed the same. Assuming that you have your settings fairly consistent with the program defaults, your screen should look similar to **FIGURE 1.1**.

On the left is still the familiar toolbar. Chapter 2 will go over some hidden features of these tools. Remember, a tool of some kind is always selected as you work on your image. If you're squeamish about an accidental editing mess, switch to something harmless like the Hand tool (H) for safely moving your cursor around for benign clicking between operations.

FIGURE 1.1 Here's my own workspace. This is a modification of the Essentials workspace with a couple extra panels added to it.

MENUS

OPTIONS BAR

TOOLBAR

PANELS

On the right side you will still find your panels for layers, color selection options, adjustments, brushes, and other nifty items (**FIGURE 1.2**). Don't neglect the panel menus that open when you click their controls; these are always located in the upper-right corner of a panel. Take note of some of the new layout and panel shortcuts. If you're unsure of a control, just hover over it to see a pop-up reminder of its name after a second and a half.

If your workspace is missing any of the tools or panels shown in Figure 1.1, you may need to reset your workspace by choosing Window > Workspace > Reset Current Workspace. (A great thing about Photoshop is the ability to reset things when they get wonky.) Or, you can choose a new workspace from the drop-down menu in the top-right corner (**FIGURE 1.3**). If you're unsure which workspace you're in, this drop-down will tell you. The defaults (depending on your Photoshop version) are Essentials, Photography, 3D, Motion (for animation/video), and Painting. Each workspace selection brings up an arrangement of various tools and panels optimized for getting you started with a specific kind of editing. *Essentials* is a good one to begin with as it has a relatively small number of panels good for a little bit of each kind of editing (**FIGURE 1.4**).

FIGURE 1.2 The panels may look different than in earlier versions, but they're still located on the right in Photoshop.

FIGURE 1.3 It's a good idea to reset your workspace in case someone was on the computer before you.

FIGURE 1.4 The panels in the Essential workspace offer a little bit of everything.

Common to all workspaces is the options bar and above it the top menu bar (**FIGURE 1.5**). Learn the shortcuts for most of these operations to increase your efficiency, productivity, and general awesomeness as a Photoshop master. Take a good look at the menu shortcuts, and try to memorize a new operation or three each time you open up Photoshop. You'll be an expert in no time!

FIGURE 1.5 No version of Photoshop is complete without the menu bar.

- **File** contains all the usual suspects for opening and saving, as well as provides access to Adobe Bridge (**FIGURE 1.6**). If you have version CS5 or earlier, don't forget to save your work insanely often with the Ctrl/Cmd+S shortcut. Newer versions have frequent auto-saving as a default. For the most part auto-save is a lifesaver, but it can sometimes be a hindrance depending on your file size and workflow. Auto-saving a large composite can take some time, and you cannot save again while another save is in process. I turn off auto-save so that I can have more manual control over when to save, but that's me. A new feature in CS6 and CC, background saving is a multitasking genius as Photoshop saves all those stunning layers and edits of yours while you continue working.

- **Edit** is the place for executing and reversing procedural edits (**FIGURE 1.7**): Copy, Paste, Paste in Place (use this when exact position matching matters), and Undo. Step Backwards enables you to undo multiple steps. Quite often just one undo is not enough, and opening up the History panel for your edit history can get in the way at times. Step Backwards is perfect for following those breadcrumbs back a few quick steps! Puppet Warp is somewhat out of place in this menu but amazing. Like the other transform features, it lets you warp a selection of pixels, but by placing your own puppet string pins throughout the image (hence the name). We'll dig more into this kind of warping in later tutorials.

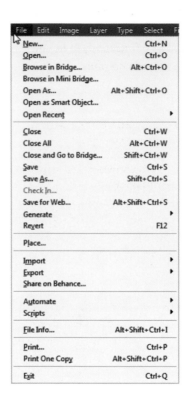

FIGURE 1.6 The File menu's Open Recent option enables you to pull up everything you were working on from the previous session, which I find very useful.

- **Image** allows you to adjust a layer's individual color balance, curves, orientation, color replacement, and a slew of other destructive edits—once you do them and move on, that's how they stay (**FIGURE 1.8**). We will go over how to do most of these things nondestructively in subsequent chapters, but these are still fun to try. I use Image Size and Canvas Size frequently in my own work and knowing the shortcuts is helpful.

- **Layer** allows you to alter and organize your layers. Grouping, flattening, merging, renaming, and much more are all packed into the menu. It's a good place to start, but Chapter 3 discusses layers in depth, including shortcuts and other improved ways to work.

- **Type** has some nifty options for working with text. We won't use this menu very much in this book, but apply some digital courage and play around with it when you have a chance!

- **Select** is another menu that you will quickly learn how to shortcut right out of use. (See the sidebar "Menu Shortcut Cheat Sheet.") In case you prefer menus, however, it does have manual ways of deselecting and modifying your selection with a transform and the like.

FIGURE 1.7 The Edit menu shows common shortcut goodies plus some great transform features such as Puppet Warp.

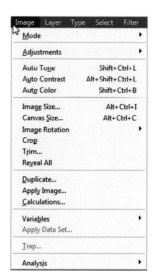

FIGURE 1.8 The Image menu gives you access to various image adjustments, most of which I'll go over how to accomplish nondestructively.

- **Filter** can alter layers with a mind-blowing array of effects (**FIGURE 1.9**). From blurs to noise reduction, this menu is invaluable for advanced editing and masterful composites. You'll use this menu in the tutorials. For now, take note of a few effects that may sound interesting and plan to return!

> **NOTE** Each version of Photoshop has a different arrangement and selection of filters, be sure to learn your own.

- **3D** is great for bringing 3D content in addition to 2D images. I rarely use it for my own composites, but your mileage may vary if you're a 3D modeler or work with one. (If you have an older version of Photoshop, by the way, you may not even have this menu.)

- **View** contains the usual Photoshop controls for toggling visual elements such as rulers, guides, snap-to features, and other layout tools.

- **Window** is your life-saving go-to menu for bringing up the full capacity of Photoshop and all those beautiful panels (**FIGURE 1.10**). So whether you accidentally turned off one or you just don't have the panels you need, you can toggle their display from here. One selection I find useful for tracking (and sometimes reversing) my work is History, the equivalent to aspirin for headaches. The Brushes panel is handy to have open as well. Figure 1.1 will show you where I like to dock them under their minimized icon 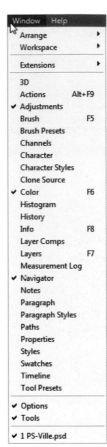.

- **Help** gives you quick access to Adobe's extensive and exceedingly helpful application documentation. If you need more background on a tool than this book provides, I definitely recommend you consult the Help menu, as well as the large library of online help from Adobe.

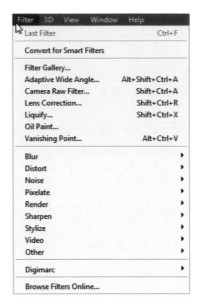

FIGURE 1.9 Filter is a standard go-to menu for tasks like adding blur and even lens correction.

FIGURE 1.10 Window allows the toggling of visible panels such as Adjustments, Color, and Layers if they disappear on you!

MENU SHORTCUT CHEAT SHEET

Shortcuts can save you time and help you work efficiently, but aren't always obvious. Here are some common shortcuts used throughout the book, arranged by menu. Learn them! Your workflow will be glad you did.

File:
- Save: Ctrl/Cmd+S
- Save As: Ctrl/Cmd+Shift+S
- New: Ctrl/Cmd+N
- Open: Ctrl/Cmd+O
- Exit: Ctrl/Cmd+Q

Edit:
- Copy: Ctrl/Cmd+C
- Copy Merged: Ctrl/Cmd+Shift+C
- Paste: Ctrl/Cmd+V
- Paste in Place: Ctrl/Cmd+Shift+V
- Undo: Ctrl/Cmd+Z
- Step Backwards: Ctrl+Alt+Z/Cmd+Opt+Z
- Fill: Shift+F5

Image:
- Invert: Ctrl/Cmd+I
- Curves: Ctrl/Cmd+M
- Image Size: Ctrl+Alt+I/Cmd+Opt+I
- Canvas Size: Ctrl+Alt+C/Cmd+Opt+C

Layer:
- Group: Ctrl/Cmd+G
- New Layer: Shift+Ctrl/Cmd+N
- Clipping Mask: Ctrl+Alt+G/Cmd+Opt+G
- Merge Down: Ctrl/Cmd+E

Select:
- Deselect: Ctrl/Cmd+D
- Select Inverse: Ctrl+Shift+I/Cmd+Shift+I

Filter:
- Apply Last Filter: Ctrl/Cmd+F

View:
- Zoom in: Ctrl/Cmd++
- Zoom out: Ctrl/Cmd+-
- Rulers: Ctrl/Cmd+R
- Snap: Ctrl/Cmd+Shift+;

Window:
- Brush: F5
- Color: F6
- Layers: F7
- Hide/Reveal panels: Shift+Tab
- Hide/Reveal tools, Option menu, and panels: Tab

Help:
- Online Help: F1

File Format Advantages

Let's talk about shoes and file formats. Believe it or not, file formats are like shoes: The best one is the one that suits the road or project you're on. The shoes I need for heavy-duty work aren't the same as those most comfortable for hiking or the ones that shine and impress on a job interview. From JPEG to Camera RAW to PSD and PSB to TIFF, file formats each fit best to different purposes, as well (**FIGURE 1.11**). Here's the skinny on each of the formats I most commonly use for compositing (or see **TABLE 1.1** for the abridged edition):

- **JPEG**: Lightweight but comfortable. JPEG (.jpg, .jpeg, .jpe) is the most common file format supported by digital cameras, phones, and tablets. These compressed files sacrifice image data in the name of space saving. When working with JPEG files, do not compress them for compositing work; *always* save them at the maximum quality level (12) in Photoshop. Anything less will continue to compress your image, simplifying the data in subtle yet damaging ways that add up to big and bad changes over time and repetition. Saving at quality 12 will keep the file size from getting any smaller, even with frequent saves. In addition, JPEG files are flattened, meaning they cannot save your individual Photoshop layers for later editing—as if the laces become glued onto your shoes after you tie them. I don't typically

FIGURE 1.11 JPEG, RAW, PSD, PSB, and TIFF are the main, most commonly used formats for compositing work; the remainder are useful for special purposes but won't be covered here.

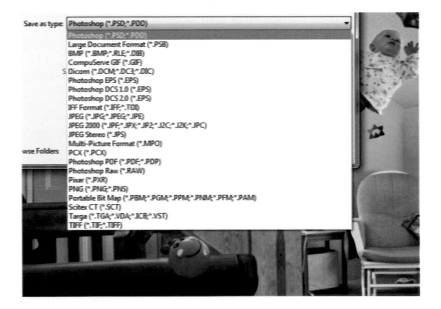

work with a JPEG file except at the very beginning and ending of a project. If I am editing nondestructively with layers, the composite will need to be saved as a different file in the interim even if it was originally a JPEG.

- **RAW**: Versatile shoes that look good and are exceptionally functional. RAW format is an umbrella term for a range of file formats that contain an awesome amount of data. For example, Nikon uses the extension .nef, while Canon saves them as .cr2. Each manufacturer of high-end cameras has a proprietary version of this advanced file format that saves far more information than can fit into a skimpy compressed JPEG file. More data saved means more options for your composite. Whenever possible, shoot in just RAW or RAW *and* JPEG on your camera, assuming you have the memory

TABLE 1.1 The Tradeoffs of File Formats

	JPEG	RAW	PSD	PSB	TIFF
Pros	Small file size Easy to transfer and view on any machine Perfect for source imagery photographs Quick saving Can upload anywhere	Contains far more information than JPEG as it is an unprocessed file (no white balance, sharpening, or compression added). Not compressed; lossless file data Nondestructive editing Beautiful and flexible image files	Made for Photoshop specifically Can save layers, adjustments, styles, and more Contains images brought into it as layers; saves as a single file Can be brought into other Adobe applications	More heavy duty file size capability than PSD with same advantages Can save files larger than 2GB	Versatile file format for many applications Can save uncompressed data up to 4GB Can save layers, adjustments, masks, and more Can easily save as a high quality *flattened* file
Cons	Compressed file; data loss Cannot save with multiple layers Can lose clearly noticeable quality if saved lower than 12 No nondestructive flexibility within the image	Larger file sizes than JPEG (roughly by a factor of 5+) Can require special and up-to-date software to view latest RAW formats Not viewable on machines without RAW readers Not all cameras can shoot in RAW	Massive size, not easy for transferring Can take longer to save In most cases, not viewable without Photoshop or a similar editor Not fully backwards compatible	Same as for PSD Massive file, requires much storage and memory space Often slow to save	Does not save *everything* a PSD or PSB file does Layers may appear flattened when outside of Photoshop

space. Shooting in both allows for flexible editing with JPEG backups that will always work even without a camera RAW update. Plus you can always archive away your smaller JPEG files, but RAW images may not fit. While very powerful, size is the RAW format's one major drawback. So much awesomeness is hard to contain in a small package. **FIGURE 1.12** shows an image shot on my Canon 7D; the CR2 (RAW) file is 24.6MB, while as a JPEG file it consumed only 6.79MB. Fortunately though, memory is continually getting cheaper, and what you'll gain in image quality as a RAW file is worth spending a little more money on hard drives and memory cards for your camera!

- **PSD:** Photoshop's happy hiking shoes. Simply called Photoshop format on the Mac, PSD (.psd) is Photoshop's native file type and is well designed for saving your big composite files. Because it is Adobe's proprietary file type for working specifically in Photoshop, PSD format can save layers, adjustments, masks, and more for later editing. The drawbacks include not being laterally compatible with other applications. Even backwards compatibility can be an issue if saved with some fancy new effects.

- **PSB:** Big outdoor boots. When your heavy-duty composites grow too large to fit into a mere PSD wrapper (larger than 2GB), Adobe has your extra-large, supersize file covered. Just save it as a PSB (.psb), and you are good to go, girth and all. This does have the same drawbacks as a PSD as well, and will often take much longer to save if in fact it is larger than 2GB.

- **TIFF**: Generic-brand shoe that is great for a wide range of uses; equally at home working or well shined. Technically, TIFF format (.tif, .tiff) can save much of the same information as the PSD format, including layers, masks, and adjustments, but it is generally more accessible

FIGURE 1.12 This image was shot in both "Large" JPEG (a 6.79MB file size) and a camera RAW (a whopping 24.6MB).

for other applications. Just be sure to look into the TIFF saving options that appear in the prompt window after you choose to save; each option is for a specific purpose and file advantage. If you no longer need to edit your layers, you can flatten them into a high-quality TIFF file, which is great for an impressive delivery compared to a JPEG file. TIFF files don't discard data when compressed in the same way that JPEG images do, even when the TIFF files are flattened; this coupled with the ability for saving layers and masks makes them very alluring for a working and editing format. TIFF is a favored delivery format for a variety of graphic fields. With that said, when I am working just in Photoshop and Adobe Bridge, I don't often need to work outside of PSD or PSB files. Still, it is always great to have an equally robust but more accessible option when collaborating.

> **TIP** Simply changing a file's name and extension will not change its format and may prevent you from opening the file by confusing your system. Only change the file format by choosing File > Save As and selecting a different format from the menu.

Organized, Clean, Efficient

Stay organized! What a supremely helpful statement, huh? Really though, when your composites begin to get more and more complicated, finding the right layer, mask, or panel is incredibly important for time and sanity's sake. You want to get lost in the creativity, not frustration!

One of the best tactics is to create an efficient workspace free of superfluous panels. Sometimes a lot of panels are needed, but sometimes they really just get in the way; so be sure to organize and arrange them in a way that is helpful, efficient, and clean. You can always reset or switch a workspace, or you can add or subtract individual panels using the Window menu. Once you get a configuration of panels and tool arrangements you find useful and efficient, save it by selecting New Workspace under the top-right drop-down menu (**FIGURE 1.13**). Name it something memorable; for example, mine is currently called I Heart Compositing.

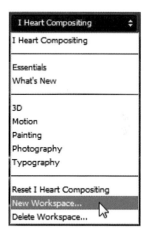

FIGURE 1.13 Save your workspace once you get a panel configuration that you enjoy.

TIP If your panels are taking up too much room, click double-arrow icon to collapse them to their minimized state.

Here are a few other quick tips for saving your life (or at least hours of it):

- Label your layers! During Chapter 3 and the later tutorials, you'll learn why this is so useful. For now, just do it. Really. Double-click the layer name to rename it something useful.

- Group your layers. If you have a section of several layers all adjusting lighting, for example, group them into a folder named Lighting (Ctrl/Cmd+G).

- Color code your layers. Seems a little anal-retentive, and that's because it is. But it's really helpful too. Again, see Chapter 3 for more details.

- Save all your materials and files in one folder if you can, and use names that are helpful. Saving your file as Master_Blaster_Final.psd is all fine and good—except when it's probably not your final version. If you work in versions or on different machines, number versions sequentially and stick to it.

- Evaluate and discard truly unneeded layers. This one is extremely hard for me to do. I confess, I am a digital hoarder: well organized, but chronic at saving everything. Photoshop files are terribly wonderful for feeding my layer-saving-addiction (often working with 200+ layers), but there can be a definite downside. Photoshop files save and work so much better without the extra unused layers, so it's worth the effort to force yourself to discard things every once in a while! I know, it's just so painful! On the flipside, though, if you think you really will need it, don't toss it!

Workflow Inspiration

Ever been completely in the groove? Not just with Photoshop, but with anything; things just work the way you want them to—smooth, fun, and ever addicting? Workflow is a lot like getting into a good groove of complete creativity. Less romantically, however, workflow is also a term used for a style or ordering of operations and certain procedures. Usually it is used in terms of generating efficient, accurate, and controlled results.

Good workflow is all about optimizing and making things easier for you, and every Photoshop master has his or her own workflow. With that said, I will give you the methods and secrets to my own workflow in the making of some of the images that might have convinced you to purchase this book.

Workflow is also ever evolving with each new version or program addition. Consider some of the later tutorials, for example. My workflow has evolved since the images were first created. In most cases, I will point out and even critique previous workflow styles and give tangible examples for learning from my former caveman habits.

So follow my lead, but always be on the lookout for your own groove! There are ten ways to do any one thing in Photoshop, so find the ones that either make it easier or just make you happy and in control!

CHAPTER 2

Hidden Basics

COVERED IN THIS CHAPTER

- Move tool and hidden transform features
- Selection tools and tips
- Healing and cloning tools
- Content-Aware Move tool
- Uncommon uses for common tools
- Better alternatives to other tools

Making masterful Photoshop composites is largely about knowing and using your tools well. That, and knowing how to be clever with them. Very clever. MacGyver clever. Once you learn and understand the hidden features of each tool, you can combine them to enhance your projects in endlessly creative ways.

This chapter takes a look at the main tools and clever techniques that I personally find useful. Think of it as a tool reference guide for the upcoming tutorials, which are based on my own composite creations and workflow.

For you pros already confident with your tools, feel free to jump ahead to the more hands-on lessons in later chapters. But remember, too, what MacGyver could do with the humble paper clip. Take another look at these basics, and you may find a few unexpected uses of your own.

▶ SERENE DANGER (2014)

Inside My Toolbox

All artists have their own set of favorite, go-to tools for projects. For example, the Photoshop tools I use for the vast majority of my workflow are the:

- Move tool (V)
- Selection tools: Marquee (M) ▦, Lasso (L) ⌁, Magnetic Lasso (L) ⌁, Wand (W) ⚡, Quick Selection (W) ⌁
- Brush (B) ⌁
- Bucket (G) ⌁
- Eyedropper (I) ⌁
- Healing tools: Healing (J) ⌁, Spot Healing (J) ⌁ Content-Aware Move (J) ✂
- Clone Stamp (S) ⌁

Don't let the brevity or simplicity of the list fool you: These commonly used tools hide quite a bit of power and can combine to create complex projects. Take a closer look at each to see how they can team up with your own favorites to enhance your workflow.

All About the Move Tool

The Move tool (V) can do so much more than simply relocate objects: Scaling, skewing, rotating, flipping, warping, layer selection, and even duplicating are all packed into this Swiss Army knife of a tool.

Before you begin pulling out its hidden surprises though, be sure to click the Show Transform Controls check box `✓ Show Transform Controls` on the options bar (right below the main menus)—small box, big differences! After you toggle on this box with a check, your layer's image will sprout handles, which are the keys to manipulating the Move tool's hidden features (**FIGURE 2.1**).

NOTE The Move tool cannot move a locked layer, such as the Background layer. If you want to move the locked Background layer, either make a copy of it (Ctrl/Cmd+J) or double-click the layer's thumbnail in the Layers panel, then press Enter when the Rename window comes up. Enter will quickly close the window and unlock the layer. (Chapter 3 will discuss layers more fully.)

The nearby Auto Select check box may look tempting, but think twice before you toggle it on. Auto Select enables you to use the Move tool as a toggle for selecting layers by clicking their pixels (again, Chapter 3 will more adequately dig into layers). This *can* save time in certain circumstances such as when layers are separated well and you have a clear line of sight to the layer you want. It can also be quite annoying as it will select only the topmost layer you click within the image—whether that's

FIGURE 2.1 The Move tool's transform controls are the little square handles at the edges of the image.

the desired layer or not. I find more control in manually selecting each layer I want to transform by clicking it in the Layers panel on the right.

> **TIP** Select a different layer you want to move that is below another by right-clicking within the composite on an image using the Move tool. A pop-up menu will give you the option of switching to another layer or group by choosing its name from a list! This can definitely come in handy when trying to move the correct object below another without making an accidental mess.

Transforming with the Move Tool

So, you toggled on Show Transform Controls; the transform handles and bounding box are visible around the image, now what? Double-check what you are actually transforming! Transforms are dependent on both your selection within the image and your layer selection in the Layers panel, so always double and triple-check which layer you are working on. Remember, a highlight means the layer is selected. Likewise, if you switched from a selection tool with a selection still active (it's surrounded by marching ants), that selection will be transformed instead.

As for the nifty transform handles, take it slow; the hot spots for different transformations can be slippery to pinpoint. In short though, once you see the symbol for what you would like to do as a transformation, click and drag accordingly. Hover near a handle to see icons representing the actions available from that point. **FIGURE 2.2** shows all of the possibilities (visible all at once for reference only) available when hovering around just a single corner. The four possibilities are:

- **Move:** Indispensible for compositing work, this is the basic Move tool function. Click within the transform bounding box and drag in the desired direction. (We'll do more with this in a bit.)

- **Scale:** This symbol appears directly over the corners and means you can resize and scale the selection. It will also let you stretch or squish the image (often by accident), so unless you want your image to lose or gain a bit of weight, hold down Shift as you drag to constrain the horizontal and vertical ratios. Shift-dragging will scale the image while keeping the height and width proportional. Make sure to let go of Shift *after* you let go of your dragging, otherwise you may still end up with a squashed image. A good way to remember keeping it in proportion is to hold down Shift *first* and *last* and you'll always be distortion free.

> **TIP** Transform control hotspots are touchy, so go slow if you're having trouble.

- **Rotate:** This symbol enables you to rotate your selection. For full control, just click and drag. Hold Shift while you drag to snap your rotation to 15-degree increments. Shift-dragging is helpful for getting things rotated perpendicular and still level-ish, while free rotating is perfect for eye-balling just the right angle of an image.

FIGURE 2.2 Hovering around the transform corner handles provides a slew of options. Although displayed here in a group for illustration purposes, the options actually appear individually.

- **Stretch:**  This individual side transform handle (accessible from hovering over any edge along the bounding box) will stretch your selection in the indicated direction of the cursor arrows (it's fixed to the direction of just the one side you clicked). Be very careful with Stretch as it typically makes the selection pretty distorted—not usually what you want, unless you're designing a fantastically cheesy B-movie poster.

After scaling, rotating, or stretching you must commit to (accept) or cancel the results. To accept the transform modifications, either press Enter or click the Commit button in the options bar below the main menus ✓. Cancel your transformation by pressing Escape or clicking the Cancel button ⊘.

Hidden Transforms

Beyond the basic transforms, the Move tool offers some additional options that are quite amazing (assuming you still have Show Transform Controls toggled on). To begin the transforming magic, left-click a transform handle; Photoshop must think that you are initiating a transform of some kind before it will allow you to see the hidden goods. Now right-click the image and behold a slew of awesome things you can now do to the layer (**FIGURE 2.3**).

FIGURE 2.3 Reveal hidden transform options with a right-click on the selection.

TIP You can also press Ctrl/Cmd+T from any tool to begin to transform a selected layer. It's good to have alternatives like this but overall I find the Move tool much more efficient for transforming. Having a tool dedicated to an action that I use all the time fits in nicely with my own workflow, but for others, the Transform shortcut works just fine!

- **Flip:** Flipping a layer selection is invaluable for a number of reasons. Using the Move tool to flip you can see exactly what is being flipped while retaining the ability to do the other transformations as well. From the context menu you can choose to flip the image horizontally or vertically, specifying the direction (left or right, up or down) when asked. (You can do the same from the Layer menu, but it's slower.)

- **Warp:** Warping is another useful process available from the context menu. Selecting Warp enables you to stretch the image with a rule-of-thirds grid; simply drag the grid in the desired direction (**FIGURE 2.4**). Sometimes images don't fit quite right as you piece your layers together, and subtle warping can be just the trick for this. Ever wish you could jam a jigsaw piece into place when you wanted to? Warp it! (For even more amazing warping and puzzle piece jamming ability, try Puppet Warp in the Edit menu).

- **Perspective:** Matching a layer to fit a composite's perspective can come in handy for those composites with obvious vanishing points that are easy to match up. For example, Perspective can help you match a texture to a side of a building that is shot at an angle. Click and drag a corner transform handle to alter the amount of vanishing and scaling occurring (it will adjust two corners simultaneously to make the vanishing effect), then use the middle side handles to slide the edge in the direction consistent with where the edge follows. Match the angles and line up the severity of the vanishing point using the acuteness of the perspective.

> **TIP** You can create a fully customized perspective by transforming a single handle point at a time: Holding down the Ctrl/Cmd key will enable you to transform just one handle point and enter a fantastic pseudo-perspective editing mode (**FIGURE 2.5**). This can help fit images together properly, especially if your images are flat and need to fit, say, on a side of a building. Moving these handle points individually will let you capture just the right transforming perspective.

One-Click Copy

You can easily duplicate any layer selection with the Move tool by holding down the Alt/Opt key and dragging the selection to a new location, just like you are moving it around (**FIGURE 2.6**). Slick and easy. Consult Chapter 3 for more options for duplicating entire layers in a similar way.

FIGURE 2.4 Warping is endless fun and great for getting that perfect fit.

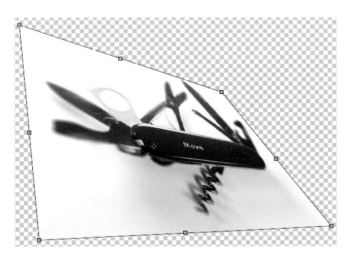

FIGURE 2.5 Holding down the Ctrl/Cmd key allows you to grab just one corner handle.

FIGURE 2.6 It's easy to get carried away with duplicating using the Move tool as it's *so* simple. (Yes, I made some scaling and blending mode changes for this image, as well. You'll learn more about these in later chapters.)

Selection Tools and Tips

The ordinary Marquee Tool (M) ▣ is my go-to tool for basic selecting a portion of a layer for copying (Ctrl/Cmd+C), and pasting (Ctrl/Cmd+V), as well as moving (hold down Ctrl/Cmd for moving on the fly) or limiting an effect or mask to a certain area (**FIGURE 2.7**). One life-saving operation of the Marquee tool is copying *and merging* multiple layers within the marquee selection. To make a merged copy of *all* layers, including adjustments, masks, and so on, select the top-most layer and press Ctrl/Cmd+Shift+C to copy and merge your composite nondestructively. Pasting the copied content back into the composite with the top layer selected gives you a fully rendered flattened image while still keeping your individual layers intact and thus nondestructive. From here, you can always give your eyes a fresh look and perspective

by flipping the flattened layer horizontally using the Move tool. Going back and forth between two seemingly simple tools can render a wide range of options with very little effort, but with worthwhile results. This layer is used mostly as a temporary and reference-only copy as any work done directly to this layer will not be nondestructive in the true sense—but it still does not touch the rest of your layers, thankfully!

> **NOTE** Whenever selecting, copying, or anything else, always check which layer you are working on!

A relatively recent addition to Photoshop and a great partner for the Marquee and other selection tools is the Content-Aware Fill option (not to be confused with the Content-Aware Move tool). It's always mind blowing how this feature works, even when it goes wrong (such as putting a building or tree in the sky)! When you need to remove something from a shot, such as a rock or an ogling tourist, and want to flow the background into the resulting space, Content-Aware Fill is just the ticket. The

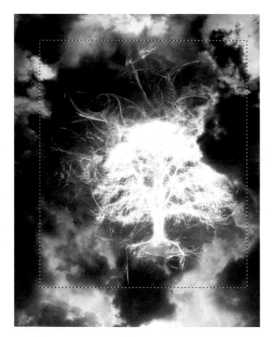

FIGURE 2.7 Marquee has several shapes as presets; this is the rectangular Marquee selection.

FIGURE 2.8 To clear the way for my compositing plans, I want to remove the rocks from the water.

best way to explain how the Content-Aware Fill feature works is with an example: **FIGURE 2.8** is a nice enough scene, but it could use some improvement and cleaning up before I build a composite on top of it. Specifically, I want to remove some rocks because they'll be in the way of what I plan to composite.

Because this will be a destructive edit (meaning it makes changes I can't undo later), I first copied the layer so I'd have a backup. After selecting the rock with the Marquee tool (you can use any selection tool you prefer), I right-clicked the selection and chose Fill from the context menu (alternatively you can press Shift+Backspace/Delete) (**FIGURE 2.9**). In the resulting Fill dialog box, I made sure that the Content-Aware option was selected from the Use drop-down menu, then clicked OK (**FIGURE 2.10**). Finally, I simply watched Photoshop calculate a new background from other parts of the image.

Using this technique I was able to remove all the rocks and produce **FIGURE 2.11** in under a minute. For a full-scale project, I typically would add some additional fine-tuning to this base image with clone stamping and healing.

TIP Keep your selections tight. The larger the selection area you use for Content-Aware Fill, the larger the sampling area Photoshop will use, which increases the potential for undesired fill results.

FIGURE 2.10 In the Fill dialog box, choose Content-Aware from the Use drop-down menu.

FIGURE 2.9 Content-Aware Fill works best with smaller selections like this rock. It starts to get a little too creative with larger selections as it samples from a larger area.

FIGURE 2.11 Removing rocks is easy with the help of Photoshop. Compare these results with where I started in Figure 2.8.

A Pair of Lassos

Very similar to the Marquee tool, the Lasso tool (L) adds the ability to draw your selection organically (although I find drawing with a mouse rather like drawing with a potato and much prefer using a Wacom tablet). As you can with the Marquee tool, you can copy and paste with the Lasso tool, but you're not restricted to selecting only a single blocky shape. From the Lasso tool, you can even switch over to the Move (V) tool to relocate or transform your selection.

> **TIP** The Lasso tool's ability to select custom shapes pairs wonderfully with the Content-Aware Move tool (J). See the "Healing and Cloning Tools" section for more information.

The Lasso tool's sibling, the Magnetic Lasso (L) seeks out contrasting pixel edges of the content you are lassoing and pulls the selection boundary to cling to the edges at points, much like a magnet. It works pretty well for situations that require a little finessing or control but that still have clear edges (**FIGURE 2.12**). By clicking once, you initiate the magnet selection process, then the tool will try to find those edges wherever you move the mouse. Click as you move your cursor around the edges of your desired selection to add custom points to your selection and include fine details that the Magnetic Lasso might skip on its own. To finish you can double-click, press Enter, or complete the selection by clicking the point where you started. Increasing the Frequency setting in the options bar will increase the accuracy by adding more points to the selection as you move the cursor around. Increase the contrast to make the tool more discerning of contrasting edges. The Anti-Alias default keeps the selection relatively smooth, so keep that one on.

> **TIP** If your mouse goes astray and a Magnetic Lasso selection begins to deviate from your intent, you can back up through the selection points by repeatedly pressing the Backspace/Delete key.

FIGURE 2.12 The Magnetic Lasso automatically clings to the contrasting edges around the rocks. By clicking, I can add additional points to the selection around areas that may need more attention.

A Quick Selection

The Quick Selection tool (W) is fantastic, especially when you're in a hurry. Like the Magnetic Lasso tool, this one will look for the nearest edges based on contrast within the intended image selection. With this tool, however, you can paint your selection with a resizable brush and be a little more discerning. If you want the selection to be an even more refined and accurate edge, you can both shrink your brush size with the Left Bracket key ([) and continue to go over the same material. To remove an area from your selection, press and hold the Alt/Opt key as you paint. A minus sign will appear inside the brush to indicate you are now subtracting from rather than adding to the selection. Repeatedly alternating between adding an area to a selection and subtracting that same area will make Photoshop more discriminating about what it adds with each pass.

> **TIP** If your Quick Selection brush is too small for you to see the plus or minus inside of it, take a look at the options bar on the far left. A plus sign next to the Quick Selection symbol ![icon] indicates you're adding, while a minus indicates you're subtracting from the selection.

The Magic Wand Tool

The Magic Wand tool (W) ![icon] is helpful for making a selection of similar pixels, such as a blue sky, a fairly uniform background, and other easy gradients. If you want a complex object selected, by selecting the more uniform background first with the Magic Wand, you can then right-click and select the inverse (Ctrl/Cmd+Shift+I) for a very clean and inclusive selection of the complex object against a plain background (or you could do the opposite if you want to discard the plain red ball and keep the complex background). When the other selection tools are having a tricky time, the Magic Wand can often do the job. Later in the book, you'll see this tool in action to create some magical scenarios.

The options bar presents some additional settings for the Magic Wand to help you fine-tune the results. The two that I use frequently are the Tolerance level and the Contiguous check box (**FIGURE 2.13**), which can make brilliant differences that completely alter the kind of selection you will get.

Tolerance refers to the range of *similar* pixels nearest to the selected likeness of the spot being clicked on (set on a scale of 0 to 255); changing tolerance will change

FIGURE 2.13 The Tolerance setting and Contiguous check box help you refine the Magic Wand tool's results.

FIGURE 2.14 Blue sky is a common visual element that needs to be masked out for a number of reasons; the Magic Wand tool can work wonders for this.

what is allowed for inclusion in the selection. Less tolerant, such as 10, means it will be more exclusive and discriminating of pixels, while more tolerance, such as 200, translates to more inclusive of pixel variations into the selection.

Consider the common blue sky in **FIGURE 2.14** and all the shades of blue it contains. When I set a low tolerance of 10 then sample a few spots of sky by clicking, the Magic Wand selects only a narrow band of nearly that exact same blue. A Tolerance setting of 100, on the other hand, selects anything slightly related to the blue family sample (**FIGURE 2.15**). It's up to you to decide which is best: an extended family get-together or a small private gathering.

FIGURE 2.15 Increase the range being selected by adding additional samples.

FIGURE 2.16 Turning off the Contiguous toggle let me select all the separate pools of gold reflection even if they weren't touching.

The *Contiguous* check box indicates whether pixels of a common color need to be touching or not to be included in the selection (**FIGURE 2.16**). When Contiguous is checked on, only neighboring, touching pixels will be included. When it's off, any pixels within the selected color range will be included. In Figure 2.16, Contiguous is off, so all the pools are selected. With the toggle on, only the large pool in the foreground would qualify. Either way, the Magic Wand tool rocks!

Refining Selections

Refining your selection can be a huge timesaver if you don't want to painstakingly paint in a mask for what wasn't selected or was selected poorly (hair is a frequent offender). That's where the Refine Edge button [Refine Edge...] (found in the options bar) comes in. Click it to open a pop-up menu full of powerful sliders that will help you shift and soften your selections and edges (**FIGURE 2.17**).

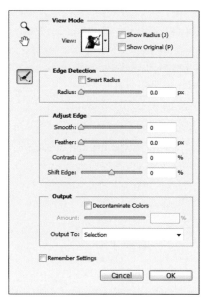

FIGURE 2.17 The sliders in the Refine Edge pop-up menu are just the thing for getting a perfect selection.

In the View section, you change the visible background to better select areas that may have been missed or not selected tightly enough (**FIGURE 2.18**). Eliminating any selection halos and leftover pixels is intrinsic to good compositing practice, and the various views are a huge help. I like to switch back and forth between a few of these backgrounds to make sure everything is selected properly:

- Black background (B) is good for finding those leftover light halos that tend to hang on for dear life.

- White background (W) is excellent for spotting left-over, unwanted pixels

- Layer (L) shows everything outside of the selection as erased so you can better determine how it's going to look if and when you mask it.

The Adjust Edge section contains four sliders:

- **Smooth:** Making your selections a little rounded and smoothed out can really help with rough edges. This slider drastically helps pat down some of those wrinkles in the selection edge.

- **Feathering:** Feathering softens and blurs a selection's clean but abrupt edges. The Feathering slider tells Photoshop how many pixels in which to transition from full opacity to zero opacity, in other words how much blur there is. The larger the pixel range, softer the feathering (**FIGURE 2.19**).

- **Contrast:** Increasing the contrast tells the selection to be more discerning with edges within the selection.

- **Shift Edge:** Shift Edge tightens the selection's edge by the specified amount. After feathering my selection, I frequently use this helpful slider to bite into the selection to get rid of any funny looking halo glow (**FIGURE 2.20**).

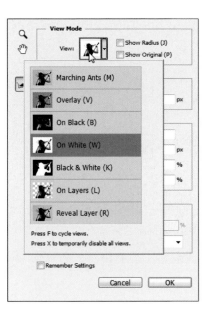

FIGURE 2.18 When refining the selection edge, you can look at the selection against a few different background options.

FIGURE 2.19 Feathering is great for matching the blurriness of the selection to that of the original image. Anything too sharp will look fake. Same goes for anything too soft as well. Find that "just right" sweet spot.

FIGURE 2.20 After making something a little soft with feathering, you often need to tighten the edge to bite a little bit more into the selection to avoid giving the image a slight halo.

NOTE Do not forget to deselect (Ctrl/Cmd+D) when you are finished editing or using a selection! This can be an annoying "gotcha" that's hard to get out of, especially if your selection is so small it's nearly invisible.

Refine Radius Tool

Ever wonder how to select pesky hair without just chopping it all off? Whether you're working with a fluffy cat or a conditioned model, the Refine Radius tool is engineered for just this hairy quandary. When you make a rough selection of hair, be sure to expand the selection boundary a little beyond the main body of hair (**FIGURE 2.21**); later you can whittle it down like a pro with Refine Radius.

> **TIP** Sometimes you will need to select well beyond the main body of hair for better refinement, other times you can simply select just the body of hair and get incredible results; this changes a little with each circumstance and hair situation.

To start whittling, click the Refine Radius button ☑ in the Refine Edge pop-up menu (to the left of the sliders), then paint over all parts of the hair, even those wispy pieces flying around and anything that shows the bland background through it. Painting over these areas will systematically tell Photoshop to find small strings of contrast (such as hair) and include them as part of the selection while leaving out the more solid background chunks. After you paint over all of the hair with the Refine Radius tool, you can sit back and watch as Photoshop does its magic and produces an incomprehensibly *amazing* selection of the hair (**FIGURE 2.22**). It won't always be *absolutely* perfect—but what hair cut ever is? Especially compared to using the clipper sheers or having to manually paint in the hair selection with a clunky tool. After using the Refine Radius feature, you can easily put just about any new background behind that hair (**FIGURE 2.23**) and be ready for the masking tips in Chapter 4; as you can see I quickly placed this selected figure into the scene I removed rocks from earlier.

FIGURE 2.21 Here's a very rough, very quick selection of the hair.

FIGURE 2.22 The Refine Radius tool definitely refines your selection as advertised.

FIGURE 2.23 Now you can put in any kind of background you want without chopping off a majority of those flowing follicles! With a couple other adjustment layers added to the mix, just about any refined selection can fit right in.

TIP Apply the Refine Edge slider changes by pressing OK before using the Refine Radius tool for something like hair selection. If you are doing hair selections, you need to refine the edge with the sliders first, so that the hair is also not adjusted along with the rest of the edges.

NOTE For hair in front of busy backgrounds (as opposed to solids or gradients), this tool may not know which parts are hair and which parts are the background. If you have a hard time discerning, so may this tool. Avoid this issue whenever possible and shoot in front of something more uniform.

COMMON TOOLS, UNCOMMON USES

Even the most mundane, familiar tools can have unexpected uses. Here are a few of my favorites:

- **Smudge tool:** Beyond simply using various brush shapes and sizes to smudge pixels, this tool can be very useful for smudging on masks, offering especially refined control to get things just right. Rather than painting back and forth with black and white on a mask, smudge the mask into place.

- **Bucket tool** (G): Besides filling large areas quickly, this tool is handy for quickly blocking out a mask or selection.

- **Eyedropper** (I): The eyedropper color picker is simple, yet very effective in assisting some seamless edits. Need an exact color? Grab a sample to paint from with the Eyedropper. If you need a color average from a certain area, try selecting a sampling size radius from the options bar. I tend to keep it tight for most work with a radius of 3 by 3 or even the exact Sample Point option (this is the default with a radius of 1 by 1).

- **Crop tool** (C): This tool is useful for early prepping of images for composites, but I especially like the Crop tool's built-in horizon straightener for prepping landscapes. Click the level-like Straighten button within the options bar and then drag across a canted horizon to crop a much straighter version of the image. (For more severe angle alterations, look into using the Adaptive Wide Angle filter demonstrated in Chapter 8.)

Healing and Cloning Tools

Many times images require a lot of repair and alterations, but with the healing and cloning tools you can remake anything anew. Clustered behind the Band-Aid icon in the toolbar, the Healing tools (J), as well as the Clone Stamp tool (S) a few icons below, are especially handy for prepping an image or background for seamless compositing. Sometimes a layer contains a small irregularity or something unwanted that mars the shot; rather than throw away the entire layer because of one little eyesore, reach for the healing and cloning tools: Spot Healing, Healing, and Clone Stamp!

> **TIP** Each of the healing and cloning tools can be applied nondestructively when used on a blank new layer above the content being healed or cloned, just make sure Sample in the options bar is set to Current and Below! All painting with these tools will be done to the new layer and still sample from the ones below it.

Spot Healing Tool

Ever had a zit appear at a shockingly bad moment? You know, the day before a big date or on the morning you have to step in front of a camera? The Spot Healing tool is perfect for zapping it and many other blemishes in your image with just a single click. This highly sophisticated tool is able to analyze and blend pixels around the area you click, deleting an element of high contrast and replacing it with the textures, tones, and color of what surrounds that area. Retouchers obviously use this for skin, but it works on cleaning up any number of things: walls with marks, dust spots from a dirty lens, garbage and sticks from sand, the list goes on. Anything that Photoshop can identify as a visual anomaly from its surrounding area, this tool can replace with a smooth

continuity. Don't overreach, however; although this tool is good for discrepancy cover ups and more, it does not do well near edges of drastic pixel changes. Use the Spot Healing tool on some blue sky too close to a tree line and you'll get a spot smudge instead.

Healing Tool

The Healing tool (J) serves the same purpose as the Spot Healing tool, but accomplishes it differently and is best for situations requiring more of a manual control. Rather than automatically using the area surrounding the healing brush shape, the tool relies on you to indicate the area it should sample and heal *from* (known as the *sample point*) as well as the area it should analyze and replace (indicated by the brush circumference and location). This is a two-step process. To first give Photoshop the sample point from which it should begin blending texture and tone, press and hold Alt/Opt to turn your cursor into a crosshair sample point selector (**FIGURE 2.24**), then click on a location that is to be sampled from for clear blending. (Hint: Pick a location that is clear of other blemishes and spots you intend to take out!) Release the Alt/Opt

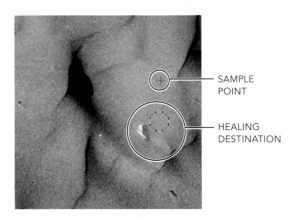

SAMPLE POINT

HEALING DESTINATION

FIGURE 2.24 Select the sample point before healing over a different area of the image.

key, and the Healing tool will then analyze pixels from the sample point once you begin brushing in a new location (**FIGURE 2.25**).

> **WARNING** Be wary of getting too close to edges where the surroundings are less than uniform as this could make a smudge as Photoshop tries to blend contrasting elements together.

Keep in mind that the sample point moves with your healing brushstrokes. When the Aligned check box is toggled in the options bar, Photoshop establishes the distance between the sample point and where you begin healing, then keeps that distance and orientation locked as you paint. This can be helpful if you need the sampled content to continue moving with subsequent brushstrokes. If Aligned is not checked, Photoshop will return the sample point to your original selection after every brush stroke. In either case, a healing stroke in a line going to the left will move the sample point in a line to the left. Healing downward moves the sample point downward. It's like leashing a robot to match your actions. Just because you *can* run the robot through a wall as you safely go through the doorway, does not make doing so the best idea. So watch where your robotic sample point ⊕ is headed before you analyze an area that could get you in trouble and make a mess!

Clone Stamp

Similar in many respects to the healing tools, the Clone Stamp tool (S) also takes content from an area you specify, but does not blend it in the same way. As the name implies, it clones! This tool is great for more precise cover-ups when you want something replaced rather than just blended and smoothed over. The same rules apply as with the Healing tool: It needs an Alt/Opt click to select a

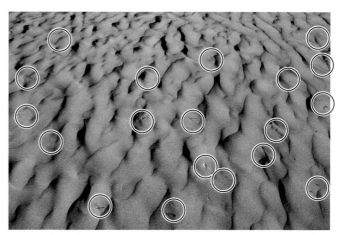
BEFORE HEALING

AFTER HEALING

FIGURE 2.25 Compare the original beach (top) to the result of cleaning up with the Healing tool (bottom).

sample point, but Clone Stamp will completely replace the content you paint over, so be mindful of where you are taking from. Even slight differences in value from the sample point and brushing area will show up dramatically in a new location, often requiring more work or a different sample point. This tool will also track your spatial relationship even after the first stroke if you check Aligned in the options bar.

Content-Aware Move

First available in Photoshop CS6, the Content-Aware Move tool (J) is great for making swift alterations. With it, you can move and simultaneously blend selected material into a new location of your choosing. With Content-Aware Move active, simply make a selection, then move it to your desired location; Photoshop will automatically apply Content-Aware Fill to the selection's original location, filling it with the surrounding material like the selection was never there. If you can easily select and separate an object from its original scene, it's a good candidate for the Content-Aware Move tool. The tool is not perfect for every situation, however, as selections and other layer content can change how it fills and blends the content (**FIGURES 2.26A** and **B**). For best results, try these quick tips:

- In places with very different backgrounds, keep selections as close to the edges of the object as possible. Depending on your selections and refinement, the blending will vary. Tighter selections means less wiggle room for Photoshop to have creative license with blending. Looser selections can work better in times of very similar backgrounds, which generally have a greater chance for success.

- Move the selected content to new locations that have a similar background, such as horizon lines, background colors, and other contrasting elements. When you place a selection in a drastically different scenario, the chances of it not looking quite right increase.

- Subtlety is key! The tool is best suited for nudging elements into place and adjusting things that weren't quite right when originally shot, rather than radical relocations.

- Use this tool for setting up a clean background scene image by moving things into more optimized positions. This is like re-arranging the furniture in your living room to fit that new couch you'll be putting in.

(A)   (B)

Finally, be warned that this is also very much a destructive edit if done without changing a couple settings in the options bar, so it's a good practice for this and other healing and altering to use a copied layer (Ctrl/Cmd+J) just in case.

The options bar has some other slick features to use with the Content-Aware Move tool including Mode, Adaptation, and the nondestructive feature of this tool: the Sample All Layers checkbox. Here's a quick breakdown of what these can do:

- **Sample All Layers:** When toggled, the Sample All Layers option is truly incredible and is the solution to using the Content Aware Move tool nondestructively. When a selection is made, create a blank new layer and move the selection with this new layer still active in the Layers panel. Sample All Layers will enable Photoshop to take everything within the selection from all layers, blend the selected content into the new location it has been moved to and fill with Content-Aware—but all onto this new layer. Aside form analysis, it doesn't even touch the other layers (**FIGURE 2-27**)!

- **Mode:** The two choices for this setting are Extend and Move. Move is ideal for times that you need to relocate the object elsewhere, whereas Extend is designed to extend a shifted over portion of something that has the potential to be repeated for greater length.

- **Adaptation:** Once you make a move, you can have Photoshop reinterpret the selection on a scale of Very Strict to Very Loose. Very Strict keeps closely to the selected area and doesn't get as inventive around the selection edges or with the main content, unlike the other extreme. Very Loose gives a long lead of the leash in regards to making something blend (even distorting parts of the selection to fit better). In general though, tighter selections will need tighter adaptation, looser selections need looser adaptation.

FIGURE 2.27 Creating a new layer you can use Content-Aware Move to move selected content onto the empty layer keeping your workflow nondestructive.

EFFICIENT ALTERNATIVES

As you know, you can accomplish any one task in Photoshop in nearly ten ways—some efficient and some more laborious. Here are a few alternatives to using some standard tools that have dramatically increased my efficiency, accuracy, and nondestructive composite flexibility:

- **Hand tool:**  Instead of clicking in the toolbar, press and hold the Spacebar to turn the cursor into the Hand tool for as long as you hold the key.

- **Magnifying:** Never mind the toolbar or the keyboard shortcuts. My favorite way of magnifying is holding Alt/Opt while scrolling with the mouse—no clicking involved. Hold down the Alt/Opt key to hover temporarily over a spot you want to magnify, then scroll upwards with your mouse to zoom in. Zoom out by

holding Alt/Opt and scrolling in the opposite direction. This method is touchy the first few times you try it, but, wow, does it save some time in the long run!

- **Dodge and Burn:** Never use these tools; they create destructive edits. Instead, I use a low-opacity, black-and-white brush on a new transparent layer with blend mode set to Overlay. I'll demonstrate this in Chapter 3.

- **Erase:** Erase creates destructive edits. Mask instead. Masking keeps your "erasing" edits nondestructive and totally in control. Remember, using layers and masks is the true power behind Photoshop. Learn to mask well and you will do well!

Brush Your Textures

The Brush tool 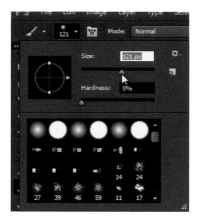 (B) is perhaps my most common go-to tool and is especially great for painting on masks and many, many other uses I'll get into later on. It's always a good idea to get familiar with how to change some of the brush properties as this is another versatile life saving ability. Seriously, I'm sure MacGyver never left home without a brush in his pocket as they have endless possibilities. Here are some common suggestions to start off:

- Change your brush size with Right and Left bracket keys (] and [). Alternately, you can always manually select the size by either right-clicking with the brush or going up to options bar for the Brush Size pull-down menu (**FIGURE 2.28**).

- Change your brush type by pulling up your Brush Properties panel. Alternately, you can right-click once again for a more limited but quicker option.

- Keep your brush hardness as close to zero as possible (available on default round brushes) as this enables you to more seamlessly edit masks and other painting without an obvious and sharp edge to every brush stroke.

And here are a few more uncommon brush tips to try out as well (most of these can be found in the Brush Properties panel):

- Dual Brush (toggled within the Brush Properties panel) can help generate better brush texture variations for just about anything imaginable (from brushing clouds to concrete and even rust). The primary brush is the main body source for each stroke while the secondary brush type (selected by clicking the Dual Brush button to the right of its check box) adds variation by subtracting from the main brush. Like biting out small pieces of the main brush, both brushes can be modified in nearly endless combinations.

FIGURE 2.28 Watch your brush size and keep your hardness down to zero whenever possible so as to avoid harsh and fake looking edges.

- Transfer is a wonderful check box to use with pen pressure if you have a tablet as it will mimic real life drawing pressure physics: The harder you press, the higher the stroke transparency.

- The Scattering check box can be a good option for bringing in even more randomness and variation to a brush. The biggest problem with default brush strokes is how easily they are identifiable, and in seamless compositing it's important to hide these seams whenever possible. Scattering takes a fan to the brush shape and generates many variations that can help make things more believable.

For each option there are countless combinations and variations with sliders and options to choose from, but in case you still don't have enough brush options, try appending even more kinds of brushes to the list by pulling up the Brush Presets panel from the Panel Setting menu and choosing another variety of brushes such as Natural Brushes 2.

The only way to get an idea of a brush is to try a few of them out and take note of where the default soft, fuzzy, and round brush is; Mr. Soft-and-Fuzzy is our friend in most painting situations (**FIGURE 2.29**)! From blending edges of masks to brushing in various details, this helps keep it from looking like a cutout collage or having very obvious brush strokes.

> **TIP** Feel free to completely create your own brush by making a selection and then choosing Edit > Define Brush Preset. Be sure to provide a descriptive name. Your selection will then show up as a brush preset you can paint with using a variety of brushing tools. It's typically best to make sure no edges are dark, however, as whatever is light within your original selection becomes transparent and whatever is dark will apply the paint or tool selected (think of dark values becoming the bristles of the brush soaking up the paint before a stroke).

FIGURE 2.29 Brushes can be a lot of fun and are always useful for a huge range of actions, from masking to texturing. Learn this panel!

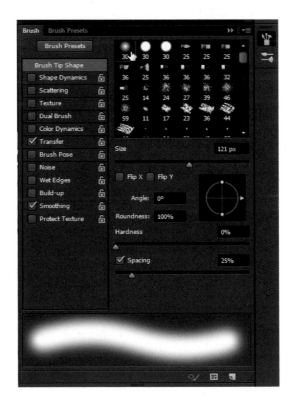

Conclusion

Tools can be tricky, and not only because they tend to change a little with each new version. Tools are tricky because of *when* and *how* they are used. Knowing the theory of how a tool works is only a small part of knowing the tools, the rest is in the hands-on practice and tackling of a broad range of scenarios. The more challenges you use them on, the more you begin to really understand their potential—the more you begin to get clever, creative, and inventive. Eventually, the tools and their various hidden features just become an extension of you and your work.

CHAPTER 3

Layers and Photoshop Muscle

COVERED IN THIS CHAPTER

- Nondestructive layer properties
- Layer organization, groups, and links
- Masking techniques and strategies
- Clipping masks
- Blending modes
- Smart Object layers and layer styles

Photoshop is all about layers. Blending modes, style effects, clipping, masking, grouping, copying, adjusting—the list of the creative potential layers offer you just keeps going. Perhaps the most powerful ability of layers is the layer mask itself and the clever ways you can use masks. The better you understand how layers behave and combine in a composite, the more effectively you can put them to work. As tempting as it may be to dive into the projects of later chapters, take a moment to not only review why layers are the true strength to composite creation, but also how to harness that strength.

Nondestructive Super Power

Layers may take time to master, but the payoff is epic (**FIGURE 3.1**). And, unlike playing with fire, layer-based edits are *nondestructive*, meaning they do not destroy or irreparably edit the original content. (Believe me, when a project suddenly goes horribly, terribly wrong, *not* having permanently edited the original content is a great thing.) You are free to edit one layer, work on another, then come back and re-adjust the first edit. Because the edits are separate, a project can have many separate layers, each with its own purpose in the composite. They can be copied, moved, altered, deleted, grouped, and so much more, while remaining nondestructive to the overall composite. Of course, every edit to a layer does change that individual layer, but keeping your edits separated as *layers* opens up the awesome potential. The concept of nondestructive

▶ ELDERS (2008)

editing is having the ability for unlimited undo options, even after saving and closing the document.

To keep things as nondestructive as possible in my own editing, I am always making copies of layers, just in case I may want to go back to a different stage of the layer or piece together different sections of it with alternative masking. Even without the compulsion of being a digital hoarder, copying is a great idea in many cases. The best way to copy, however, depends on what you are doing.

- To copy just one layer, you can drag it onto the New Layer icon 🔲 at the bottom of the Layer panel or select the layer and Ctrl/Cmd+J. Photoshop will make a new layer using the content of the layer you are dragging to the icon.

- I prefer to Alt/Opt-drag the layer up or down one new level. This method will make a clone of most layer elements, including masks, selected pixels, folders, effects, and other layers. You can use this same method of copying a layer directly on the content; hold down Alt/Opt while dragging with the Move tool to copy the content to the place you drop it—and as a new layer! This is one of those features that can be used for just about everything (like duct tape) and is worth remembering.

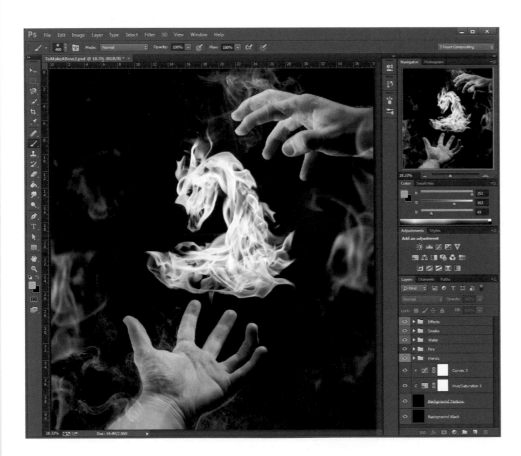

FIGURE 3.1 Although layers can give you super powers, the edits you make with them are nondestructive (as the tutorial in Chapter 8 demonstrates).

Layer Organization

Imagine putting your underwear on outside of your pants. It might create some issues in that order or, at the very least, be uncomfortable—for everyone. Layer order is equally important in composite work. The main thing to understand is that a top layer will affect the visibility of all layers below it in the stack in the Layers panel. Just as in real life, we see whatever is on top first and more clearly than anything else. If you want one layer to be shown above another, make sure to drag it to the proper place in the layer stack—put your pants *over* your underpants. Thanks.

If you do need to reorder your layers, simply drag each layer within the stack in the Layers panel. As you move up or down in the stack, a thick line will follow the Hand tool, indicating the layer's new position when released (**FIGURE 3.2**).

FIGURE 3.2 Drag a layer to move it in the stack. A faint double-lined bar will appear between two layers indicating where the layer will be placed when you release it.

Names and Colors

A key part of keeping layers organized in the proper order is to give layers easy to identify names and even colors (**FIGURE 3.3**). Whether you're working with 10 or 100 layers, the importance of naming cannot be overstated. If the Socks layer must be beneath the one containing shoes, you need to know which is which in the stack. Image thumbnails can be hard to track down (just like real socks), so use descriptive names and name layers as you add them. Trying to organize and rename once deep into a project is never as easy as it sounds.

> **TIP** To make your layer icons larger or smaller, right-click in an empty gray spot below the last layer, then choose a size from the context menu. (If there is no room below the layers for clicking, you can access the same thumbnail size options by clicking the Options icon ≡ in the Layers panel then choosing Panel Options from the resulting menu.) Changing the size can be helpful to see which puzzle piece is what as sometimes even descriptive naming is just not enough.

FIGURE 3.3 Keep your layers labeled, color coded, and in the right hierarchy as you work.

To rename a layer, double-click the letters of its default name. If your clicking is off by one pixel, Photoshop will want to annoyingly do something else such as add layer styles (press Escape if that happens and try again).

The latest version of Photoshop CC enables you to search (filter) for and display specific types of layers, so you can concentrate on only specific kinds of layers at once. Name your layers as you create them, and you can then easily search by those names using the Filter Type option. Be wary of the Filter Layer toggle █ as it may not show all the layers you are expecting to see if you accidentally activate it. Red means it's activated and filtering; when in doubt, you can turn it off and go find your layer the old fashion way. One interesting use for filtering layers is that you can separate by a type of layer (such as adjustments), and then use the group command Ctrl/Cmd+G to group selected layers together. Once out of the filtering feature, these layers will be contained within one group, but be warned: doing so will take them out of their original order.

Color coding your layers can make them easier to spot for any kind of searching. To choose a layer color, right-click near the visibility Eye icon. This brings up a context menu from which you can select a color for that layer (**FIGURE 3.4**).

Group Folders

Even color-coded, clearly named layer stacks can become unwieldy. Stacking multiple layers together into a single group you can easily handle is perhaps the single most important organizational ability within Photoshop. Think of the layers as sandwich ingredients held within the bread—er, group name. Grouping enables you to have delicious, complex composites without the mess of eating it all separately (**FIGURE 3.5**).

Even though they work like stacks of ingredients and bread in a sandwich, visually groups look like folders in the Layers panel. When you need to see the contents of a group, you can expand it to reveal all layers inside, or you can minimize them to show just the folder name, color,

FIGURE 3.4 Right-click to the left of the layer thumbnail for a quick way to color code your layer.

FIGURE 3.5 All three layers of this meager meal are now placed in a Group folder and can be moved, masked, and transformed altogether.

and mask if the group has one (**FIGURE 3.6**).

To create a group folder for layers, click the folder icon █ at the bottom of the Layers panel. Alternatively, you can select multiple layers that you want to be grouped together and press Ctrl/Cmd+G to create a new folder and fill it in one move. Groups can be especially helpful for clustering together large numbers of similar layers. Be sure to rename your group from the default and keep it organized as you go. Don't confuse a BLT with a Veggie-Deluxe—name as you go!

FIGURE 3.6 Collapsing group folders helps keep your layers from getting mixed up. Always keep the Layers panel neat and efficient whenever possible.

TIP Be careful when moving layers near groups. As you drag the layer, you can place it in the group folder inadvertently, rather than just above or below the group. It's easier in these cases to just move the entire group folder out of the way rather than moving the individual layer and risk it being swallowed.

Link Layers

One last small feature with a big impact is the ability to link a selection of multiple layers. This can be handy when you need to move or transform blocks of related layers that are scattered throughout the Layers panel because of the composite's depth hierarchy rather than neatly collected in one group. Select multiple layers by Ctrl/Cmd-clicking their names to piece together a medley of layers, then click the small Link Layers icon 🔗 on the far left at the base of the Layers panel. Once you link the layers, what you do to one will affect them all. For example, move one with the Move tool to move them all together. Transforming in all its varieties can also be done to multiple layers simultaneously if they are linked. To unlink the layers, again select their names in the Layers panel and click the Link Layers icon. Take note that the link icon is not visible if one of the linked layers is not active.

TIP Temporarily disable a link by Shift-clicking on the Link icon to the right of the layer thumbnail in the Layers panel. This way you can disable the links, make an individual edit, then re-link immediately afterwards.

Create, Delete, or Lock Layers

In case you're rusty on some of the very basics, here's a quick reminder. To create a blank new layer, simply click the Add New Layer icon on the bottom of the Layers panel 🔲 or press Ctrl/Cmd+Shift+N and click OK on the pop-up prompt. We will be creating many such new layers throughout the book, so keep this shortcut handy in your brain. Fortunately, deleting layers is just as easy. Select the layer you want to trash and click the trash icon in the lower right corner of the layers window 🗑. Pressing Delete on the keyboard or dragging the layer to the Trash icon will also delete the selected layer. If you don't want a layer to be accidentally deleted or edited, click its Lock icon 🔒 in the Layers panel. Sometimes layers get caught up in a selection or moved by accident and not discovered until later; locking can be a great way to insure this doesn't happen.

Masking

Masking is the power behind seamless edits, localized adjustments, and the ability to piece anything together at will. What do you do when you want to hide your sandwich from a hungry friend? Throw a napkin over it so he can't see it. Masks are like that napkin: They render what's below them invisible. Leave a corner of BLT sticking out and your friend will spy (and maybe swipe) your bacon. Leave a corner of a layer unmasked, and it will be visible in your composite, potentially with equally unpleasant consequences.

Just as your sandwich is safe under that napkin for you to eat later, masking is like nondestructive erasing. To mask a layer, select it, click the Add Mask icon ▣ at the bottom of the Layers panel, then grab a brush (B). The white rectangle linked to the right of your selected layer's thumbnail will display the mask as you paint it over your layer, meanwhile anywhere you paint black will become invisible (**FIGURE 3.7**). If you mask a portion of a layer that you shouldn't have or that you later need visible, you can easily retrieve the parts you need by painting white on the layer's mask. This simple yet handy ability becomes exceedingly versatile as your artistic ideas continue to get more ambitious.

Remember, when you paint on a mask, you have no color options just values (blacks and whites, darks and lights, 256 shades of gray for an 8-bit image to be exact). You can, however, control the opacity of the black or white as you paint, which in turn determines the opacity of the mask. Changing the opacity or value of your Brush tool will change the opacity of the mask you paint (50% gray is equal to 50% opacity).

> **TIP** Although you can use grays to paint on a mask, I find it significantly easier and quicker to paint with black and simply change the opacity of the brush. Pressing numbers 1 through 9 jumps the opacity a level from 10 through 90%, respectively. Pressing 0 jumps the opacity to 100%.

Just like any other pixels, black and white mask pixels can be selected (with selection tools), transformed (with the Move tool), moved, copied, adjusted, smudged, and so on, giving you endless control over nondestructive erasing. In addition, you can separate the link between the mask and its thumbnail by hitting the small chain link between them. This will allow the layer and mask to be

FIGURE 3.7 The Entire Sandwich group folder is being masked out with black. Everything in white is visible; everything painted black is invisible.

moved and transformed independently from one another, a very useful tool from time to time.

> **WARNING** Unless you have a mask actively selected in the Layers panel (signified by a thin white frame around the thumbnail), painting and any other alterations may be accidentally conducted on the layer content itself—yikes! So be sure to click on the mask thumbnail before working on the mask.

In my composites, I use masks to not only blend multiple images into one, but also to apply adjustment layers, such as Curves (see Chapter 4 for more on adjustment layers), to just *one* area of the image. So in short, masks are not limited to just image layers, but can also be applied to adjustments as well. For example, in **FIGURE 3.8** I combined a picture of Bell Meadow and a Yosemite mountain with a city scene I shot in Montreal. Finding three shots that matched in lighting and perspective, all I needed to do was mask out what *didn't* fit the scene. **FIGURE 3.9** shows each layer and its mask; notice how the background city shot didn't need a mask because other layers were placed above it. (In Chapter 9 you can try your hand at re-creating this image to practice your masking skills.)

FIGURE 3.8 Three well-placed layers with good masking can completely alter a scene.

In **FIGURE 3.10** I selectively applied adjustments to certain areas of a composite. Specifically, I used a curves adjustment layer and its mask to lighten the center of the image only—a simple, yet powerful technique. This will come up repeatedly in the tutorials and inspirational projects, so get ready to call on these features.

FIGURE 3.9 I painted masks for the Meadow and Mountain layers of the composite in Figure 3.10.

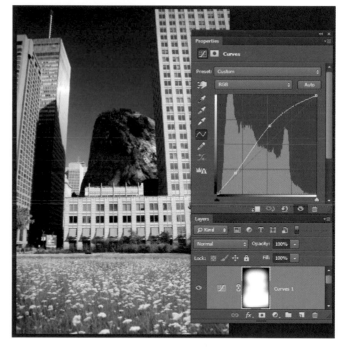

FIGURE 3.10 This Curves adjustment layer affects only the middle section as the black of the mask erases the lightening effect.

WARNING If you accidentally select the image thumbnail instead of the mask's, you will experience a horrible paint blotch on that image layer—probably not the best looking paint blotch either. Simply undo (Ctrl/Cmd+Z) the mistake, and make sure to select the mask thumbnail before painting again. It will have a thin white border indicating it is active.

Masking Hidden Features

Perfecting your masks takes some practice to get right, however there are some great hidden features and techniques that can help:

- Refine your selections perfectly (covered in Chapter 2) then click the Add Mask icon to mask out everything that was outside of that beautiful selection of yours. Take note that selections, even ones being refined, stay as selections until you click the Add Mask icon.

- Press the X key to switch between your primary and secondary color selections (black and white by default when selecting the mask of a layer). Reset your default black and white color selections by pressing D or clicking the small black and white icon at the bottom of the toolbar ▣. This enables you to efficiently paint your mask back and forth with black and white until it is perfect.

- Alt/Opt-click the Add Mask icon to create a new mask for a layer that is already inverted to black. This lets you paint in what you want to see of the layer using white. It can be helpful at times to start with everything visible if there are only small parts that you actually *do* want visible.

- Press the Backslash (\) key to display the masked-out area in an obnoxious red overlay (**FIGURE 3.11**); this is good when checking for leftover, accidentally non-masked pixels you thought were gone. Make sure to always keep your masking clean and intentional. All those accidental faint pixels are like grease that can add up by the end and make for a grimy composite.

TIP In the Mask Options section of the Mask Properties panel, you can change the mask's overlay from the default bright red to a preferable color.

- Clicking a layer's Visibility icon 👁 off and on repeatedly while looking at the composite will reveal what's been completely masked out successfully and will instantly show areas that you may have missed or that still need work. With the layers disappearing and reappearing, it becomes easier to see the flaws of a mask. Similarly, you can enable and disable just the mask itself by Shift-clicking the thumbnail of the mask (notice the small red X over the thumbnail when disabled).

FIGURE 3.11 The Backslash key helps you find those pesky places that need going over on your mask by showing everything masked in bright red.

- Color Range is a phenomenal feature for complex masking (**FIGURE 3.12**). As you might guess, it lets you select a range of color to then add to or subtract from a mask. Placed within the Mask Properties panel (double-click on the layer's mask over in the Layer panel to pull this up), this feature enables you to choose colors to add to (make sure Invert is checked in the dialog box) or subtract from the mask (toggle off Invert). Although you may not be able to *paint* with colors onto a mask, that doesn't mean that you cannot *select* a range of colors from the layer that you want masked out and invisible (say blue sky surrounding a red balloon). Using color range you can click the blue sky and have it instantly disappear from the view. Part of this feature is a slider called Fuzziness that increases or decreases the variation tolerance—do you want that exact blue masked, or all things that are bluish? The fuzzier, the more general the range.

> **TIP** In the Color Range dialog box, select the Add to Sample icon ✎ to choose multiple sample colors for the Color Range effect. This works well when you need to mask out multiple color ranges, such as all the blues and all the greens from an image.

- Just above the Color Range button, the Refine Edge button is a nifty tool for improving the border edges of your mask. Just as you used it on selections in Chapter 2, you can use Refine Edge to adjust the edges of the mask.

- Scrub off "digital grease." By this I mean clean up all the hard to find pixels that gunk up a composite, layer by layer (**FIGURE 3.13**). Digital grease clings to those hard-to-find leftover places that didn't get masked out at full opacity as first thought—like the greasy residue that clings to the corners of a roasting dish. Always do

what you can to remove digital grease as you work. There's nothing worse than going layer by layer late in a composite looking for what causes some unnatural sharp edge or greasy smudge.

- When masking subjects or other objects in a composite, be sure to paint with a brush softness that is equivalent to the edge blurriness or sharpness of the image. If you are masking a crisp image, make your brush small and crisp, if masking something with soft focus, use a matching soft brush.

FIGURE 3.12 Double-click a mask to bring up its properties. Clicking the Color Range button enables you to specify a color selection to use for custom masking.

FIGURE 3.13 "Digital grease" like this may seem obvious against a white background, but with complex composites, it simply makes the composite look grimy and can be hard to track down.

FIGURE 3.14 These two adjustments layers are clipped to the Mountain layer and will mask the visible pixels in that layer only.

Clipping Masks

A clipping mask is a mask that is attached to and used by other layers, which sounds complicated but is easy to understand if you think in physical terms. Imagine several pieces of paper stapled together (the attached layers). On one layer you draw and outline (the shape of your mask), then you cut the entire stapled packet along that outline (the effect of your mask). Adjustment layers (covered in Chapter 4) have a built-in clipping feature to attach themselves to the visible parts of another layer, but you can clip any regular layer with pixel content to another's mask (and still retain the first layer's own mask as well).

A layer that is "clipped to another layer" or "using a clipping mask," means the layer interacts with and affects only the layer directly below it (**FIGURE 3.14**). So if you wanted to make a Curves or Color Balance adjustment layer affect *only* a certain layer and keep it nondestructive, using the clipping mask is the tool for the job. Plus if you previously made a mask for the layer being clipped, it will stay within those boundaries as well (essentially being double masked). You can even have a stack of multiple clipped layers all only affecting the bottom of the stack. I can't imagine working without clipping masks, and you'll try them out in Section II's tutorial projects.

To use the clipping mask feature, select the layer you want to clip and press Ctrl+Alt+G/Cmd+Opt+G to affix the clipping mask to only that layer directly below it. Alternatively (and sometimes easier as a workflow), Alt/Opt-click between the two layers to clip the top layer to the bottom masks just the same as the keyboard shortcut. Adjustment layers come with a shortcut button in the Adjustment Properties panel, which can be another handy alternative. Just be sure to have the clipping layer above whatever you want it to affect!

> **TIP** In the latest versions of Photoshop CC, you can even use a clipping mask applied to a group folder and all of its contents. This profound improvement in efficiency instantly shifts many roundabout workflows into obsolescence.

Blending Modes

Whether you want to burn and dodge, change colors, or make a layer's dark pixels invisible, reach for a blending mode feature to turn your cleverness and creativity into a truly amazing, seamless, or stunning image. Blending modes instruct Photoshop to interpret a layer's pixels differently than simply levels of color and opacity—this gives you immense control (**FIGURE 3.15**).

A blending mode generally requires two layers, because in order to see the effects the layers must be interacting with each other in some way. For example, a layer set to Lighten blending mode tells Photoshop to interpret it as something that only adds lighter pixels to what is visible beneath it, ignoring all darker pixels. Apply the Color blending mode to a layer, and Photoshop will ignore light and dark values of that layer, applying only the layer's color to the composite and replacing all other colors from layers below.

To apply a blending mode, simply select a layer and choose a mode from the drop-down menu of blending modes that resides at the top of the Layers panel. By default, it's set at Normal, the boring blending mode that performs standard pixel interpretation. Normal mode is like vanilla ice-cream: tasty in most situations, but definitely not for every combination. The blending modes I most commonly use are Overlay, Color, Hue, Multiply, Screen, Lighten, and Darken. In the sections that follow, take a closer look at their strengths and how to use them.

For all blending modes, the Opacity setting can be a lifesaver for lessening the visibility of a selected layer by a percentage. Let's say you want a Color blending mode layer (more on this in a moment) to alter the color of the composite, but it ends up looking just a bit like Technicolor overkill. Changing the opacity of the entire Color blending mode layer can help you find just the right balance for blending the new and old together. In the case of **FIGURE 3.16**, the bread needed to be warmed up, as it was not quite as appetizing with a cooler coloring. If you decide to play with some extreme layer effects, go ahead. You can always scale them back in opacity if you find the results too extreme and the results are nondestructive.

FIGURE 3.15 With so many blending modes to choose from, the combinations are nearly endless.

(A)

(B)

FIGURE 3.16 Here you can see the Color blending mode at 100% opacity (a) and then reduced to 22% opacity (b). At 100% it was quite painful to look at, but scaling back the opacity helped make it look a little more believable as well as tastier.

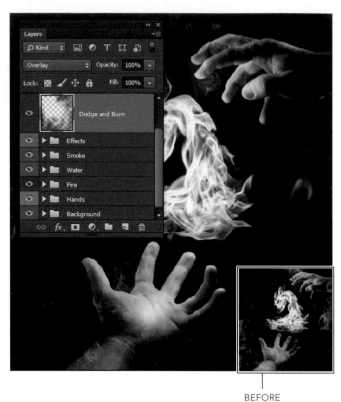

BEFORE

FIGURE 3.17 Change a new layer's blending mode to Overlay to dodge and burn nondestructively by painting with black and white.

Overlay Is Versatile

Overlay is the go-to blending mode that I use most often, outside of the default of Normal. From dodging and burning to color filtering, this one allows for ultimate control and versatility of your composite, especially in regards to lighting effects. With a mathematical complexity that I'm not going to get into, this blending mode uses a layer's pixel values (lights and darks) to accentuate the composite's shadows or highlights. Anything neutral such as middle gray is completely ignored.

Dodge and Burn Nondestructively with Overlay

When used with black and white, Overlay mode provides a nondestructive alternative to the Dodge and Burn tools. Editing with the Dodge and Burn tools directly on an

original layer is a destructive process; however, you can alter or remove Overlay mode's edits because they are on a separate layer that does not permanently affect the rest of the composite.

To dodge and burn with Overlay, first make sure your foreground and background paint colors are set to black and white (D). Create a new layer, set it to Overlay mode, and then simply paint with a lowered opacity (start with about 10%) on the new layer with white to lighten (or dodge) overly shadowed areas or with black to darken (burn) areas that are too bright (**FIGURE 3.17**). Because the changes are on a separate layer, you can easily remove them if you change your mind (select the layer and press Delete, or cash in your one allowed use of the Eraser tool). I'll use this blending mode throughout the book as it is a standard lighting control effect.

TIP Be careful with your opacity as you paint. For subtle burning and dodging, very low paint opacity is always best (under 10% to start). If you use a tablet, set the dynamics to pen pressure and you will have another level of dodge and burn control.

BEFORE

FIGURE 3.18 Overlay blending mode at 20% or less makes for a great photo filter with your color of choice, giving you complete control over the composite continuity.

TIP You can reset your black and white defaults by clicking the small Color Reset button ⬚ beneath the Magnifying tool on the toolbar (or press D). Press the X key to bounce back and forth between primary and secondary color selections, just like when masking.

Use Overlay as a Color Photo Filter

Painting with color does something else entirely with Overlay mode: It blends the color you apply to a layer with the colors already present in the composite to add both hue and vividness without muddying the overall look of the composite (**FIGURE 3.18**). I often use this flavor of Overlay to make a vibrant and dynamic image with strong color continuity.

For a number of reasons, I have never liked the built-in Photo Filter adjustment layer effects that come with Photoshop. Instead, I commonly use Overlay as a color Photo Filter. Using the blending mode set to Overlay has allowed for greater control with better results. Here's what I do:

1. Add a blank new layer to the composite, and drag it to the top of the stack.

2. Apply a medium to light, vibrant orangish-yellow color with the paint bucket (G).

3. Change the blending mode to Overlay.

4. Lower the layer's opacity to between 10% and 20%.

Chapter 7 and subsequent tutorials will give you more opportunities to try this technique.

Color and Hue

Good composites are all about controlling your image and layers. A big part of this is controlling color, and the Color and Hue blending modes enable you do just that to the extreme. Add a blank layer and change its blending mode to Color. Now any colors that you paint on the layer will supersede all other colors of layers below. In addition to altering the color of the composite, Color mode maintains nearly the exact values of the layers below as well. Say you start with an image of jeans that are dark blue. Paint your Color layer a variety of red, the jeans will now appear red, but keep the same darkness and lightness of the original jeans—those worn edges at the pocket seams will still be lighter than the center and the decorative stitching will still stand out (**FIGURE 3.19**). It doesn't matter whether you painted a dark or light red, Photoshop ignores values (lights and darks) on a Color layer. Another feature to Color mode is the saturation. Photoshop matches the exact saturation level of the color you are painting (vibrant versus more neutral), rather than sticking with the original composite material below it. This blending mode is quite a lot of fun and has many uses as you will see in the coming chapters. My favorite use is to get color controlled and totally under my thumb. From the reds and yellow of fire, to the green of trees, this feature can make just about any item really pop in just the right way.

For more naturalistic color alteration, use the blending mode called Hue. With Hue, you again paint color on a layer to alter the layer or layers below, but Hue matches the saturation levels of the original content. Now you have believable color alterations with fairly little effort (**FIGURE 3.20**). Catalog designers use this technique to show a variety of color options, basing them all on a single product shot.

FIGURE 3.19 Color blending mode instantly adds vibrant color of your choice to wherever it is painted on the layer.

FIGURE 3.20 Hue blending mode keeps the inherent saturation of the layers below it and only alters the hue.

Multiply Without Math

Definitely one of my favorites, Multiply mode enables you to combine layers by adding the darks of one layer to the darks of others. This has an effect that the added layer becomes partially transparent, but it darkens the composite by adding darks with each layer addition set to Multiply. This can be handy if you want to combine a layer and need added shadows or textured dark spots (**FIGURE 3.21**).

Screen

Screen mode can be useful for adding vibrancy and layering the lighter qualities of a layer. This blending mode works as the direct opposite to Multiply: Where multiply darkens the composite with each addition, Screen lightens with each layer that has lighter qualities. For those pyromaniacs out there, yes, this is perfect for adding light flames to a dark composite! This is the main technique used in Figure 3.1 and Figure 3.21.

Lighten

Similar in many respects to Screen, Lighten mode adds the lighter elements of a layer to the composite. The key difference, though, is its comparison of the lights and darks to those of the composite. If the Screen layer has parts that are lighter than the pixels of the composite below it, then it will remove those lighter elements visible with full opacity (lacking the change in transparency range that Screen provides). Try adding stars to a very dark composite (or one made to look dark like this scene) and change the stars blending mode to Lighten. Only the light stars will come through (**FIGURE 3.22**, which also contains some additional masking done to keep the stars from joining with the buildings).

FIGURE 3.21 Choose the Multiply blending mode to add layers as darkening texture effects, such as the bark layer used on top of the wrist layer.

FIGURE 3.22 Here you can see the Lighten mode in action: I added stars to a sky that originally did not have any.

Darken it Down

Darken blending mode does the opposite of Lighten. Say you have something with a white background and you want only the things that are not white to be visible. Rather than deleting or masking or doing any other action that is a time-consuming pain, try changing the blending mode to Darken. All that light background will disappear like you're keying out a green screen.

Smart Objects and Styles

Masking and blending modes can take you only so far in a large-scale composite. Sometimes you need to dig in and resize, reshape, or otherwise transform layers, maybe even apply some special effects. Smart Object layers and layer styles can help you.

Smart Objects

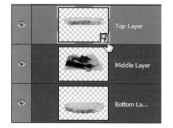

FIGURE 3.23 A Smart Object layer is indicated by a small icon in the lower right of the thumbnail. This layer is now ready for nondestructive transforming and filtering!

Smart Objects are yet one more powerful tool in Photoshop for working nondestructively (**FIGURE 3.23**). With layers converted to Smart Objects you can nondestructively scale, transform, use various filters on, and warp a layer without permanently changing its pixels. This means you can shrink it down, click the Commit button (the check), then scale it all the way back to its original size without loosing a single pixel of detail.

Pick a layer that you want to alter nondestructively (preferably a layer without a mask as the conversion will apply the mask), right-click its name, then select Convert to Smart Object from the context menu. Going up to the Filter menu will also allow you to convert a selected layer to a Smart Object with the Convert for Smart Filters option. Both ways will allow you to apply most filters nondestructively (where you can keep returning to them, change parameters, mask them, or even turn off their visibility), as well as scale and transform to your hearts content!

If for some reason you ever want to paint directly on the layer that's a Smart Object or directly edit the pixels in some fashion, you will need to rasterize the layer. Do this by again right-clicking the layer's name in the Layers panel, then selecting Rasterize Layer from the context menu. Once you instruct Photoshop to rasterize the layer, however, the changes cannot be undone. In addition to transforming, Smart Objects are useful when you want to apply Smart Filters to a layer. These filters are a subset of those available to *simple* layers, but have the added benefits of frequent returning and altering of the filter parameters and never loosing detail or quality of the original. Smart Object layers do have limits to their intelligence: They still don't allow for the full range of edits that rasterized images do. So if you are painting, cloning, healing, and so on, the image will need to be rasterized before you can manipulate it in those ways.

Layer Styles

Layer styles enable you to nondestructively apply some neat effects options to the pixels of a selected layer. To display a menu of your options, click the Effects icon $fx.$ or double-click off to the side of the layer name. Such effects as drop shadow and outer glow can be very helpful from time to time. I use Outer Glow to simulate fire, lava, and on occasion some magic twinkle dust (or other mysterious glowing substances). Within the layer style options are ways to alter the color of a gradient for such things.

Located in the on the Layers panel beneath Opacity, the Flow slider is a useful companion to layer styles. Like the Opacity slider, the Flow slider enables you to adjust the opacity of a layer from fully opaque to fully transparent; the difference is how Flow handles layer style effects. Flow enables you to decrease the opacity of the layer, while still keeping the opacity of the layer styles unchanged—definitely a neat feature. I use this at times when I want the effect of an outer glow without having to show the actual painted parts—the glow of the sun without the sun itself! This means you can apply a certain effect just in the parts you want them.

Conclusion

As you will soon find out in Sections II and III, the versatility and nondestructive control available through layer use is what makes Photoshop the powerful program that it is. From layer organization features, editing the smart way, to blending modes, nothing is impossible or unnecessarily destructive, even when it seems like it should be!

CHAPTER 4

Favorite Adjustment Layers and Filters

COVERED IN THIS CHAPTER

- Curves
- B&W adjustment layers
- Color balance
- Hue and saturation
- Smart Filters
- Blurring
- Sharpening
- Reducing Noise
- Camera Raw filter

Remember your first few composites—those roughly cut and pasted, disjointed collages? Whether we like to admit it or not, we all go through this stage before honing our eyes and skills to craft an element of photorealism into our work. That element is what elevates a composite from a mere copy-and-paste-fest to a seamless new reality. The craft behind it is largely the craft of using filters, adjustment layers, and their masks (**FIGURE 4.1**). These features represent their own art form when used by a pro. Endlessly useful for a multitude of situations, they can be the difference between realizing your vision and consigning yet another project to the digital scrap heap of "not quite right."

Rather than giving you a hasty flyby of every adjustment layer and filter, this chapter will push deep into my four favorite adjustment layers (along with their subterranean features), as well as the Photoshop filters that I find come in most handy for composite work. This focus will get you going for most situations and provide a solid base for the more complex tutorials and projects in Sections II and III.

▶ Four Tears of Victory (2009)

FILTERS

ADJUSTMENT LAYERS

ADJUSTMENT PROPERTIES

FIGURE 4.1 Filters and adjustment layers are essential for blending very different image sources into a seamless composite.

Adjustment Layers

When working nondestructively, adjustment layers are the professional way to go rather than choosing the destructive adjustments available from the Image menu. By making your adjustment as a dedicated layer with an accompanying mask (**FIGURE 4.2**), you can later fine-tune or remove your changes without any permanent alterations or loss of quality. Just like standard layers, adjustment layers affect the layers directly below them in the stack and can be independently altered by themselves. When you just want to adjust a single layer, you can restrict an adjustment layer to a single layer or group by clipping it to the layer placed directly below it (as covered in Chapter 3). As a standard feature, every adjustment layer comes with a clean white mask for safe and nondestructive adjusting.

Although the Adjustments panel (choose Window > Adjustments to bring this up if it is not open) offers many choices, each with its own specialty, I have come to rely on four adjustment layers in particular. Whether piecing layers together seamlessly or correcting for some shortcomings of an image, I use Curves, Black & White, Color Balance, and Hue and Saturation most heavily.

Curves

Of my top four, Curves is perhaps my most used adjustment layer and is by far the most versatile, as well. It is my go-to when something is just not looking right or when I need more control over the general lights and darks of an area, when I need to isolate a tone, and much more. A Curves adjustment layer enables you to nondestructively shift tonal attributes of an image, making specific tones lighter or darker.

The controls you need are housed in the Curves Properties panel (**FIGURE 4.3**) The horizontal and vertical gradient strips along the bottom and left side of the Curves control represent the range of possible tones (from darks through midtones to lights) in an image. The diagonal line (the "curve") represents the value of each of the tones in the gradients as they compare to each other. Notice that when you first apply a Curves adjustment layer, any point on the line corresponds to the same tone on the horizontal gradient (the scale for tones in the starting, or input, image) as on the vertical gradient (the scale for tones in the adjusted, or output, image). You've not adjusted anything, so the values are the same along both gradients. Click the line to add a control point, and drag the point upwards. Notice that because the point is higher, it now corresponds to a lighter shade on the vertical

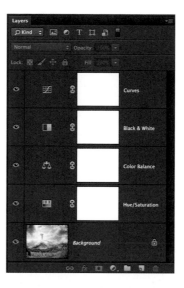

FIGURE 4.2 Each adjustment layer includes a mask for immediate nondestructive erasing of the adjustment.

FIGURE 4.3 The Curves Properties panel contains both the controls to adjust the levels of darks, midtones, and lights in an image and a histogram that graphically represents the quantity of those tones present.

gradient than on the horizontal gradient? By dragging up, you've lightened the original tone at that point, as well as along the curve. Dragging a control point down does the opposite.

For example, in **FIGURE 4.4**, I shifted a wide range of tones lighter by lifting the single control point (perhaps not the best aesthetic choice, but a good demonstration); to see how this works, pick any point along the new curve line and compare where it lies along the horizontal gradient (the original tone) to where it aligns with the vertical gradient (the new, adjusted lighter tone). This is a good way to remember how Curves works by default: Pull a point higher means lighter, pull it lower means darker. (Note that this default changes; it inverts when you work on a grayscale image, or you can change it to match RGB.)

> **NOTE** You can use Curves for adjusting color, as well, although I prefer to use a couple of the other adjustment layers and their sliders for this work. If you choose to try Curves for colors, however, I definitely encourage you to try individually adjusting red, green, and blue separately rather than using the default RGB, which controls them all in equal amounts. Change the color by clicking RGB in the Curves Properties panel and select one of the other additive primaries.

Curve Strategy

With a better understanding of the technical theory of Curves adjustment layers, consider some practical tips for using curves to their full potential:

- Don't try anything too radical. For example, curves with a very exaggerated S shape (such as doubling back on themselves as in **FIGURE 4.5**) create an inversion for some tones of the image, causing lights and darks to switch places with each other. (Try pressing

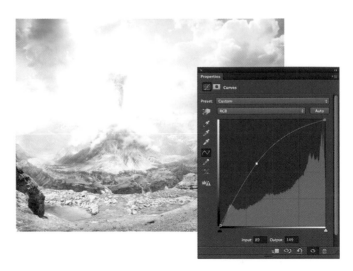

FIGURE 4.4 Pulling a curve's single control point upwards or to the left shifts the tonal values lighter and keeps the lightening effect proportional with all nearby tones as they are gently elevated along the curve.

FIGURE 4.5 Curves that get too exaggerated end up looking pretty awful (like a posterizing effect) or produce inversions of lights and darks as shown here. Keep your adjustments gentle and controlled instead.

Ctrl/Cmd+I on an image layer to see the full effect of this.) The power behind Curves adjustment layers is in the subtlety and gentleness of the curve that you make.

- Use two points to create a fully controlled contrast adjustment. Click to add two control points along the curve line, one toward the bottom darks and one towards the lighter end. Slightly drop the darks control point downward and similarly bring the highlights control point upwards for a punchier look!

- Use no more than three control points along the curve whenever possible. I usually stick to adding just one or two unless I am trying to isolate a very specific tonal adjustment. The more points you make, the higher the chances are that the image might begin to look "off" or inversion begins.

- Isolate a tone by using the Sampling tool ⬚ , (found to the left of the Curves histogram in the Curves Properties panel) to click on a specific area or tone in the actual image. You will see a phantom control point along the curve line demonstrating where the value falls. With a click, you can add control points for whatever distinct tone you clicked on within your image. This can be helpful for those times when you need to find a specific value and shift it lighter or darker.

- Use the mask provided with the adjustment layer to isolate your Curves adjustment to specific areas. Suppose you want to lighten one area to draw further attention to it, but you don't want it to lighten the edges of the image. As you adjust, focus only on the critical areas, then paint black on the layer's mask to remove the changes from areas you wish to be

POWER OF THE HISTOGRAM

Understanding the histogram, found behind the curve line in the center of the Curves Properties panel (Figure 4.3), will give you better control when working with Curves adjustment layers. The histogram is much like a speedometer in a car, giving you a readout of simple data on which you can base adjustments; knowing the current reading can help you adjust your speed (or image tones) to the desired level. (Unlike a speedometer, however, the histogram does not respond interactively as you raise or lower a point on the curve.)

The data that the histogram represents is the full tonal range from dark to light of an image, presented as a series of peaks and valleys; the higher the peak, the greater the quantity of the corresponding tone it represents, which is shown below it in the horizontal gradient. The histogram is helpful because it shows the relative quantities of each tone present, from all the deepest, darkest pixels (starting

at the left by default) through the midtones to those spots of pure white (far right by default). If an image is heavy on dark pixels, the histogram will be more mountainous at the dark end of the bottom gradient. Likewise, a higher percentage of lighter pixels produces peaks towards opposite end of the gradient.

Keep in mind, however, that histogram shapes have no bearing on the quality of the image. Two images may be equally stunning but be represented by vastly different histogram shapes. With that said, you want to avoid having a histogram that does not take up the full range, ending short with a completely flat valley after a hill at either end of the spectrum, because it will appear washed out (lacking the contrast of full black and full white). These images will need further adjusting to increase contrast, such as with Curves or Levels to regain a fuller gamut of tones.

unaffected. Alternatively, you can also make a selection before adding the adjustment layer, and Photoshop will automatically adjust only the selected area, applying a mask to everything outside of the selection.

- Use a pair of Curves. One Curves adjustment layer can be helpful for controlling, say, the darks, but when you try to get the highlights right in the same curve, it changes too much or is harder to control. Adding a second Curves adjustment layer that finesses another portion of the image, such as the lights, will keep a more even tonal adjustment than trying to do it all in one go and getting dramatic with the curve shape.

- Clip the Curves adjustment layer to a single layer below it so that you can affect that clipped layer only. This is so important for composite work where images are taken from a wide variety of sources that you must match the lights and darks consistent with the background (**FIGURE 4.6**) or each other. To clip the adjustment layer, either click the clipping icon ![icon] at the bottom of the Adjustment Properties panel or Alt/ Opt-click between the adjustment layer and the layer directly below it.

Black & White

Although not specifically designed for the purpose, B&W adjustment layers can replace hours of traditional black-and-white dodging, burning, and filtering to a swift move of the slider. True, this adjustment layer will turn the content black and white, but you can control the lights and darks of each color of the original image separately to enhance certain features once in grayscale. To begin, simply click the B&W Adjustment Layer icon ![icon] in the Adjustments panel; from the Black & White Properties panel that opens you can adjust the values of each color individually (**FIGURE 4.7**). Suppose you want a green

SEVERAL PIECES THAT ALL MATCH

TOO DARK TO FIT IN

FIGURE 4.6 Adjust an individual layer by clipping the adjustment to it and then matching the lights and darks to the others around it; in this case, the piece was much too dark and needed a Curves adjustment layer to lighten it up.

FIGURE 4.7 The mix-match of lighting amongst the elements ended up just being too overpowering in the image (left), so I added a B&W adjustment layer (right) to alter the saturation (by lowering opacity) and values of separated colors.

(converted to a mid-gray) to become an even lighter gray; find the green slider, and move it to the right to shift all the related greens lighter.

At lower opacities, the Black & White adjustment layer is phenomenal for subtly controlling saturation and the lights and darks of certain colors. (I rarely use it full force, which produces a black-and-white image.) The power of moving around the darks and lights for each color has far reaching benefits. For example, I photographed the elements of Figure 4.7 with a wide range of lighting color temperatures, edited them together with a certain vibrancy in mind, then decided I needed to tone down the colors instead. Adding a B&W adjustment layer, I lowered the opacity to under 40% until it curbed the

saturation. From there, I further adjusted the colors to lighten the yellows and darken the reds and blues slightly to create a more contrast in the composition.

TIP The Black & White Properties panel's Slider Modifier icon (![icon] above the sliders) is especially helpful for times when you need to modify a specific color family quickly. Simply click the icon, then click and drag directly within the image to sample a color. Sampling a color within the image tells Photoshop to find the closest matching slider in the panel (just one at a time); move the cursor back and forth to adjust the color slider in the same way as using it directly.

Color Balance

As an adjustment layer, Color Balance is a good choice for blending in layers whose colors don't match those of the other elements in a composite. Perhaps the images were shot on different light settings, different cameras, or just have a different color palette in general. With a Color Balance adjustment layer, you can easily correct moderate differences. The Color Balance Properties panel contains three sliders: one ranging from cyan to red, one from magenta to green, and the last from yellow to blue. **FIGURES 4.8A** and **B** are a good example of better blending two images with Color Balance. The woman with the sword was too warm in color compared to the cooler background, so shifting the sliders over to the cooler sides (more cyan, blue, and just a hint more of green) helped dramatically with fitting the two images together. The sliders start out neutral at the center, so you easily can go back and forth to finesse the colors.

Although Photoshop offers many other ways (some a lot more refined and exacting) to help with color balance, this adjustment layer does a fairly decent job and is so straightforward and quick, it works with very little effort or tweaking, making it my go-to choice in most cases.

Hue/Saturation

As my first choice for quick color shifts and general desaturation, a Hue/Saturation adjustment layer is also great for altering a selected color using color range (revisit Chapter 3 for a reminder) and shifting the color to an entirely new hue. Combining simplified features of the Color Balance and B&W adjustment layers, Hue/Satura-tion includes a very basic, yet quick-to-use Saturation slider and can be good for simple neutralizing or color shifting. I find this adjustment layer especially valuable when I need to shift over a specific color. For example,

(A)

(B)

FIGURES 4.8A and **B** Color Balance is not especially refined, but is quick, efficient, and works wonderfully for most color discrepancies. When I first composited the figure with the background, I discovered I photographed her with warmer colors compared to her new, cooler surroundings (a). To cool the subject down and match the scene, I applied a Color Balance adjustment layer (b).

in **FIGURE 4.9** I needed a small green object down by the crib to help complete a compositional triangle of color. I added a Hue/Saturation adjustment and mask color range to shift just the juggling ball by the crib to the proper green.

> **TIP** You can shift or neutralize a specific color range within the Hue/Saturation adjustment layer even without using a mask. In the Hue/Saturation Properties panel, simply select a color from the second drop-down menu (set to Master by default). You can even restrict or expand the allowed color variation using the bottom color gradient, specifying only yellow, only red, or only colors between yellow and red, for example—endless possibilities for color shifting and saturation control.

FIGURE 4.9 A Hue/Saturation adjustment layer and mask using Color Range (see Chapter 3) works especially well for isolated color changes; you can alter a selected color or restrained portion of the image. Here I changed the ball from red to green.

Featured Filters

Somewhat related to adjustment layers are filters that can be applied to a layer. Both filters and adjustment layers can dramatically alter the look and feel of an image, helping with seamlessness or adding a nice visual effect. Filters don't have a dedicated panel though, and instead live within the Filter menu (see Figure 4.1). Although many of the filters by themselves end up looking too canned and obvious for most uses, there are the few described in the next sections that stand out as invaluable for composite work. Filters such as Smart Sharpen and Reduce Noise can help with quality differences and, like color adjustments, help match images from different sources. Blurs also come in handy as an effect when you need more control of the depth, mood, or motion. In Chapter 9, you'll use them to create sunrays, while Bonus Chapter 16 demonstrates using filters to soften glare.

Smart Sharpen

What makes the Smart Sharpen filter smart is its ability to control simultaneously the amount of sharpening, noise reduction (Photoshop CC), and compensation for various kinds of blur, from motion blurs to lens blurs (**FIGURE 4.10**). This combination of strengths is more versatile than other sharpening methods (like Unsharp Mask) and is very useful when you need to match one picture element to another, as illustrated in Chapter 14.

When using Smart Sharpen, either on ordinary layers or as a Smart Filter on Smart Objects, keep a few tips in mind:

- Avoid halos created from too large a Radius and too high an Amount of sharpening applied. This not only looks bad, but it's a tell-tale sign of amateur sharpening or that you did not zoom in close enough to see what was happening. When the radius size is larger than the blurriness you start to increase the contrast for parts that you shouldn't be increasing, parts that don't need it. Combine this with a sharpening amount that goes a bit overboard, and you have yourself a mighty halo on the outside of your edges. Start with a radius that matches the blur radius (typically 1 to 3 pixels for my own setup), then boost the Amount slider until edges pop without a dramatic light halo. For Photoshop CS6 and older versions, this usually meant

under 100%, but the CC version of this feature can easily push to 300% without overly adverse effects.

• Zoom in close to see what's being sharpened and what the effects are in regards to halos and noise, then zoom out to make sure it's actually having a good sharpening effect in a general sense. It's always a balance of too much and creating bad halos versus not enough and having very little sharpening taking place.

FIGURE 4.10 Smart Sharpen enables you to compensate for multiple kinds of blur and gives you greater flexibility than other sharpening methods.

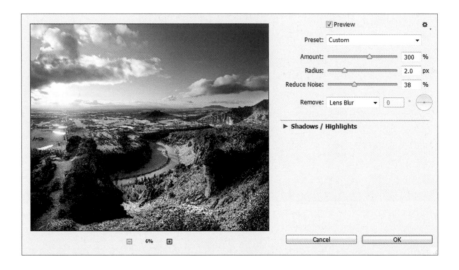

SMART FILTERS

When it comes to filters, *Smart* is just another way of saying nondestructive. You can edit the settings of Smart Filters at any time after applying them to a layer or remove them entirely without permanently changing the underlying layer. You can apply Smart Filters to Smart Objects only, however, so you must first convert your layer to a Smart Object. To do so, choose Filter > Convert for Smart Filters. Once the layer you wish to filter is a Smart Object, Photoshop will consider almost any filter you apply to be

a Smart Filter (and create a separate mask, thumbnail, and Visibility icon for the filters being applied to the layer in the Layers panel).

Be aware, however, that a few filters, such as Liquify, Vanishing Point, and some of the newer specialized blurs in CS6 and CC, cannot be applied as Smart Filters. Still, for the rest of the goodies packed within the Filter menu, clicking on Convert for Smart Filter is the nondestructive way to go—the smart way to go!

(A)

- Click and hold on the Preview image to the left of the sliders to see its original state, then release to see the effect of the current Smart Sharpen settings. This is great for toggling a fast before-and-after comparison.

- Use the Remove drop-down menu to specify the type of blur you're trying to remove. In most cases, the Gaussian or Lens Blur setting works best. When you need to sharpen away some camera motion, choose Motion Blur and set the Rotation dial angle using the line running through the center as a reference for the direction the motion blur is smearing (this fills in the Angle field automatically). From there, adjust the Amount slider until motion is looking a little more stationary (**FIGURES 4.11A** and **B**). Note that this does not perform miracles on unholy amounts of motion blur—it's smart, not omnipotent.

FIGURES 4.11A and **B** Fix mild motion blur with the motion blur removal option; set your angle that the blur is smearing, and work with the Amount slider until satisfied. Compare the results (b) with the original image (a), which contains a small amount of diagonal motion blur as I didn't have a tripod with me.

(B)

Reduce Noise

When compositing images from sources of notice-able quality and other differences, the Reduce Noise filter is one more handy tool in your seamless editing belt. Consistency is important for overall continuity and making those puzzle pieces blend without a trace is the challenge. Digital noise is often a hidden trip wire in underexposed images. Noise is a term used for random-ized bits of unwanted visual static. Noise occurs from taking pictures that have boosted the amplitude of the sensor's signal (results of a higher camera ISO), usually for low light situations (Chapter 5 discusses this in more detail).

There's not a whole lot to this filter, but the Reduce Noise filter does help with this noise challenge by leveling out some of the bits of contrast and static generated from sharpening a grainy image or getting rid of high camera ISO complications. Typically though, I use this filter for concentrating just on color noise (what I find to be the most important part to focus on), randomized bits of color in particular, as those are easy enough to get rid of without too many consequences such as blurring the layer (**FIGURES 4.12A** and **B**).

(A)

(B)

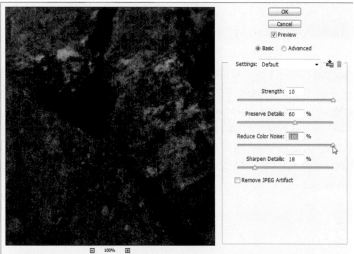

FIGURES 4.12A and **B** The Reduce Noise filter works especially well for terrible color noise generated from lightening an underex-posed or high-ISO image; here you can see the color noise in the lightened shadows of the rocks (a) being reduced (b).

Blurs

Ever notice a full sense of depth created from an image using a shallow depth of field? Some parts of the image blur as they get closer or further away. The tendency to focus our attention in just the right areas and create a sense of depth or motion are particularly helpful abilities of the various blur filters. Ever try to simulate a longer exposure with a motion blur? Photoshop CC and CS6 come with some fantastic blurs for a wide range of uses, from simulating tilt-shift lenses to natural-looking lens blurs (**FIGURE 14.13**).

FIGURE 4.13 Three blurs living under one roof is a helpful feature for getting just the right blur to an image.

The Three Latest Blurs

The three newest blur filter additions, the Tilt-Shift Blur, Iris Blur, and Field Blur, are linked together within the same dialog window and offer a wide range of control and blurring effects. The most powerful and useful for my own workflow is the Radial Blur, but here's a little information about each:

> **WARNING** All three new blurs are currently destructive edits. You cannot apply them to Smart Objects, so always make a copy of the layer you want to blur, just as a backup (Ctrl/Cmd+J).

- Tilt-Shift Blur provides a nice mirrored gradient transition of blurring, much like the shallow depth of field when shooting something small, such as a miniature model set. This can be a nice effect for those images with easy to see distances and without obstructions (**FIGURE 4.14**).

- Field Blur enables you to change the blur and sharpness. Very similar to the traditional Gaussian blur filter, Field blur allows you to set multiple blur pins each with their own amount of blur controlled independently. This is especially valuable for moments of variable blurring of a layer—such as an actual field blur simulation.

FIGURE 4.14 Tilt-Shift provides an interesting miniature look to an image making even the largest vistas feel more like a macro shot.

- Iris Blur is similar to the Field blur, but one-ups it with control and some added slick features. Rather than giving a general blur (like Field blur) and a location to apply it, this blur lets you shape it as an oval! You can set both the iris radius (oval size) and orientation while also indicating the area it begins to transition from sharp to blurry (**FIGURE 4.15**). When working with Iris blur you can also edit multiple features just within the preview area. For example, click and hold the default center focus pin to drag it to a new location, or you can add additional focus pins by clicking elsewhere in the image. Click the outer blur area ring to expand and rotate the Iris radius where the full amount of the blur-ring pixel radius is applied in force (**FIGURE 4.16**). The four middle points help you adjust the inside ring that stays absent of blur (called the Sharp area).

> **TIP** When using Iris Blur, Alt/Opt-drag the inner focus pins to move just one isolated point at a time (rather than the default linked set of all four). Some-times it's best to have the sharpness area extended in one direction a little more than another, and rather than making another focus pin, you can simply move one of the inner sharpness points for this.

BLURRING BEGINS HERE

FULL BLUR RADIUS IS APPLIED FROM HERE ON

FIGURE 4.15 The Iris Blur filter lets you control where blur starts and how dramatic the transition is from being sharp to the full blur amount (set by the Radius slider).

LOCATION OF BLUR PIN

BLUR RADIUS AMOUNT

MULTIPLE PIN LOCATIONS

FIGURE 4.16 Iris Blur is wonderfully versatile as you can control the location of the blur, the severity of the blur, and several other customized options, as well as having multiple blur locations all on one layer.

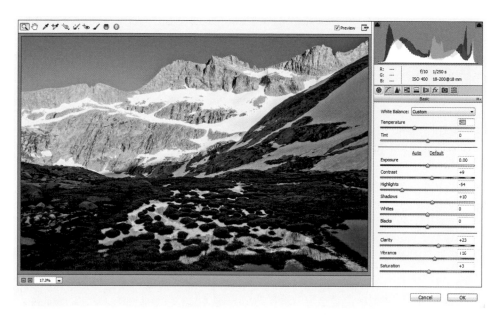

FIGURE 4.17 The Camera RAW editor is unparalleled as the newest Smart Filter; all the sliders and editing interface combined with the potential of working in Photoshop's layer environment—just brilliant.

Filter with Camera Raw Editor

The Camera RAW Editor enables you to make nondestructive adjustments on RAW images for everything from color temperature, lights and shadow, clarity, to specialized curves and other color control elements. Chapter 5 will highlight some of the key features of editing in RAW, but no discussion of useful filters would be complete without mentioning you can use the Adobe Camera Raw (ACR) Editor as a Smart Filter (**FIGURE 4.17**).

Conclusion

With these four adjustment layers and a handful of filters, you can do nearly all the major edits needed for seamless work—from matching any layer's look with another to synching lights, darks, and color. You can correct a multitude of discrepancies and even improve the overall look and feel of a composite with greater depth or motion. As you will see in later chapters, these adjustment layers and filters will help tremendously in just about any situation.

NOTE Even though the ACR interface is the same as that for editing RAW files, the filter is not a complete RAW Editor replacement. Using this filter may not have the same flexibility (such as when working with JPEG files), as the information in the files it will be working with is much more limited in general than in an unprocessed RAW file.

CHAPTER 5

Photography and Compositing

COVERED IN THIS CHAPTER

- Types of cameras
- Camera accessories
- Manual exposure controls
- Editing RAW files in Photoshop's ACR editor
- Shooting various subjects for a composite archive
- Lighting strategies for a composite

▶ ETHEREAL, 2008

Photography is the backbone to compositing, and there's nothing like shooting all your own material for a project. It gives you total control over your creativity, so you are not bound by the parameters or dependency of always using stock photography. Consider *Ethereal* (at right) for example. Shooting my own clouds and manually controlling the exposure for each shot enabled me to expose for exactly what was needed in each cloud—it all added up in the end. Whether you use a point-and-shoot to capture texture images or a DSLR for important subjects, having complete control over the process will help you improve the quality of your composites and save editing time by taking the best photographs possible. This chapter covers some basic manual exposure mechanics and provides strategies for photographing with the composite in mind. Build a quality photo archive, and you'll be ready for any imaginary possibility.

Types of Cameras

There are countless types and varieties of cameras out there these days, from easy point-and-shoot models to fully controllable DSLRs. Smartphones now offer built-in gadgetry and optics that may rival many early-generation DSLR camera bodies. And technologies are continually getting more impressive. The options can be overwhelming. If you are poised to purchase a new image-capture device for composite work, knowledge of your options and their strengths will help you determine how each relates to your needs. Categorizing digital cameras is an

ever-moving target with hybrids of already hybridized varieties—Smartphones with replaceable and add-on lenses, full-frame compact system cameras, and so on. You'll be able to make sense of them all, however, once you understand the three basic categories:

- Simple point-and-shoot cameras

- Compact system, or bridge, cameras

- Digital single-lens reflex (DSLR) cameras

The sections that follow will examine some of the ins and outs of your general camera body options, specifically in relation to composite work.

Point and Shoot

Point-and-shoot cameras are easily portable and fully automated, which makes them great for spur-of-the-moment shots and grabbing textures nearly anywhere any time. They're also handy for getting an entire day-lit scene, such as a landscape, perfectly in focus. Smartphone cameras are improving at both of these tasks, but are still on the lower end of the point-and-shoot scale. For seriously heavy uses, I prefer a dedicated camera with its better focus (such as macro possibilities), optical zoom, memory options, battery life, and processing times. Nearly a third of the shots I end up using for a composite are taken with a dedicated point-and-shoot camera. They are just so great at getting everything in the straightforward scene crisp and clear, which makes for very useful source imagery. For example, I took **FIGURE 5.1A** with my point-and-shoot camera, capturing the full depth of the scene nice and sharp for later use in a fantasy landscape composite (**FIGURE 5.1B**).

Standard basic model point and shoots are limited by the very things that make them quick and easy: their fixed lens and lack of manual control for exposure (although many high-end point and shoots do offer increasing

(A)

(B)

FIGURES 5.1A and **B** Point-and-shoot cameras are designed to make an image look good with little to no effort; I snagged this shot (a) on my little Canon PowerShot SD1000 while hiking in Switzerland and used the water and rocks for a fantasy landscape composite (b).

exposure control now). In general though, point and shoots just don't have the range of creative flexibility as the other camera types because they're designed primarily for quickly and easily capturing memory snapshots. If, for example, you need a very specific background shot of, say, an indoor scene containing high amounts of contrast and at a certain shutter speed, these may not be the cameras for the job. You'll need at the very least either a bridge camera or better yet, a DSLR. Even the entry-level DSLRs and advanced bridge cameras allow for pretty wonderful flexibility and control with focus and exposure—plus RAW capabilities. Where point and shoots excel is for stocking up on textures to fill your archive. I always have one on me just in case I come across something with potential.

> **TIP** Make the most of your point and shoot by regularly using the few quick settings it does provide, such as the macro (usually a flower symbol), action shooting (a person running), and landscape (mountains) modes. These are designed to optimize the exposure quality for each specific type of shot (but may restrict other settings, such as shooting in RAW).

Compact and Bridge Cameras

Positioned between point-and-shoot cameras and DSLRs in both camera size and capabilities, this category is simply exploding with variety. Compact, or bridge, cameras are also a perfect fit for many compositors, offering more flexibility than a point-and-shoot or Smartphone camera, but less intimidating complexity in regards to gear and price than a DSLR. Bridge cameras function much like their big brother DSLRs in regards to features and settings, but are mirror-less relying just on the display screen rather than a traditional viewfinder. Although many of these cameras still have a fixed lens, loads of new hybrids combine interchangeable lens capabilities with point-and-shoot sleekness. These are truly the best of both worlds if you aren't shooting at a professional level but still want to capture a wide range of quality imagery, often with RAW and full-frame capabilities. Simply put, this is an awesome balance of manual control and fast-and-easy shooting.

> **NOTE** Each kind of camera has a different size category of sensor, which affects not just megapixel capabilities, but image quality as well. Full-frame sensors are larger (as their name implies) than the other standard sizes, such as the APS-C sensor in my Canon 7D, and generally capture higher quality images. To learn more, I recommend Ben Long's *Complete Digital Photography* (Cengage Learning PTR, 2012) for a full breakdown of sensors, lenses, and the rest—plus just about everything you'd ever need to know about digital photography.

DSLR Cameras

Digital single lens reflex cameras, more commonly known as DSLRs, provide the ultimate creative control. Their most obvious feature is their ability to support multiple lens sizes and types for all kinds of situations. Equally important, DSLRs give you incredibly easy manual control over aperture, shutter speed, focusing, color balance, and more. For the best of both worlds, many offer camera-assisted modes that enable you to manually control aperture or shutter speed while the camera optimizes other settings (although this ability is no longer exclusive to DSLRs). I use my DSLR to capture the key components of any composite, especially for shooting subjects and wildlife, which often require both creativity and better control (and quality).

For instance, with a DSLR you have the potential to get much better optics as mentioned, but also a larger f-stop range, and a larger sensor in most cases, along with better processing power, autofocusing options, and metering capabilities (not to mention no shutter lag). In short, I personally could not get along without a DSLR of some kind, but these cameras are not your run-of-the-mill, snatch-and-grab image takers. They require a little time to adjust before shooting and are impossible to hide while out in public; everyone around you will take note of your shooting. The primary benefits of creativity and control are well worth the extra time and weight to me. Like a skilled painter choosing various paints and brushes for just the right creative situation and look, we as photographers can choose just the right creative settings for exposure controls, focus, and post-production capabilities by shooting in RAW with a DSLR camera. **FIGURE 5.2** shows the kind of base image you can capture with a DSLR and telephoto lens; this could be a good setup for any number of composites and was shot on an APS-C size sensor exposing specifically for the highlights of the clouds. Having this kind of DSLR control is especially helpful in getting the kind of look and material you need to build your composites.

Which Is Best for Composite Work?

If you can afford it, consider dual camera ownership: a high-end point and shoot for unobtrusive, spur-of-the-moment image capture and a powerful DSLR for circumstances when you need increased control and data. In most cases, a point and shoot won't slow you down with lens cap fiddling, sensor cleaning, full manual control over aperture or shutter-speed control adjustments, or focus ring twisting, so you may be more likely to use it frequently and, therefore, capture more potential variety as it goes where you go all the time as its meant to fit in your pocket or bag. When you're not in a hurry and need

FIGURE 5.2 Shooting with a Canon 7D DSLR camera provides a range of lens capabilities and exposure controls, as well as RAW files for more post-production editing flexibility.

to execute an exact exposure, mood, or other creative flare, turn to your DSLR, which will offer all the control you need. If the point and shoot is your sketching charcoal, a DSLR is the fully stocked painting studio.

If you're on a budget, however, and must choose just one camera for all kinds of composite work, a bridge camera has the potential to meet a range of needs. If you're considering one, make sure it captures in RAW format. Being able to shoot RAW images opens up a range of flexibility and quality control that leaves mere JPEGs in the digital dust.

Whatever direction you may be leaning towards, definitely consult reviews and side-by-side comparisons. Digital Photography Review (www.dpreview.com), for example, has all the latest specs, reviews, and comparisons you could ask for. Also I highly recommend visiting your local photography store to get a hands-on feel for equipment; what may sound nice as a technical stat list, just may not be intuitive to you in the hand.

Lenses and the Effects of Sensor Sizes

Your choice of lens can affect the image you capture as much as your choice of camera—as can the size of the sensor. Measured in millimeters, lenses excel at different tasks depending on their size, or *focal length*. For example, short focal-length lenses, such as 8mm to 18mm on my Canon 7D (APS-C sensor), are best for wide-angle shots, while focal lengths of 70mm and longer are designed for telephoto work. When considering what size or how many lenses you need, keep a few guidelines in mind:

- Normal lenses (35mm for APS sensors, 50mm for full frame, as the full frames crop the image less) are those that closely resemble how our eyes naturally see the scene. These are great when you want to capture an image that makes viewers feel as if they were actually there or at least looking at the scene through a window.

- Wide-angle lens (8mm to 18mm, 15mm to 28mm for full frame) arc useful when you're shooting in tighter spaces and simply can't cram everything into the scene otherwise. A wider angle of view allows for greater flexibility with what can be included within the frame. To capture all the elements I wanted to be included in the background of the composite in **FIGURE 5.3**, I needed a 15mm lens with me and my gear shoved into the corner. These kinds of lenses are also good for developing a certain stylization, because the images may appear slightly distorted and warped looking. Be prepared to shoot with a wide-angle lens if you are matching another shot that was clearly also shot with a wide angle. Matching the focal length measurement does wonders for the final product. When the focal lengths of source images don't match, our eyes may

FIGURE 5.3 When you don't have enough room in a scene to capture everything you need, shooting with a wider angle lens like this 15mm on a APS-C (not full-frame) grabs just enough to make it workable.

not know exactly *what* is wrong with the composite, but they will definitely pick up that *something* is wrong!

- Telephoto or long lenses (70mm and larger) magnify parts of a scene for a zoomed in look, as in Figure 5.2. Telephoto lenses are especially handy for capturing distant subjects or far away details that you intend to add into a scene at a similarly distanced placement. A telephoto lens lets you get nice and close without scaring off the wildlife, for example (or getting eaten).

Even when captured through the same lens size, images still can have a different field of view depending on whether or not you have a full-frame sensor camera body or not. Full-frame cameras have a larger sensor area and can capture the full image being brought in by the lens, whereas the APS-C sensor like my 7D (not full frame) more or less crops the image because of the smaller sensor size. Cameras such as point and shoots (and especially those in camera phones) often have much smaller sensors, and therefore typically can't compete with quality compared to the larger sensor sizes.

> **TIP** If you can afford the expense, high-quality lenses are definitely worth their typically heavy weight, especially lenses with low-light capabilities (f-stops close to 1.4). Called fast lenses, these can still shoot fast shutter speeds even in low light, providing greater shooting capabilities for a range of lighting scenarios.

Control Exposure

Buying a bridge or DSLR camera is one step towards getting higher quality shots. The other is to break out of Auto mode (meant just for average conditions) and take control of your camera's three fundamental settings: shutter speed, aperture, and ISO. Once you understand each of these, as well as how they work together with *reciprocity* (a give and take more or less of each exposure control), you can customize how your camera captures an image and better gather more effective source material for your composites.

Shutter Speed

The shutter speed setting controls the length of time that your camera's sensor is exposed to light for a shot and is measured in factions of a second (or whole seconds for longer exposures). If you want an image to have motion blur, keep the shutter open for a longer time with a *slower* shutter-speed setting (such as 1/4 of a second). For example, nighttime photographs of star trails across the sky and silky-looking running water shots (**FIGURE 5.4**) both

▶ **FIGURE 5.4** Water turns to silky streams of blur when photographed with a slow shutter speed, such as the almost one-second exposure used here.

FIGURE 5.5 At 1/4000 of a second, there's not much a fast shutter speed can't catch clean and sharp.

use slow shutter speeds for long exposures (hours long for the night shot). Likewise, if you want a sharper image, say to catch a bird's wings in mid-flap as in **FIGURE 5.5**, shoot with a faster shutter speed (faster than 1/125 for capturing moderate motion). Depending on the camera and subject matter, settings slower than 1/60 of a second (often shown on the camera as just 60), may produce some motion blur during hand-held shooting on most stock lenses and setups. (If you have rock-solid hands,

however, you may be able to get a decently sharp image with 1/30 of a second on certain camera setups.) To avoid accidental motion blur, either use a tripod or increase your shutter speed if light and other exposure settings allow it (such as changing aperture, ISO, or both).

TIP If your lens (or camera body) offers image stabilization (sometimes called optical stabilization), use it for those times that you must have a slower shutter-speed to get the exposure you want. This will let you shoot at slower speeds for hand-held shots for instance, but won't let you freeze action in the same way as a faster shutter speed. Also, be sure to take off the image stabilization when shooting a single scene to be composited in multiple shots because they may be cropped slightly differently from one another otherwise.

Aperture

Think of the aperture setting as the size of the pupil of the camera lens' eye. Dilated, wide pupils let in a lot of light; constricted, smaller pupils allow less. The area of light being let in is based on the size of the aperture radius, which allow us to control the *depth of field* of an image, meaning how much of the image is in focus. When a narrow fulcrum of light passes through the aperture opening of the lens it provides a greater depth of field, meaning everything near and far is nice and sharp. A wider area of light passing through the aperture produces a shallower depth of field, meaning only one single distance is in focus; this is because there is a wider splay of light rays being focused on the sensor, reducing the depth of field as only some of those rays can be fully brought in focus.

Measured in *f-stops*, the aperture setting enables you to control the depth of field in your shot (**FIGURES 5.6A and B**). A large f-stop number, such as f/22, means a

(A)

(B)

FIGURES 5.6A and **B** Smaller aperture diameters, such as f/11 used in 5.6a, put your entire scene in pretty good focus; larger aperture diameters, such as f/4 used in 5.6b, provide a narrower depth of field, focusing tightly on near subjects and blurring beyond.

smaller aperture size (so less of an area for light to pass through) and a greater depth of field. Conversely, a low f-stop, such as f/1.4, has a larger aperture (letting in a larger area of light) and only a narrow distance from the lens is perfectly sharp.

> **NOTE** An f-stop refers to the focal length of the lens (say a 50mm lens) divided by the aperture diameter measured in millimeters. So a 50mm lens with an aperture diameter set to 25mm wide is a ratio of 1:2 and is known simply as f/2 (focal length over 2).

In general though, when you need to let in more light to the camera, you have the option of a longer exposure (shutter speed, which controls motion blur), or changing the aperture's f-stop, which controls depth of field—so it is always a trade off (such as when shooting indoors without a lot of available light).

ISO

The third fundamental setting is ISO, which controls the camera's light sensitivity by boosting the signal from the sensor before it gets recorded. The higher the ISO number, the more boosting effect on the signal. Increasing light sensitivity in this way, however, comes at the price of *noise*, small, unwanted bits of randomized light and color contrast visible in your image. Low ISO settings, such as 100 to 200, produce less noise, while higher settings, such as 1600 and above produce greater amounts of noise (because the faint noise of the sensor is boosted along with the desirable parts of the signal as well). When available light is especially low and changing the shutter speed or aperture would cause too much blur, you can try changing the ISO to get the shot you want (**FIGURE 5.7**).

FIGURE 5.7 I raised the ISO to 1600 to get the proper exposure of the stars. Thankfully, the resultant noise almost blends in with the stars.

Master the Exposure Trinity

Mastering the exposure triangle of shutter speed, aperture, and ISO is all about *reciprocity* balancing of the ways we control a properly exposed image. To attain the right look and exposure, you must achieve the proper ratio of give and take among the three exposure controls, which together are called the *exposure trinity*.

Assuming you have a properly exposed image when looking at your camera's light meter (you can see mine in **FIGURE 5.8**), if you then change one of the three exposure controls, you must compensate by changing another to retain the same good exposure reading (reciprocity).

SHUTTER SPEED

LIGHT METER

F-STOP

ISO

FIGURE 5.8 Here's a shot of what my own manual exposure controls look like on the Canon 7D with a properly exposed and very well-lit scene.

My Canon 7D, like many cameras, operates in 1/3 stops, meaning if I move the dial controlling the shutter speed one dial click for a faster shutter speed, the camera's light meter shows that the exposure moves by one-third of a full stop to the left (saying I am under-exposed by 1/3 stop) and tells me I need to change either my aperture one click or my ISO by one click to compensate for the shift in shutter speed. This is the idea of reciprocity, change and compensation.

> **NOTE** Each camera maker has their own set intervals between stops that may be different than my own setup—so definitely read the manual of whatever camera you have.

Here's where the fun strategy comes into play and why it's always a give and take. If you want an image with greater depth, you will need a high f-stop and will have to compensate with slower shutter speed to let in a longer amount of light (reciprocity). Now let's just say though that there's a complication and you also have to freeze some moderate motion in this shot. Now you need both a higher f-stop (for depth) as well as a faster shutter speed (for frozen motion), both of which restrict the amount of light hitting the sensor—so then you may have to resort to boosting your ISO to compensate for both of the others (but sacrifice quality by adding more grain to the shot). Makes perfect sense, eh?

Although straightening out the exposure trinity may sound a bit complicated at first, there are many resources out there that can help you get a full grasp on the concept of exposure and reciprocity. For example, I recommend starting with Jeff Revell's *Exposure: From Snapshots to Great Shots* (Peachpit, 2014). Exposure control is really the power of complete image control and makes all the difference for ensuring you are getting what you need—and is well worth learning!

Accessories

Some accessories are nearly just as important as your camera for getting good material for your composites. Here's a very brief breakdown of my favorites and how they can help raise your shooting from adequate to stellar.

Tripods Stand on Their Own

Get your hands and camera on a solid tripod for those moments when you need a sharp and controlled image. In low light, for example, a tripod is invaluable; with its added stability, you can take a longer exposure (because you don't have camera motion as with handheld shots), avoid noise, and still get away with a decent depth of field. As you shop, keep a few tips in mind:

- **Levelers and a locking system.** Having your gear smash to the ground defeats the whole stability advantage. Look for a tripod head rated for your camera's weight that also has easy and secure ways to lock it down. Levels on the head ensure you get the straight shot you want.

- **Soft padding grips on the legs.** Put grips on your tripod if you are planning to shoot scenes outside in the cold for hours at a time. Touching a bare metal tripod may seem like a minor thing, but believe me, shooting in the cold can suck the heat right out of you (**FIGURE 5.9**).

- **Balance weight and stability.** Make sure you choose a tripod that's both light enough to carry a distance, yet sturdy enough for rugged use and the weight of your camera and lens. The material that a tripod is made

FIGURE 5.9 Hiking through the snow to shoot scenes like this in the middle of nowhere requires a combination of rugged and smart gear; foam grips on my tripod's top legs makes setting up in the cold easier.

out of matters a great deal in terms of cost, weight, and strength, so be sure to get one that suits your needs. Metal tripods can often have greater stability, but do weigh more, while carbon fiber tripods can be packed to just about any high peak.

- **Tripod heads.** Where the camera attaches and balances on the tripod is also important. Something that I find invaluable in a tripod is a quick release system for fast attaching and release for moments that I want to switch to hand-held shooting. Also having levelers on the head itself is invaluable for getting your image looking level without the need to crop in post-production. I find having handles for tightening and loosening the head rotation comes in handy for fine finessing where the camera is pointing and oriented.

Intervalometers and Filters

An intervalometer is handy for those times you simply don't have enough hands to do it all. Basically, an *intervalometer* is just a remote trigger with a built-in timer. More powerful than the simple timer function of your DSLR, these devices can shoot in steady intervals, leaving you free to be in front of the camera posing for or positioning source elements. For example, every floating object in **FIGURE 5.10**, as well as those in the composites in Chapters 7 and 11 were taken as separate shots using an inexpensive intervalometer connected to my DSLR on a tripod.

Filters can also be helpful accessories. For example, a polarizer does a wonderful job of cutting glare and minor reflections. A decent quality UV protection filter for each lens is also a fairly important but minor investment if you plan to do crazy outdoor excursions for a lot of your shooting. When shooting hazardous environments, whether hiking in the mountains or avoiding ferocious pets, I've seen these little filters continually

FIGURE 5.10 Automate your picture taking by attaching an intervalometer to your DSLR; here you can see mine working with my Canon 7D setup.

save expensive lenses as they take the hit or the grit, dust, mud, and so on—keeping the expensive lens glass behind it nice and safe.

Edit in Adobe Camera Raw

As mentioned earlier, shooting in RAW format allows for unparalleled nondestructive flexibility. The Adobe Camera Raw (ACR) editor in Photoshop enables you to easily and efficiently work nondestructively with various unprocessed file formats from all the major camera brands. (Each manufacturer uses its own proprietary variation of storing the same RAW data, as you remember from Chapter 1.) To access the ACR editing window, first browse for the image or images using Adobe Bridge (always a good place to start with photographs in general). Double-clicking a selection of RAW images will ferry them quickly into the RAW editor, which is a default part of Photoshop but more like an anteroom. As mentioned in the previous chapter, Photoshop now has the ability in CC versions to access ACR editing environment as a Smart Filter—which opens the door for all kinds of new workflows and possibilities.

NOTE If you have the latest camera but an earlier Photoshop, you may need to download a camera RAW update for Photoshop. Sometimes camera manufacturers release their hardware before Adobe releases a patch to work with the data from them, so you may have to wait out a delay of a couple months for the best support. A workaround is converting all files to DNG first, then you can edit in the ACR editor.

FIGURE 5.11 shows the Photoshop CC version of the ACR editing environment—don't worry if your version looks different. Sliders frequently change both name and position with each version, but even so, most of the capabilities stay the same.

FIGURE 5.11 The ACR is perfect for such critical adjustments as exposure, white balance, and color. This image was originally a little underexposed and lacked contrast and strong color, so moving the sliders around I was able to compensate for the original shot.

Adjust with Sliders

From color temperature to filling in shadows, Adobe Camera Raw (and the RAW format) enables you to edit all of these pieces nondestructively by saving the relevant slider setting and raw editing data in a separate external file called an XMP file with the same file name and .xmp suffix (GreatShot.cr2 and GreatShot.xmp, for example). If you ever make an edit and then want to move the image with the accompanying edits in tow, make sure to grab both files (the RAW file and the XMP) before the great migrating.

I tend to stick to a general workflow of changing color temperature first, then the exposure, next shadows (as I like to fill a bit more detail), highlights, then contrast, and the rest as needed. In this order I can change the main pieces with dependable results and aesthetics that feel balanced. Then I rely on the main editing environment of Photoshop and its layers for the rest of my adjustments. Making a few global edits before jumping into the full application and composite editing, however, is a good practice because you're working with the unprocessed file at this point and, therefore, greatest RAW quality. The sliders I use most are:

- **Temperature.** This setting enables you to cool your image down (slide left) or warm it up (slide right) from the Kelvin light temperature your camera initially set as the white balance when you captured the image (**FIGURE 5.12**). A good practice is to get the white looking fairly white, where they are neither cool nor warm cast. This feature when shooting in RAW basically negates the need for setting white balance on the camera as it can be flawlessly changed in post.

FIGURE 5.12 With the Temperature slider you can compare warm (at 9400K) and cool (at 4500K) versions of the same image.

TIP Use the White Balance Tool ![eyedropper icon] (I) to quickly pick (by clicking on) a white or neutral gray that the ACR can then use as a reference for setting the color temperature slider. This is a good place to start if you are unsure of what temperature to go with.

- **Exposure.** Just as you can set your exposure in the camera, you can also do a bit of fixing after the fact with this slider (**FIGURE 5.13**). Even with highlights slightly blown, setting the exposure a little darker by sliding –1 or –2 to the left may bring back some details. The sensor records more data than is represented visually, and the Exposure slider gives you access to it. The ACR can work in a 16-bit space while JPEGs are limited to 8 bit, meaning there is a far greater amount of information available to work with while editing (seen most clearly in exposure range and variation subtlety).

FIGURE 5.13 Before I adjusted the Exposure slider to +1.35, this shot was just a bit underexposed and muddy looking.

- **Contrast.** This slider adjusts the image contrast, and I tend to use it after adjusting my shadows and highlights. This way I get the details I want in the image, then I make them pop with a bit of added contrast.

- **Highlights.** With this slider you can lower just the highlights, rather than adjusting the overall exposure when an image is just slightly blown. This can help bring in some details without affecting any of the other tones of the image. For instance, the first RAW example image in Figure 5.10 had just a few cloud highlights that were running a little hot for my taste, so I lowered them by dragging the Highlights slider left. This is a pretty big deal as this only works with RAW images specifically.

- **Shadows.** This slider is invaluable for getting some additional post-production fill light on shadowed areas. Sometimes photographing in high-contrast situations can't be helped during a shoot, but playing with the Shadows slider (previously called the Fill slider) can help bring back some needed shadow detail.

> **TIP** If you know you will be shooting in a high-contrast environment and using the Shadows slider for bringing back details within the shadow, make sure you are shooting with as low an ISO as possible. Boosting shadows will also boost the noise within them.

- **Whites and Blacks.** These two sliders adjust the white and black points of the image, respectively. I don't usually touch these much unless an image is not even close to reaching full black or white. In effect, you can create more contrast with these sliders, but with more precision and isolation than the Contrast slider provides.

- **Clarity.** This setting can soften an image by reducing clarity (sliding to the left), or you can increase the slider to make a high dynamic range (HDR) effect. Essentially, the setting creates contrast on an area-by-area scale, which is great for wringing an extra feel of grit out of textures or making shadows and contours of an object more dramatic. Use it sparingly, however, as the effect rapidly starts looking a bit wacky and over-stylized (**FIGURE 5.14**).

(A)

(B)

Clarity	0
Vibrance	+75
Saturation	−15

FIGURE 5.14 Increasing Clarity on a RAW image uses the deeper bit depth (larger gamut of lights and darks) to add localized contrast (similar to the idea and look of mild HDR); this often results in noticeable halos around edges such as the tree line here.

FIGURES 5.15A and **B** Alter the sky's hue intensity by first decreasing the Saturation slider, then increasing the Vibrance slider to compensate for a more general area saturation effect.

- **Saturation and Vibrance.** These two sliders often work in tandem; you might take out a little bit of saturation (the hue intensity of individual pixels), and then increase the Vibrance slider slightly to compensate. Vibrance similarly affects the hue intensity, but on more of a general level, looking at groups of similar color. Rather than changing the saturation of each pixel's color, the Vibrance slider looks at areas that have color in common and increases the saturation of those colors only. Consider the sky in **FIGURE 5.15**, for example, which is made up of a variety of differing colors that add up. This pair of sliders can generally help with creating a color-consistent look to an image: Lower the saturation by, say −30, and increase the vibrancy to compensate for the desaturation. The result is smoother and averaged color that I find works well for larger areas.

TIP Once you get a single shot edited the way you want, you can save the settings as a preset to apply to other images from the same shoot just from doing it the one time. Click the Presets tab ▤ and click the Create New icon ▯ to create a new preset. Name it something memorable and descriptive, then press OK. Apply as many times as you want (even to large groups of selected images all at once).

Other ACR Features

Beyond the sliders, the ACR window holds quite a few sweet features, which will help you improve workflow and image quality before syncing the image into the composite. Below the histogram on the right of the window, the ACR provides a strip of icons (**FIGURE 5.16**). The first icon ⊚ displays the tab of sliders just discussed, which is the default view. Click the Curves icon ▦ to do a preliminary Curves adjustment to the image using a control similar but more refined to the version available as an adjustment layer within Photoshop. The Sharpening icon ▲ opens the sharpening controls, which are quite helpful for some images with a slight amount of blur to them. Although it can't work miracles, it offers a large degree of sharpening flexibility that's not afforded within a Photoshop adjustment layer. Always apply and adjust sharpening first in this nondestructive RAW setting.

FIGURE 5.16 Click these icons to access and adjust various categories of settings within the ACR editor.

NOTE You can still apply ACR settings to many images, even if they are not similarly shot, say they were from different scenes. Although it is possible to do this, the images may not look that great as each most likely started with a different look to them, and changing a slider for one may do something far different to the look of another.

Now here's the true workflow godsend of working with the ACR and Adobe Bridge: batch processing! For example, you can select all the thumbnails (either inside folders or collections) for an entire shoot's worth of images within Bridge and open them all together within ACR. Once within the ACR window, if all your images from the shoot were shot with the same settings and scene (preferably), press Ctrl/Cmd+A to select and edit all the images at once (or alternatively click the Select All icon [Select All] in the upper-left corner of the window). ACR applies every slider adjustment to all selected images involved, creating XMP files for each within the shoot's folder.

I like to start by editing an entire shoot as one large selection to get the general scene looking right, then afterwards select individual image thumbnails within the ACR to modify, touch up, and finesse the individual picture. Sometimes a subject moves into different lighting, or something changes slightly even keeping the same camera settings; it's helpful to edit all the images together, then go in and adjust the particular shot.

Shooting for an Archive

It's not always enough to take pictures for just memory or the visually artistic qualities of a scene or subject. Compositing is often its own category of shooting that comes from a combination of the other two, coalescing into a literal fusion of imagery. But building a useful archive of composite-worthy photographs takes some planning and forethought to capturing images that have great potential to be used in a number of situations. Part of this is shooting for not just subjects, but also textures—those strangely isolated water, bark, tree, metal, stucco, and other shots that are nothing overly grand on their own but that combine with other images to help you create a new concept. Shoot more variety than you may feel is necessary, and always consider your POV and how you might capture useful images that can later be combined. While photographing, keep in mind the potential for future masking, cropping, or leaving that extra room in a simple scene to perhaps add things later; the more you do, the better off you will be when that great idea hits you.

For my own archive, I never reject an image (unless it's too poorly exposed to be discernable), because every image has the potential to be useful. So set aside large amounts of storage (and backup) for an archive and follow these tips for shooting for composite work:

FIGURE 5.17 Shoot fire in the dark with a dark background and fast shutter speed that is in the thousandths of a second to avoid blur.

- **Smoke and fire.** Use a fast shutter speed and a dark background to highlight the flames while keeping them clear and sharp. Put point-and-shoot cameras in Action mode, or increase your DSLR's shutter speed in Manual or Shutter Priority mode (**FIGURE 5.17**). Lingering shutters will produce motion blurring rather than a quick freezing of a moment. For the fire images in Chapters 8 and 10, I simply waited until night for a nice dark setting, then took fast exposures of a log dosed in lighter fluid.

- **Water.** How you approach this subject depends on whether you're photographing water for texture or water for a subject, such as a lake, river, waterfall, or ocean to place in your composite (**FIGURES 5.18A** and **B**). Sometimes the approach is more of a macro mode way of seeing images (when you need to get close with sharp focus), looking at how the water texture can be applied to other situations. Other times your approach may be looking and shooting the water's big picture flow or resting state. In either case, know whether or not the water is going to be captured moving quickly or slowly, needing great depth, or shallow focus (though usually the more the better as you can simulate focus blur in post production). When shooting fast moving water for texture work, for example, keep your shutter speed just as fast as the water itself. Lighting and time of day will also dramatically change outdoor water shots, so plan ahead to achieve the mood you're after. (If you want Golden Hour light, don't arrive at high noon on a rainy day.) Reflections and coloring also come into play with water, so find the right angle and POV (or just shoot a huge variety to be safe once you start the editing process). When compositing, reflections often have to match fairly closely so try to get a range of reflections that are more or less free of artificially identifiable objects or anything that stands out too much.

- **People.** When photographing people for a composite, keep the intended background image in mind, so you can match the angle of the scene in which they will be placed. Is the background a wide-angle or telephoto shot? If you don't know exactly what the background will be, try to capture images with as little distortion as possible for greater flexibility later. A 35mm lens for an APS-C camera and around a 50mm on a camera with a full-frame sensor will get you started with an image that looks close to normal to the eye.

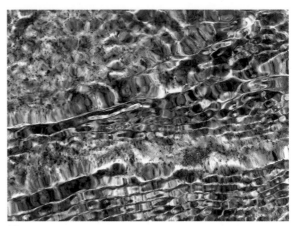

(A)

(B)

FIGURES 5.18A and **B** Take macro shots of water to use as a texture (a), as well as images with greater depth of field so you can use water as a subject in your composites (b).

Give clear direction and feedback to adults and older children modeling for you. Describe the imaginary world of your composite so they can see what you see to help remove some of the awkwardness that naturally comes from posing. For example, I told the model featured in **FIGURE 5.19** that a band of marauders with spiked cudgels was in the distance; she immediately reached for the sword and glared at them (beyond the white wall in front of her). A couple variations of this and the shots were perfect for the tutorial project in Chapter 9.

For small children, make a game of things. Capture their attention with toys in the areas you want them to look or reach for. Keep your shutter snapping quickly to capture that moment when the mood aligns. Stay flexible, and make it fun.

- **Buildings.** Variety is crucial; photograph everything from futuristic glass structures to leaning and moss-covered barns. You never know what's going to be that perfect missing piece your future composition needs, so shoot a range of angles and directions. Don't stop with straight-on street views, shoot up from the sidewalk and down off the roof in all types of weather. You never know how the buildings will come in handy—sometimes just for textures and small pieces as seen in Chapter 15 or as a backdrop in Chapter 9. Pay attention to the time of day and the reflections of sky. Because of this, clouds change the look of buildings, as do sunsets; so if you find an interesting building, pick interesting times of the day that bring out its interesting qualities (the golden hour at sundown or sunrise is a good one to start with). I photographed a cityscape during sunrise from atop a tall building, only to later find this lighting and perspective fit perfectly with a picture I took at sunrise from atop Half-Dome in Yosemite National Park. **FIGURE 5.20** shows the composite that resulted.

FIGURE 5.19 Whether your subjects are adults or children, get them playing and imagining with you; your shots will come out much stronger for it.

- **Landscapes.** These usually need to stand on their own as background shots; they typically make up the filler when used with outside composites. Shoot with an openness in the scene that has the potential for adding in other elements, like filling a spacious room with furniture. Shoot with a high numbered f-stop to make sure the entire view is in focus. You can always blur after the fact, but you can't always take out blurring that occurs in the camera.

- **Trees.** One thing about these guys, they sure can hold a pose. When photographing them, consider your point of view and lighting, which can change their look dramatically. If you already have a composite scene in mind, move around to match it. I shot the tree in **FIGURE 5.21** from a nearby hill, for example, to capture a slightly higher vantage point and make it look right for the rest of the project demonstrated in Chapter 16. If you don't have a project in mind, give yourself flexibility by capturing a variety of images—also shooting in flat lighting whenever possible will let you paint more of your own desired lighting while editing.

- **Skies.** The perfect sky rarely pairs with the perfect landscape when I'm in the perfect position to photograph it, so I collect them separately and composite them together. Tilt your head back and take pictures of interesting clouds and skies any time you see them—cloud formations, rainbows, dramatic storm fronts, captivating sunsets. Sunsets come in handy for a variety of compositing uses, from color palettes and blending mode effects, to boring sky replacements. High-contrast scenarios such as sunsets and even highlights on clouds can be hard to get right. One strategy is to always expose for the brightest elements. With a point and shoot you can usually do this by holding the trigger button partly while pointing it fully at the

FIGURE 5.20 Shooting buildings from various perspectives, even high up from the vantage of another building, as well as at unique times of the day lends itself for greater potential for an interesting shot as a backdrop.

FIGURE 5.21 Trees at least stay still, but need a good amount of coverage like buildings as lighting and POV changes the look dramatically.

FIGURE 5.22 Animals don't typically hang around and pose in the ways that you want, so when you see a moment, get as much as you can from it.

brightest area only, then without letting your finger go off the trigger, bring your camera back to the framing you wanted and click the rest of the way down (this of course works with other kinds of cameras as well).

- **Animals.** Whether you are shooting birds, squirrels, or lions, proximity and posing are a challenge. Always be ready, and start snapping the shutter, preferably a fast one, as soon as you encounter interesting wildlife. If you have the opportunity, capture multiple points of view. Peering down from a lofty human height produces a very different effect than the skink-eye-level shot in **FIGURE 5.22**. Remember, wildlife needn't be wild; local zoos, farms, and even rescue shelters can yield the beast, fur, or hide you need.

Light It!

Good lighting means good planning and control, whether it's by choosing the right time of day to photograph outdoors or creating a studio setup. Plan out the right angles to match the look of your shot to the rest of the scene. Good lighting preparation and consistency among your images lends power and credibility to composites.

For example, for the *Nature Rules* composite in Chapter 9, I needed to light and photograph a model (**FIGURE 5.23B**) to composite into an image of Montreal, Quebec, that I'd taken previously (**FIGURE 5.23A**). To help me, I enlisted my friend Jayesunn Krump, an award-winning photographer and lighting expert. We based our plan to light the model on the lighting of the Montreal cityscape, getting just enough fill and key lighting and matching the angles of each (**FIGURE 5.23C**). Taking the lighting direction into account is vital. As Jayesunn explains, "The temperature and color cast can be adjusted in post-production, but you cannot readily change the direction of your light and shadows. Make sure that your shadows all fall in the same direction and are coming from the same relative direction with a consistent intensity."

FIGURES 5.23A, **B**, and **C** Start with an idea or example of the lighting you will be matching and plan accordingly. For *Nature Rules* I used the initial city lighting (a) as a guide for the controlled studio shot (b), so the final composite blended credibly (c).

(A)

(B)

(C)

Diagraming your lighting setup can help you plan a better match. Making a top-down sketch of the lighting is just as important as sketching out your idea of the scene from the point of view of the camera. A view from above allows you to better see the lighting angles, almost as a 2D game of Ping-Pong. It doesn't need to be fancy, just play the angles! For example, **FIGURE 5.24** shows Jayesunn's lighting plan for one of his favorite location shots, *End of the Tunnel*. As he explains it, "I set up a single flash unit with a Rogue FlashBender to camera right and aimed it toward the wall next to my subject. The light was bounced off of the FlashBender and lit up the tunnel wall and the side of the subject. I really like the way the hard light filled the scene and fell off as it traveled down the tunnel."

Once you get the lighting angles arranged, you can adjust the quality of your light with *light modifiers*. Reflectors, diffusors, umbrellas, and even pieces of paper and foil can help modify and control the light to simulate various sources from harsh directional light to soft, nearly shadowless light (and everything in between). If you need to mimic clouds or other soft light, for example, try using diffusers to help spread out the area of the light source and soften the hardness of the shadows created by direct rays of light from a source point. I use an inexpensive 5-in-1 expandable reflector in most cases, but you can use nearly anything to control and shape your ambient light. Even the pros

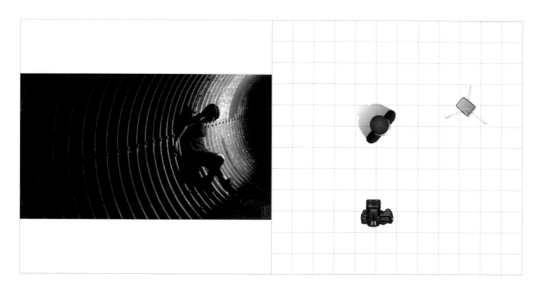

FIGURE 5.24 Whether using a Smartphone app or a paper sketch pad, try planning out the angles of your shot beforehand. This rough plan of Jayesunn's charts the angles from a top-down view.

improvise; Jayesunn recommends inexpensive and readily available white-and-black foam core, because, "the white side makes an excellent reflector and the black is fantastic for soaking up light and deepening shadows." Jayesunn's *Queen of Ruin* in **FIGURE 5.25** is a good illustration of lighting control through modifiers. "Once you have a good grasp of reflectors," he explains, "you can use the same principles to control light from a flash."

Conclusion

Strong composites come from strong photography. Get your source imagery looking good, and that's all there is to it. Okay, that's not quite *all* there is to it, but it's a good size portion of the compositing craft. Get control of your photo equipment, lighting, and RAW files, and photograph everything to build a decent photo archive. If you do, you'll be well prepared for just about any idea that happens to jump in your head. After all, compositing is really an exercise in brain-photography: Capture and convincingly create the image that's in your mind!

FIGURE 5.25 Jayesunn Krump's *Queen of Ruin* is a shot with a precisely controlled and modified light source paired with a modifier to control the lighting absorption and bounce.

SECTION II
TUTORIALS

CHAPTER 6

Prep and Organize Three Projects

COVERED IN THIS CHAPTER

- Making an extensive photo palette
- Creating an automated procedure using actions
- Rating and sorting images in Adobe Bridge
- All file prep work for Chapters 7, 8, and 9

The key to success behind every kind of composite is surprisingly simple: awesome prep work! You've already read how staying organized dramatically increases efficiency and avoids the general mayhem that can accompany a mega-sized editing process. This chapter puts that organizational theory into practice. You will learn about three categories of composites and practice the prep work needed for each. Plus, in doing so you will create the starter files you'll need to complete the hands-on tutorials in Chapters 7, 8, and 9.

Know Your Composite Style

To know how best to prepare for your composite, you need to know a little about the style of composite you're intending to make. I find composites generally fall into three categories, each of which benefits from a different type of prep work:

▶ **FIGURES 6.1A**, **B**, and **C** Whether assembled from images in a photo palette (a, *Fire Play*), shots combined from a stationary point of view (b, *Good Kitty*), or images brought into Photoshop as separate tabs (c, *Nature Rules*), projects benefit from organization and careful prep work before compositing.

- **Complex composites with multi-source layering**, such as images requiring many pieces of textures or wide ranging materials that have to be collected beforehand (**FIGURE 6.1A**). In my setups, these images require a large photo palette. A *photo palette* is a separate file that contains all the components you may include in the composite. From this palette you can then choose an entire image or only a small portion, like selecting and mixing paints on a traditional painter's palette. By arranging all your pieces in one place you can easily view your options before bringing images (or even small pieces of them) into the final composite.

(A)

(B)

(C)

- **Images mostly shot in one scene with similar lighting, positioning, point of view, and so on** (**FIGURE 6.1B**). *Good Kitty* featured in Chapter 7 is a prime example of this as all the shots needed for that project were captured at once, from one position and one lighting setup. *Adobe Bridge* is a better "palette" choice because it gives you better quality side-by-side comparisons and rating capabilities for your images. For these composites, you usually know the shots *will* fit, the question is which shots will have the *best* fit?

- **Composites needing fewer ingredients and layer options, but still assembled from several different sources** (**FIGURE 6.1C**). These composites often aren't worth the time to create a separate photo palette. Instead, search for the choice images using Adobe Bridge and *bring them in as separate tabs* within Photoshop to be used when ready. Document tabs are manageable up to a point in the workspace; my tipping point is once they can no longer be seen easily all at once. These composites are also different from those shot in a single scene because the images may be spread across multiple folders rather than contained all within one folder.

Depending on your own style, you may mostly work within one or two of these categories, but they are all valuable to know how to prepare for as projects are not usually as straight forward as you first thought. From here on, I'll be walking you through my own way of prepping and organizing for each of these composite types. Following along with each will also get you setup with the right files for the next three chapters' tutorials so be sure to get the resources needed and follow my lead here.

NOTE To access the resource files and videos, just log in or join peachpit.com, and enter the book's ISBN. After you register the book, links to the files will be listed on your Account page under Registered Products. For this chapter, you will need three folders of files (Chapter7_Resources, Chapter8_Resources, and Chapter9_Resources), because you are preparing materials for the next three tutorial chapters.

Creating a Photo Palette

For composites that are comprised of many different varieties of images or pieces of images, such as **FIGURE 6.2**, a good workflow strategy is to have all your source images in one Photoshop document area. You can then draw image elements from that document, or *photo palette*, like paints from a traditional artist's palette, picking and choosing the perfect combination. Using a photo palette will also help keep your composite document clutter free, compact, and more manageable overall. Without a palette, you're forced to choose between opening each image individually within Photoshop or bringing all the images into the final composite. Both of these alternatives can produce messy, confusing, and overly cluttered workspaces.

With a photo palette, however, you can easily toggle the visibility of each layer for identification, also see a thumbnail of the image for reference, and have it ready to select pieces from and copied at any moment. Yes, you could bounce back and forth from Photoshop to Adobe Bridge to look at whole images, but you'd also be missing the point as these larger projects sometimes require many smaller pieces and a lot of quick trial work to get the right

FIGURE 6.2 The prep work done in this section will get you ready to jump straight into playing with fire in Chapter 8, so it's well worth the time to do this right and not get burned later on!

NOTE I typically work with two screens and a lot of RAM. This set up makes the photo palette an optimal workflow choice as I have the room to spread out and can easily have two or more large projects open at once. Palettes do take both screen real estate and RAM to work perfectly, but are ideal whenever possible.

The best way to learn is by doing, so in the sections that follow you will work through creating the photo palette you'll need for the tutorial in Chapter 8 on re-creating Figure 6.2. (Be sure to download the Chapter8_Resources folder before you begin.)

Ferry Images into the Photo Palette

When loading a large number of composite elements into your photo palette (such as the fire and smoke images), you can speed up your workflow either by using automated actions from the Actions panel or by using a built-in feature within Adobe Bridge that imports a selection of images from a folder or collection as layers into a single Photoshop file. To use Adobe Bridge, select the images then choose Tools > Photoshop > Load Files into Photoshop Layers. Using the Bridge feature is quick and painless, but at the same time doesn't have quite the flexibility of the actions method. For example, you can't bring in additional selections of images or edit an image individually before quickly bringing it into the palette. The actions method is Photoshop's robotic assembly line. Basically, you record a sequence of steps as an action, assign it a name and keyboard shortcut, and then you can run the action to repeat the entire sequence with a single keystroke. Although both methods require a little preparation, they can also save you huge amounts of time in the long run.

look (just like a real artist's palette). Plus, you'd have to individually bring each image into Photoshop and the composite just to try it out, taking up precious time (even using Mini Bridge). Using a separate photo palette file, you not only keep all your images at your fingertips, you can also automate the process of bringing the images into Photoshop with actions (more on this in a moment).

WHEN TO USE ACTIONS

Actions can help you, but sometimes they offer more power than you need at a higher price of time upfront—why rent an excavator to plant a handful of marigolds? Here are my general rules for moving and copying files into another document:

- Use the Place feature in Adobe Bridge (right click an image then choose Place > Photoshop from the context menu) when you want to bring in one *entire* image (not just a piece of it) into the current composite and as a Smart Object.

- Use the Move tool if you need to move less than three images. This includes dragging the contents of one image to that of another.

- Use the Marquee tool for selecting a piece of an image in Photoshop, then copy (Ctrl/Cmd+C) and paste (Ctrl/Cmd+V) if you need to move between three and seven images.

- Record an *actions* preset if you need to move more than seven images in a row. Using Photoshop's powerful action automation is a workflow godsend for repetitive actions such as this.

To practice, in the following steps you'll create an action to copy and paste images into a *Fire_Play_Photo_Palette.psd* file, which you'll need for Chapter 8. You'll perform the copy and paste steps for the first image, and then afterwards expend no more effort than pressing a single key to bring in each subsequent image. To open the Actions panel, choose Window > Actions menu. Using actions requires very specific steps, so be sure to follow closely. If documents are in a different tab order or something else is clicked on once the actions begin, your results will definitely vary from mine. First, you will arrange your workspace for clean and easy action recording, then you will record the action:

TIP If you prefer, skip using actions by selecting the images in Adobe Bridge then going to Tools > Photoshop > Load Files into Photoshop Layers.

1. In Photoshop, create a new document (Ctrl/Cmd+N) of 8000 x 8000 pixels, so you can comfortably fit several layers side by side for comparison (**FIGURE 6.3**). Name it *Fire_Play_Photo_Palette*, and click the OK button.

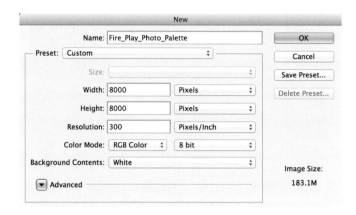

FIGURE 6.3 When creating a photo palette, use large dimensions that allow for enough room to look at several image layers simultaneously and efficiently.

2. Make sure only the new *Fire_Play_Photo_Palette* document is open. If any other documents are open, close them now.

3. In Adobe Bridge, browse to the Chapter8_Resources folder, within it open the Fire folder containing the fire images. Select all the image files (Ctrl/Cmd+A), then press Enter/Return to open them into Photoshop as separate document tabs (**FIGURE 6.4**). Do the same to bring the smoke images into Photoshop; look for the subfolder named Smoke.

> **TIP** If you shot your own fire images in RAW, select all images once again (Ctrl/Cmd+A) in the Adobe Camera Raw editor (ACR) and then click Open (after you finish with RAW edits of course) to bring them all the way into Photoshop as separate document tabs.

4. Without clicking any other document tab, open the original *Fire_Play_Photo_Palette* document using the document selector icon to the right of the tabs (**FIGURE 6.5**).

5. With the photo palette open, select the next document tab to the right of the Fire_Play_Photo_Palette tab. Now you are ready to begin recording a new actions preset.

6. Create a new action by clicking the New Action icon  at the bottom of the Actions panel.

7. In the New Action dialog box that appears, name your action Photo_Palette_Copy_Paste. (Always use descriptive names; they're more helpful for future use.) The Function Key setting enables you to specify a keyboard shortcut to use to replay the action. Choose F9 from the drop-down menu (**FIGURE 6.6**). Take note that if you already have a shortcut set to F9, Photoshop will ask whether you mind bumping it for this new version.

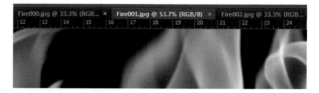

FIGURE 6.4 All open files are usually organized as document tabs beneath the options bar.

FIGURE 6.5 The document selector comes in handy when you just plain run out of room for all those tabs.

FIGURE 6.6 Creating a new action is like setting up a VCR or DVR to record a favorite show.

8. After taking a steadying breath, click the Record button to begin. From here on Photoshop will record every step you take, so be mindful what you click and change!

9. Click the Marquee tool (M), select the entire image (Ctrl/Cmd+A), then copy it (Ctrl/Cmd+C).

10. Close the document to return to the Fire_Play_ Photo_Palette tab (be careful only to close and not click anything else).

11. Paste the copied image into the photo palette by pressing Ctrl/Cmd+V.

12. Click the next tab to the right of the photo palette, and then stop recording your actions by clicking the small Stop button ■ to the left of the red Record button on the Actions panel. Your Actions panel will display your newly recorded action (**FIGURE 6.7**).

13. Try out your new action: Click the Play button in the Actions panel, and Photoshop will load the image from the tab to the right of the Fire_Play_Photo_Palette tab into the photo palette, close the image, and jump to the next image in line! For each new image, simply press the F9 shortcut to load it into the photo palette—workflow optimized, big time!

> **TIP** As a somewhat easier way of playing an action that doesn't require remembering a shortcut or clicking the play button, try turning the designated actions into a button mode display. Go to the Action panel's settings icon ▼≣ and right there at the top of the context menu is the Button mode option. Toggling this will just show the action names as easy to read and click buttons. For editing and other features, turn off the button mode.

FIGURE 6.7 After you record an action, it displays in the Actions panel.

14. Use this action for all remaining fire and smoke images, but remember not to click on any tab in a different order. An inadvertent click will tell the action to jump to where you clicked, which could mean missing an image or loading the wrong document. Don't touch anything besides F9 until all the images are loaded and the palette is the only open document.

Organize the Photo Palette

After you bring all the fire and smoke images into your palette, it's time to do a little housekeeping and optimizing for easier image selection.

1. First, select all the smoke layers in the Layers panel. (Click the *first* smoke layer, hold Shift, then click the *last* smoke layer as this will select everything between the two).

2. Put the layers into a group folder by pressing Ctrl/ Cmd+G, and name the folder Smoke.

3. Repeat step 2 for the fire layers, housing them in a group folder called Fire (**FIGURE 6.8**).

   Clearly labeled group folders can help you more easily find the type of image you need, while the next steps will ensure you can more easily see the fire and smoke images when previewed.

FIGURE 6.8 Organize your photo palette from the beginning by categorizing your images into group folders.

4. Click the white Background layer at the bottom of the layers stack, and press Ctrl/Cmd+I to invert it to black.

5. Still in the Layers panel, select all of the layers minus the background, and change their blending mode to Screen. This allows you to see them all at once as only the lighter portions of each layer are now visible and the darks of each layer are invisible (revisit Chapter 3 for a refresher on this blending mode). Because the darker pixels become increasingly transparent the darker they are, only the firelight remains visible.

6. With only fire or smoke images activated and visible at a time, use the Move tool to spread out the images for wider view of the selections, as in **FIGURES 6.9** and **6.10**.

7. Toggle which layer is active and visible by holding down Alt/Opt and pressing the layer's Visibility icon . This will allow you to see just one layer at a time as a layer solo feature (meaning that only one layer will be visible by itself). The advantage is that no other layers clutter what you are looking at within that one layer. The downside is that you must again Alt/Opt-click the Visibility icon to later re-activate the visibility of the other layers.

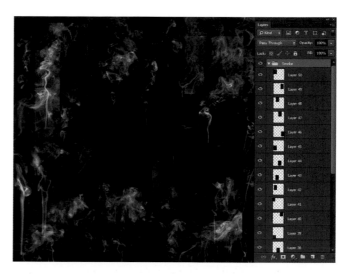

FIGURE 6.9 It's a good idea to separate out each category and scatter the layers for better picking and comparing.

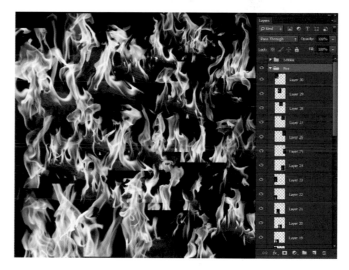

FIGURE 6.10 If the Fire folder is activated and visible, turn off visibility for the contents of the Smoke group folder so as not to get too overwhelmed.

TIP Creating a collection of various files sharing common traits within Adobe Bridge has some advantages. You can then place and view files into this virtual folder (a collection category) without moving any of the original file locations, making the files easy to find across many different folders. Select some initial files to be included within Adobe Bridge and change over to the Collections tab. Click the Create Collections icon 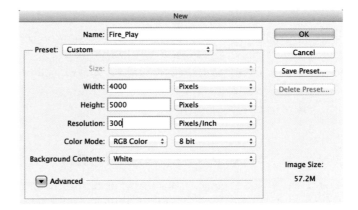 and drag future matching files into the collection thumbnail for later searching.

New Document Composite Prep

With the palette all ready to go, the next step is getting a new file document ready for your actual composite work. Although it's tempting to simply press Ctrl/Cmd+N and dive in, a little prep work will save you big headaches later. Your main composite document can benefit from the same attention you paid to organization and visibility in your photo palette. Try setting up the composite document for the project in Chapter 8 to see what I mean.

1. Create a new Photoshop document (Ctrl/Cmd+N), and name it *Fire_Play*. Set Width to 4000 pixels, Height to 5000 pixels, and Resolution of 300ppi. Select White for the Background Contents setting, then click OK (**FIGURE 6.11**).

FIGURE 6.11 When you create your main composite document, choose a size that leaves plenty of room for bringing in your high-resolution images.

2. When the document opens, immediately invert the white background to black by pressing Ctrl/Cmd+I. Having a black background enables you to later play around with various opacities within the composite and not have to worry about white showing through (like wearing white socks with fancy black pants and shoes). Go all black just in case something slips up!

3. Next, set up image folders to organize the elements of your composite and help you find your layers when the project grows complex. Create a new group folder by clicking the small group folder at the bottom of the Layers panel ▣.

4. Double-click on the group folder title to rename it something a bit more helpful, like Background.

5. Repeat steps 3 and 4 to create additional folders for Hands, Fire, Water, Bark, Smoke.

6. Color code your groups, as well: Right-click near the layer's Visibility icon ◉. From the context menu that opens, select a color for each group. When you're finished, your Layers panel will look like **FIGURE 6.12**.

   Color coding helps you find things just a little more efficiently and can keep you from putting something where it doesn't belong.

7. Save your file to the Chapter8_Resources folder; you'll need to whip out these fiery documents in Chapter 8.

FIGURE 6.12 Group your layers into folders with clearly identifiable names and color codes.

Your photo palette and composite document are now prepped and ready for Chapter 8. When you get there, you'll see how this somewhat tedious work pays off huge dividends by the end. In addition, you can apply these same methods of building a palette to a wide range of composites with similar requirements of vastly different and numerous source material.

Rating and Filtering in Adobe Bridge

When working on a project in which nearly all the components are shot in one single location with one point of view (POV), the same lighting set up, and so on, compositing becomes less about *if* images will fit in the same composite scene and more about *which* images fit the *best* for the desired composition. You no longer need to create an entire palette to visualize and test out elements, because technically they all should work in some capacity. Because the images have so much in common, it then boils down to making yes-or-no decisions on individual shots within the series. Accordingly, the prep work for this type of composite involves rating images for the best composition options and filtering out the ones that don't work as well.

Adobe Bridge offers great tools for comparing and rating images, then loading the best into Photoshop (and the appropriate composite group folder) one at a time. Think of this as drawing from a loaded deck that's filled with all aces and face cards. Play the right combination, and you'll do well. To demonstrate this preparatory process, I'll walk you through rating the image elements for the composite in Chapter 7 (**FIGURE 6.13**). You'll then prepare the composite file with the appropriate group folders, names, and ordering hierarchy so you'll be all set to jump right in and play a killer hand in Chapter 7.

Download and Filter

Assuming you're following the photography advice from Chapter 5 and shooting your own images in RAW with JPEG backups just in case, you'll need to do a bit of "pre-prep" before the main event in Adobe Bridge when preparing for your own projects. Specifically, after shooting the elements for your composite, transfer the images from your camera's card into a descriptively named folder on your computer. If you start a naming scheme from the beginning, it will be easier to keep your composite organized. Next, open Adobe Bridge, find the new folder, and filter out the JPEG images to leave only the RAW files visible (**FIGURE 6.14**). Click the Filter tab, choose File Type, then toggle on Camera Raw Image so that only the RAW images show up while browsing.

FIGURE 6.13 The image elements for the *Good Kitty* composite (which you'll re-create in Chapter 7) were all shot in one session, so the prep work will mostly use Adobe Bridge.

FIGURE 6.14 Filter out any JPEGs that made it into your folder as you want just the RAW files; in this case they are my Canon's CR2 files.

Rating and Sorting

Adobe Bridge is made for browsing, rating, and sorting images (among some other pretty cool things, such as batch processing), plus it gives you quick access to editing them directly within Photoshop as you simply double-click the image to open it. So when I first get a new batch of images straight from a shoot, I need to begin browsing through them and sort out exactly the good from the bad. The star-rating feature is all too perfect for this stage. The method I use to rate and choose the best images for a project is:

1. In Adobe Bridge, choose Filmstrip from the drop-down menu of workspaces from the options bar (**FIGURE 6.15**). Setting your workspace to Filmstrip provides a nice scrollable list, as well as large examples for better assessing and comparisons.

2. Go through your images, looking for those that have potential to work into your composite and those that just don't. You'll also find the inevitable on-the-fence images that have to be tested in certain image combinations. Rate all these images accordingly by clicking a one- through five-star placement beneath the image or by pressing Ctrl/Cmd+1 through Ctrl/Cmd+5 on a selected thumbnail (**FIGURE 6.16**).

3. Filter the images to show only the best results. For example, press Ctrl+Alt/Cmd+Opt+3 to show all three-star or better rated images. Alternatively you can go to the small star symbol on the options bar and select a rating from the drop-down menu.

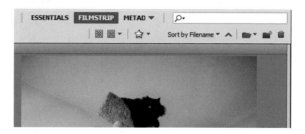

FIGURE 6.15 Change your workspace to Filmstrip for helpful side-scrolling lists and large image comparisons.

FIGURE 6.16 Rate the images in Adobe Bridge for better sorting and filtering abilities.

FIGURE 6.17
Group your similar images into stacks while working in Adobe Bridge. Here I stacked four potential cat shots together for later editing.

FIGURE 6.18 Always set up group folders to keep your image elements organized. You'll need these folders for Chapter 7.

4. With only the best of the photo-shoot showing, you can do some early grouping by category, even keeping within Bridge. For the example, I selected all of the potential cat shots for *Good Kitty* by Ctrl/Cmd-clicking, then grouped them into a single stack by pressing Ctrl/Cmd+G. This works just like grouping in Photoshop and produces a stack like in **FIGURE 6.17**. The number 4 in the upper left refers to the number of stacked files within the group. Notice how the files condense once grouped. To expand them within a grouping, click the small triangle to the right of the upper-left number.

To expedite the process of re-creating *Good Kitty*, I previously rated and sorted the necessary images (found in the Chapter7_Resources folder). To be thoroughly ready for the tutorial in Chapter 7, however, you will need to load these into a composite document.

Prepare the Composite

Preparing the composite document for a project that will rely on Adobe Bridge rather than a photo palette is similar but a bit simpler. To practice, you can create the composite shell you'll need to complete the Chapter 7 tutorial.

1. Open Photoshop, create a new document (Ctrl/Cmd+N), and name it *Super-Person*. Set Width of 3456 and Height of 5184, then click OK. Although this number may seem somewhat random, it is the full resolution of the original files. (An alternative is to simply open your intended background image and begin just as easily from there.)

2. In the Layers panel, click the Group Folder icon ▣ to create five group folders.

3. Double-click each folder's name to rename that group folder for the category of image it will hold: Reader, Super Person, Toys, Cat, Effects (**FIGURE 6.18**).

4. Save the file in Chapter7_Resources, so you can be ready to pull it open again during Chapter 7.

Using Tabs: Few Pieces, Big Payoff

Not all composites are about stitching together a plethora of *many* small pieces of similar material or about getting all material from one photo shoot. Sometimes you need only a few pieces to combine into a strong image. **FIGURE 6.19**, which you'll re-create in Chapter 9, is a good example of a composite made from a smaller group of source images.

For these cases, your prep work will focus mainly on organizing the composite file with group folders that correspond to the visual depth of the image. In this sense, some composites are more like a burrito, with the ingredients all mixed up and blended together, while others definitely need individual layering like a sandwich. In the end, paying attention to which objects must be seen in front and on top of another object then ordering your layers to match will help you finesse the composition to perfection and ensure the best results.

You can practice keeping your layers in viewing order with the source files for the Chapter 9 project. Because creating group folders always builds from the bottom-up, here is the order you should create each group folder knowing that the last group will end up on top over everything else as show in **FIGURE 6.20**.

FIGURE 6.19 Although the results look involved, the *Nature Rules* composite required very few source images and equally little prep work.

Each of these categories will have several layers and adjustments (and sometimes many such layers) that will be part of each group you just created (as you will see in Chapter 9), but what's really amazing about organizing your project by viewing-order grouping is the ability to keep the compositional placement of everything nondestructive right up until the end. Keeping each element in its own group folder based on depth will allow you to adjust, move, and transform each element until it all fits properly in the end, much like putting large sections of a jigsaw puzzle together for those final connections. Jump right in and try.

FIGURE 6.20 Here's the layer order needed for Chapter 9. Take note of which are on top and which are at the bottom as this matters in the final composite and depth.

1. Download the Chapter9_Resources file, if you haven't already. You'll find all the source images for the Chapter 9 composite are in their respective subfolders: Subject, City and Mountain, Sky, and Textures.

2. Create a new document (Ctrl/Cmd+N) and name it *Nature_Rules*. Set Width to 2667 pixels and Height to 4000 pixels to match the original composite's dimensions (although any 2 by 3 size ratio will do). It's always a good practice keeping the resolution at 300ppi in case you ever want to print your work. Click OK.

3. In the Layers panel, create six group folders, renaming them in the following order: Sky, Mountain and bg City, Main City, Meadow, Subject, and Effects. Notice that the first folder you created (Sky) appears at the bottom of the layer stack in **FIGURE 6.21**.

4. Save this project file in the same Chapter9_Resources folder to make sure all the source images and prepped files are altogether—no panicked hunting it down in a few chapters! Keep it easy to find.

FIGURE 6.21 These groups will help keep the composition adjustable right up to final effects.

Conclusion

I can't overstate the importance of having an image that is well organized from the start. Going back through my older projects is like looking at work done by someone stumbling in a dark room. Although the end results still looked fine, nothing in my old composites makes any kind of sense organizationally and the time I needed to make those old relics was ridiculous—exponentially longer than my current well-lit workflow. The hours of editing and finessing were a chaotic and frustrating experience I urge you to avoid partaking of yourself. Instead, embrace my revelation of the importance of being properly prepared early in the project. Think about what your project will involve—a complexity of images from disparate sources, many images shot from under the same conditions, or relatively few source images—then choose the best method of prep work for the task ahead. In all cases, use group folders to give your Layers panel structure and organization. Imagine your composites are like a bike trip: Do the heavy uphill peddling first and you'll find the rest to be downhill coasting and a lot more fun.

CHAPTER 7

Making a Super Composite

COVERED IN THIS CHAPTER

- Quick and thorough selections
- Masking with subtlety
- Curves for lighting changes
- Color matching adjustments
- Composition balancing
- Using Adobe Bridge for multiple images
- Clipping to a group folder
- Using Clone Stamp nondestructively

A successful composite is all about verisimilitude: Even though we know it's not, we should feel the image is real. The composite should encourage us to suspend our disbelief and be enthralled with what we see. To do so, the image has to look just "right" and not distract with technical tell-tales. Photography's realism can lend credence to the new reality you construct from pure imagination, but it's no replacement for good Photoshop skills. Exceptional masking, color adjustments, curve adjustments, lighting, and even cloning all play a part in convincing viewers to believe.

Seamlessness and continuity are your foremost goals. In this project, based on an image from my Raising a Super-Child series (**FIGURE 7.1**), you'll practice making good selections for well-crafted masking, refining color and curve adjustments, balancing light for eye-flow, and even cloning pieces that need to be hidden or reconstructed. With these elements in your control, who needs super powers?

Begin with the Background

Planning ahead pays off: Open the *Super-Person.psd* composite file you created in Chapter 6, and you'll be all ready to start this chapter's example project. As you remember, the group folders for the composite (starting from the bottom of the layer stack) are Reader, Super Person, Toys, Cat, and Effects.

▶ **FIGURE 7.1** In *Good Kitty*, I gave my son super powers and our cat one more thing to put up with. When you combine multiple everyday shots into a new world like this, be mindful of continuity and seamless compositing.

If you did not complete the prep work in Chapter 6, take a few moments to do so now. You'll find instructions on how best to prepare files for a composite like this in the section "Rating and Filtering in Adobe Bridge."

NOTE To access the resource files and videos, just log in or join peachpit.com, and enter the book's ISBN. After you register the book, links to the files will be listed on your Account page under Registered Products.

To begin the composite, lay down your foundation: the main background image. When choosing a background, make sure it contains the essential base elements for your scene, but is otherwise clutter free.

1. In Adobe Bridge, browse to *Reader.jpg* in the Chapter7_Resources folder. Because everything is happening around and on top of the jaded parent reading in the corner of the empty room, this image works well as the main background.

2. Right-click the thumbnail for *Reader.jpg*, then choose Place > In Photoshop from the context menu (**FIGURE 7.2**) to load the image into the active Photoshop document (*Super-Person.psd*) as a Smart Object.

   Using Place from Bridge works for the composite background image because you want the entire layer and not just a piece of it. If you used Place for all the layers and depended on large masks to hide the unwanted portions, the file size would get dramatically more cumbersome because you'd be saving quite a bit more data that you don't even need. So use the Place technique when you need an entire image or at least the majority of it.

3. Place the new layer into the Reader folder at the bottom of the layers stack. Again, this will be the base image so all other layers must be above it to be seen.

TIP For my workflow, I prefer the manual control of copying and pasting every layer. As an alternative, however, you can work straight from Bridge: Open all the images at once in Adobe Camera RAW editor (ACR), crop and adjust them, then close to save the RAW edits. To bring them in Photoshop as layers, select all the image thumbnails within Bridge, right-click one of them and choose Tools > Photoshop > Load Files into Photoshop Layers from the context menu. The images will open in the current Photoshop document as individual new layers, which you can then move into place.

FIGURE 7.2 Right-clicking a thumbnail and choosing Place can save time and keep your workspace fairly tab free.

Paste the Pieces in Place

With the background in position, you can roughly block out the positions of the composite's other elements by pasting in the various pieces. After loading the pieces, you can make selections and masks as needed. One reason for holding off on the selections and masking until later is that not all the objects may work within your composite—a fact you may not discover until you start positioning (and repositioning) the pieces. Why put all that time and energy into selecting and masking, if it's potentially a no go for that element? Sometimes you may need to do a rough initial mask right after bringing in an element, especially if it has parts that will interfere with seeing other elements at the same time. Don't, however, waste too much time with masking until you get the pieces in and know they will work with what you have in mind. (For the example, I've simplified the process enough that you can mask afterwards with little problem.)

1. Browse to the Toys folder of the Chapter7_Resources folder, and open *Rabbit.jpg* as a separate tab (**FIGURE 7.3**).

2. Use the Rectangular Marquee tool (M) to draw a small rectangle selection around the bunny. (To make the necessary portion easier to select, I've blurred out the irrelevant areas.) Copy this section with Ctrl/Cmd+C.

3. Before you paste, click the Toys group folder back inside the main composite file so the layer you're about to add will end up where you want it. Now use Paste in Place (Ctrl/Cmd+Shift+V) to paste the bunny into the composite in the same position it occupied in the original, thus matching the location exactly.

For a project like this in which all elements were shot in the same room under similar conditions, Paste in Place is a good way to add each object as it makes sure the lighting and backgrounds match appropriately. With a good selection, you can always move each object, but this method provides a good initial reference for matching and adjusting the pieces to perfection (**FIGURE 7.4**).

FIGURE 7.3 To help you make your rough selections more quickly, I've isolated the relevant areas and blurred the rest of the source images.

FIGURE 7.4 Paste in Place is the ultimate way to get the pieces in the right spot without having to bring in cumbersome full images, nor having to nudge the small piece into position until it fits.

FIGURE 7.5 Block out the main objects and their original placement before further alterations.

FIGURE 7.6 Select the rabbit with the Quick Selection tool (W), but be careful not to include the hand.

4. Repeat steps 1 through 3 for the remaining elements from the Toys, Toddler, and Cat folders (**FIGURE 7.5**). Feel free to try your hand at some detail work with the ring-stacking toy on the floor (*Objects_and_Toys_5.jpg* through *Objects_and_Toys_14.jpg*, which I skipped in my own version). Also, make sure that the Cat and Toddler layer are in their own group folders—and don't forget to label your layers as you work!

Remember, this is just a starting point for editing your composition; you can shift elements around more to your liking later.

Select then Mask

In most cases, it's a smart idea to get a good selection before masking anything (Chapter 11 covers some of the exceptions). Small objects, especially, benefit from this approach, which is why you'll be working next on the selections then the masks for the floating toys.

The composite may still look pretty "off" at this phase, but don't lose heart. Because you're focusing on selections and masks only, the ever-changing lights, darks, and colors won't match yet. The day I had for shooting was partially cloudy, making shooting "consistently" a moving target as the natural light I wanted varied wildly from moment to maddening moment. The result, as you can see, is that even with studio lighting fairly consistent coming from the left, each shot has its own subtle variation. You'll adjust the finer points to match the background lighting in the "Use Curves for Color" section. For now, concentrate on getting some good selections and masks. For each object, it's a good idea to turn off the visibility of the others around it as you work on this part.

1. Begin once again with the rabbit toy: Pick up the Quick Selection tool (W), and drag it around inside the bunny body to select it (**FIGURE 7.6**).

> **TIP** If the Quick Selection tool proves too difficult to use against a similarly colored background, try the Magnetic Lasso tool.

2. If the tool mistakenly grabbed some of my hand or the back wall as part of the creamy rabbit fur, press and hold the Alt/Opt key to toggle Quick Selection to subtraction mode, then Alt/Opt-drag to deselect unwanted areas. Work a little at a time, toggling between selecting and deselecting.

With each pass of this back and forth process, Photoshop refines its edge detection, trying harder to see what you might be seeing.

NOTE If you're not getting the results you want, don't hesitate to try another selection method (see Chapter 2 for more). Find the one that works better for your techniques and workflow. Whether you're lightning fast and accurate with the Magnetic Lasso or prefer to paint what you want with the Quick Selection mask (Q), find your groove.

3. After everything is selected, click the Refine Edge button in the options bar to open the Refine Edge dialog box. Here you can make adjustments to avoid two of the most common masking problems: the abrupt sharp edge and the halo surrounding the object you are trying to select.

4. In the Refine Edge dialog box, change the Feather slider to about 0.8 to soften those hard selection edges just enough to match the natural blur of the image. Any variation from the natural lens blur will contribute to making the composite look fake, like a collage cut out with dull scissors, rather than like a seamless composite (**FIGURE 7.7**).

5. Set Shift Edge to −40 to pull the selection edge inwards by 40%. This will help avoid a halo of unwanted background pixels, which would become intrusively obvious if you moved the bunny to another location. Click OK when you're satisfied with the selection.

TIP For selections that get a little choppy with sharp and inconsistent edges, try slightly increasing the Smooth setting within the Refine Edge dialog box. This will help even out these small variations by averaging the path of the selection edge. Use Smooth in moderation, however, as too much can start making a big, rounded blob of a selection!

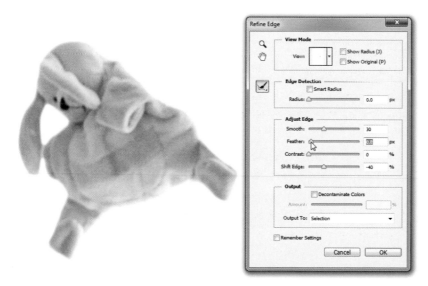

FIGURE 7.7 Change your Refine Edge settings to make a more seamless selection.

Task Masker

With the initial edge refining done, your next task is to get the mask looking sweet and seamless. Because you took the time to perfect your selection, this part will be easier: Simply apply a mask, then paint with black for the remaining parts that need some fudging.

1. Click the Add Mask icon 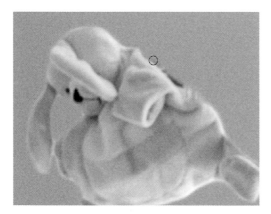 at the bottom of the Layers panel to convert your selection into a mask. The result may not be perfect, but it's a pretty good start that you can paint into shape.

2. Choose a soft, round brush with Size set to 10px and Hardness to 0. With full-opacity black, paint away the parts that stand out, such as the area with a little pink from my hand (**FIGURE 7.8**).

3. As is sometimes the case, Shift Edge took a little bit too much off in a few other areas, so you need to paint those back in with white. Keep the same brush properties, but press the X key to switch to white. Paint the necessary areas back in. If you return too much, just press X to swap to black to paint it out again.

FIGURE 7.8 Paint out the remaining pieces that still draw attention, like the pink halo that remains from my hand.

That's one toy done! Repeat the selection, refining, and masking steps for each of the flying objects. Don't worry that you can't totally mask out the hand holding the bottom of the cat's scratch post, you'll address this with the Clone Stamp tool in the "Clone This" section. For the cat's hair and the post's carpeting, try the Refine Radius tool found in Refine Edge dialog box. Originally designed for selections like hair, it does fairly well on a range of materials with fine details along the edge. (Chapter 9 digs into this tool in detail.)

> **TIP** To isolate the layer you're working on and better see your adjustments, turn off the visibility for other layers by clicking the Visibility icon . I recommend this, especially for parts that overlap and conflict.

Kiddos and Shadows

The toddler truly does have super powers in this composite: His mask must be seamless and believable to sell the image's conceit. If it isn't, the entire image falls down around him. Luckily, getting this crucial piece right is easier than the rest of the masks in many ways.

For your own project, always be on the lookout for the critical pieces that break the verisimilitude of the scene. Perhaps the most common example within composite work is the shadows around the feet of a subject. Unlike with floating objects, which usually do not cast any obvious shadows, our eyes instantly know when shadows of something touching the ground are off. In these cases, we need to take a different approach to masking, something a little smoother and trickier: a transitional mask that is painted rather than selected.

1. Without selecting anything at this point, add a mask to the Toddler layer using the usual Add Mask icon ▣.

2. Pick up the same soft, round brush but change its Size to 100px in the options bar and paint black on the mask to soften all the visible edges. After getting rid of the hard edges from pasting, change the brush size to 500px. This larger brush enables you to paint with an even softer radius that provides an even feathering and transition from one image to the other as you mask—the larger the soft radius the smoother the transition. Paint with black the outside of the toddler and his shadow using the mask of the layer. Be extra careful *not* to mask out part of his shadow or hands, however; this would undercut the realism you're after (**FIGURE 7.9**).

(A)

3. Decrease the brush size again to 300px (press the [key), and paint around the fingertips. You need a small enough brush to get between the elements you want (the hands) and those you don't (the didgeridoos they reach for), but a large enough diameter for a soft transition from the Toddler layer to the background.

> **TIP** While photographing my son Kellen for this project, I quickly learned that making an awesome game out of the session is the way to go. Catching the right mood is vital. If your toddler model isn't feeling it, don't even think about trying to shoot. Reschedule, seriously.

(B)

FIGURE 7.9 Mask out the hard edges created from pasting with a soft brush at 100px (a), then get the smooth transitions just right using a carefully finessed brush with the size of 500px (b).

Adjust Curves and Color

As mentioned earlier, despite careful planning for consistent lighting when shooting source images, sometimes you can end up with minor and even dramatic variations between shots. Even with a consistent lighting setup inside, ambient natural light may change as the day progresses. Or maybe your studio is like my house, where a heavy power load in another area noticeably drains the lights (Tip: Never attempt a photo shoot while your washer and dryer are churning.) You could correct these differences in the Adobe Camera RAW editor, true, but what if you don't have that option? Perhaps you're working with JPEG files supplied by a client. Curves and color balance adjustments are the answer. Remedying exposure inconsistencies is an incredibly important skill to develop, and the Super-Child composite gives you plenty of opportunities to practice.

FIGURE 7.10 Notice how the lighting in the Toddler layer differs from that of the background? With one Curves adjustment, it will become nearly invisible.

1. The toddler commands the viewer's focus, so concentrate on fitting that layer into the composite first (**FIGURE 7.10**). Click the Toddler layer, and add a Curves adjustment layer ▨ from the Adjustments panel.

2. Clip the adjustment layer to the Toddler layer so that it does not affect any other layers during the adjustment: Click the Clipping icon in the Adjustment Properties panel ▱ or Alt/Opt-click between the Curves adjustment layer and the Toddler layer. You will notice the cursor change from the pointer hand to a slashed down arrow next to a white rectangle (newer versions) when you hover between the layers; when you see this curser change it means that once you click, it'll clip that adjustment layer to the toddler layer.

3. Add a Curves control point in the middle and make a gentle adjustment upwards. Take a look at **FIGURE 7.11** and notice how little is changing, yet that masked edge simply disappears (well, aside from color differences).

   To better finesse the Curves control point, click a point to turn it solid black (which indicates that the point is selected), then use the arrow keys to nudge it into just the right spot. To match the example's settings, enter 172 in the Input field (represented by the bottom gradient) and 192 in the Output field (represented by the side gradient); you will find these fields directly below the Curves control panel and the histogram graph (you may need to expand the panel size to see these).

FIGURE 7.11 Without much movement to the curves control point, you can successfully make the dark edges along the mask disappear.

FIGURE 7.12 Make sure that both adjustments layers are affecting only the Toddler layer by clipping them to it.

Color Control

Curves help immensely, but aren't the total fix. The color is still a bit off. When the reading dad was photographed, the light was a warmer temperature than when the toddler was photographed. The difference isn't dramatic, but like most things when compositing, it all adds up in the end! You can correct for this sort of color shift with a simple Color Balance adjustment in no time at all.

1. Add a Color Balance adjustment layer by clicking the icon 🎚 in the Adjustments panel. Make sure this layer is above the Curves adjustment layer. As a rule, I try to always adjust color after a Curves adjustment because adjusting lights and darks will also affect the color with saturation changes.

TIP To use a Curves adjustment layer without it changing the saturation along with the contrast, switch its blending mode to luminosity. This doesn't give as refined control as a Color adjustment layer, but it does provide fantastic consistency with the existing hue and saturation.

2. To clip the Color Balance adjustment layer to the Toddler layer, select it then press Ctrl+Alt/ Cmd+Opt+G or use whichever clipping method you prefer for your workflow (**FIGURE 7.12**).

3. Within the Adjustment Properties menu (double-click the Color Balance adjustment thumbnail image to pull this up), make sure the Tone drop-down menu is set to Midtones, then shift the colors sliders to make the cools in the Toddler layer become just a hint warmer. Watch the wall along the edge of the mask as an indicator as you adjust. If one layer's wall is a little more yellow, then the other layer's has to match (even if these are masked out because you're not adjusting only the walls for better matching here, but the subject as well). For the example, I settled on +4 for the Cyan-Red slider, 0 for Magenta-Green, and −8 for the Yellow-Blue slider, moving it closer to yellow (**FIGURE 7.13**). Clicking the Visibility icon 👁 repeatedly on the Color Balance adjustment layer will give you a closer look at the before and after for this adjustment.

FIGURE 7.13 A slight adjustment to the color balance of the Toddler layer matches it with the background.

Fix a Group of Toys

That's the lighting and color fixed for one source element, but still lots to go, right? Yes, but here's the good news: In Photoshop CS5 and later, you can clip an adjustment layer to an entire group folder, meaning you can adjust the layers it holds all at once instead of one at a time. This solution works for the Toys folder because all the toys were shot while the sun blasted through that side window, flooding the room with light. The toy layers all needed to be knocked down some shades and desaturated at the same time. Although a couple layers in there still may need further adjusting, clipping Curves and Color Balance adjustment layers to the Toys group folder will improve the layers to a pretty close match of the background image.

1. The rabbit is once again a good starting reference. Even when you plan to alter an entire group, it's a good idea to focus on one layer that is representational of the lights, darks, and coloring of the others. Start by temporarily disabling the mask of the rabbit so you can better see that background wall you need to match up. Shift-click the Add Mask icon of the rabbit in the Layers panel. A red X appears across it, indicating that it is temporarily disabled (**FIGURE 7.14**).

2. Add a Curves adjustment layer (click the Curves icon ▦), and place it directly *above* the Toys group folder; now your adjustment will affect all the toys in the group rather than just one literate rabbit. Clip this layer to the group folder by pressing Ctrl+Alt/ Cmd+Opt+G.

NOTE Since Photoshop CS5, users have been able to clip a layer to a group folder, unlocking new and exciting workflow possibilities. If you have an older version, simply copy your adjustments from layer to layer (Alt/Opt-drag the adjustment to the other layers, or use the Clip icon ▣ within the Properties panel and clip them (Ctrl+Alt/Cmd+Opt+G) as you go. The method is a little bit of a pain but still very workable.

3. Open the Curves Properties panel (double-click the Curves adjustment layer thumbnail), and create a control point in the very center with one click along the diagonal line. Drag the point straight down until the rabbit's background wall matches the values (lights and darks) of the background image. You will notice again that changing the curves also changes the color (unless of course you change the blending mode to Luminosity, but there will still be slight adjustments to make regardless because the brighter lighting also made the toys more saturated to begin with). So, after adjusting the Curves ignore the bad saturation for now, just focus on the darkness of the wall (**FIGURE 7.15**).

FIGURE 7.14 Temporarily disable the rabbit's layer mask by Shift-clicking the mask.

NOTE Lights and darks can be difficult to separate from hue and saturation if you're not practiced in discerning. Just know that there can be two very different saturation levels, and both still have the same value.

4. To make that wall a lot less yellow, create a new Hue/Saturation adjustment layer (click the ▣ icon in the Adjustment panel), place above the Curves adjustment layer, and create a clipping mask as explained in step 2. With this new layer you can quickly control the saturation for all the layers in the Toys folder.

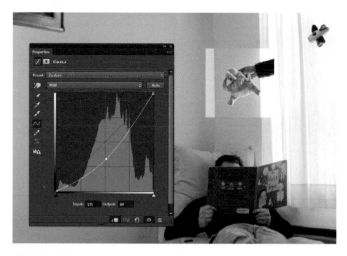

FIGURE 7.15 Match the values with curves first before adjusting color; make sure that the walls have the same lightness or darkness.

5. Double-click the new layer to open its Properties panel, then move the Saturation slider to the left to −46, which seems to be the sweet-spot for controlling that vibrant yellow that came out of the previous Curves adjustment (**FIGURE 7.16**). Enable the rabbit's mask once again with a Shift-click, and take a stroll around the composition to check the other toys and flying objects. Aside from a couple smaller adjustments, this worked pretty well!

TIP I often pair Curves with Hue/Saturation adjustments layers as either linked layers or in their own group folder with a single mask. They work exceptionally well as a team, one always compensating for the other and both super quick to adjust.

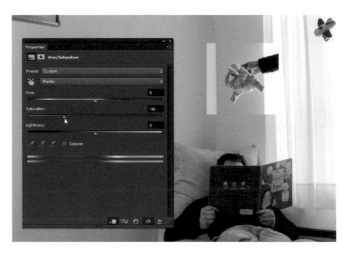

FIGURE 7.16 Using a Hue/Saturation adjustment layer is a quick way to control saturation changes that are heightened by a Curves adjustment.

COMPOSITION

Once you finish masking and adjusting, take a moment to think about your whole composition before you begin finessing the smaller details. Evaluate the overall busyness and general *eye-flow*, meaning where the viewer's eye starts and moves around the image as if reading it and discovering details and meaning. Mainly, I'm looking for balance. For the *Good Kitty* composition, for example, I decided:

- The focus should be around the toddler, so any clutter right around him was too distracting.

- The placement of the garbage truck originally competed with other elements, but was also a perfect object to relocate elsewhere for better balance.

- Positioning the ukulele partly out of the frame created more of an open composition, hinting that more of this scene was floating just out of view. Containing all elements too perfectly within the frame can look "off" and is a hard problem to pinpoint at times.

- The picture frame enabled me to add an intentional collision as a pressure valve to everything else being very neatly spaced for the most part. Even just throwing in one or two items that aren't perfect can help viewers believe what they're seeing.

Clone This

Despite careful planning, something else occasionally goes awry in a shoot, something that can't merely be masked out or adjusted. Heavy objects—such as a cat balanced on a scratch post—often need properly leveraged support, and your hands or props can't always be tucked away out of sight from the camera. For these situations, turn to the Healing tools. Specifically, by cloning content onto a blank new layer, the Clone Stamp tool provides a nondestructive way of fixing the hands or other unexpected objects that show up. To fix the scratch post, for example, try using the Clone Stamp tool to paint some cloned bits of post on an empty layer above the original content.

1. In the Layers panel, click the Layer icon  to create a new blank layer on which to do your clone stamping. Name the layer New Clone, and place the new layer directly above the Cat layer within the Cat folder. Because you're going to use Clone Stamp on this new layer, you can instantly trash it and start again (or use the Eraser as an undo tool) if the operation goes wrong.

2. Alt/Opt-click between the layers to clip the New Clone layer to the Cat layer and ensure both layers use the mask you created for the scratch post in the "Task Masker" section (**FIGURE 7.17**).

3. Grab the Clone Stamp tool, and using the drop-down menu in the options bar, specify which layers you want the tool to affect. Change from the default setting of Current Layer to Current & Below [Current & Below]. Now you can clone from the current layer (which is empty) and layer below. Keeping your work as separate layers as much as possible is always the best practice.

FIGURE 7.17 To keep the edits nondestructive, you will use the Clone Stamp tool to paint the cloned content on a new layer (New Clone) that is clipped to the original (Cat).

FIGURE 7.18 Pick a sample point location that is very similar for a seamless effect.

4. Set your sample point by Alt/Opt-clicking once in an area similar enough that it will work painted over the problem spot. For the example, I clicked directly above where the hand was gripping the scratch post as this area is very similar and free of fingerprints (**FIGURE 7.18**).

5. With the sample point set, begin painting over the hand area on the scratch post. I paint in small strokes or dabs so that they are controlled and nothing accidental gets cloned (such as the same hands, only further down!). Watch where that sample point target is moving along with each stroke. Set a new sample point and continue cloning if you run out of clean material.

> **TIP** Toggle Aligned Sample on in the options bar if you want the Clone Stamp tool to keep the sample point consistently spaced from your cloning, where it follows at an equal distance set by you. Uncheck Aligned Sample if you found a single spot you want the sample point to return to after each stroke/click. This can be helpful for times when there is just a small area available to clone from. Rather than resetting the sample point, keep Aligned Sample off.

Further Alterations

You can clone the rest of the scratch post's corner to fix where the hand holds it on the bottom, but this will take a little more craftsmanship (**FIGURE 7.19**). Here are some good strategies for fixing this large section and others like it:

- Change the sample point frequently, and piece it all together without too many cookie-cutter instances.

- When you find a clean area with a fair amount of stroke room around it, set your sample point then go to the options bar and uncheck Aligned Sample. (This may or may not be toggled on, so always double check which way you are using this tool). With Aligned Sample off you can paint in new spots while having your sample point return to the original spot after every stroke.

FIGURE 7.19 Keep clone strokes small and vary the sample point, and you'll be surprised what wasn't actually there to begin with.

- To better see what you are actually cloning, expand the mask on the layer below, especially if you have it clipped. You can do this by switching over to the paintbrush and adding some white to the needed areas.

- For areas looking a little too blotchy and uneven, try changing the Clone Stamp Opacity to 20% and go over a larger area using a sample point with lots of room for tracking. This will even things out and give you a cloning airbrush effect.

Fine-Tune Lighting and Effects

As the final touch to my composites, I fine-tune the lighting for better emphasis and eye-flow within the composite. Frequently, areas of the composite compete for attention or, perhaps, lack enough contrast, and final lighting effects can be the subtle changes that make the difference between bland and eye-catching—and believable as well! To practice this, you'll create six effects for this final Effects group folder. These effects are definitely within the vein of my own series aesthetic that generally has strong contrast, muted yet warmer tones, and controlled vignettes (**FIGURE 7.20**).

FIGURE 7.20 I include this standard set of lighting and effects layers with each composite in some form.

1. Darken things down and up the contrast: Create a new Curves ▧ adjustment layer within the Effects group folder (**FIGURE 7.21**), and paint with black on the mask just in those places that you don't want this darkening effect to affect. Typically, this means masking out the things that are already pretty dark, such as the cat, shadows, and the toddler's dark pants. These already have just enough detail and don't need darkening. On the curve line itself, create a control point in the middle and drag it gently downwards.

2. Repeat step 1 to control the lights. Again, paint with black in all the places that don't need lightening. I painted out everything that stood out as a little too light, such as the scratch post highlights, the curtains, and the slight vignettes (created in step 1 by adding in a little more darks) I wanted to stay dark. Much like moths we're always drawn to the lighter elements. Knowing this, I used a lighter center and darker outer edges to control eye-flow to the subjects and floating objects.

3. Again in the Effects folder, create a custom lighting layer with an Overlay blending mode to provide nondestructive dodge and burn painting ability (more on this in the next chapter). Mainly I use this effect for focusing eye-flow by lightening up the center with soft low opacity islands and

FIGURE 7.21 Use Curves to gently get the darks and lights the way you want them; I usually start with the darks.

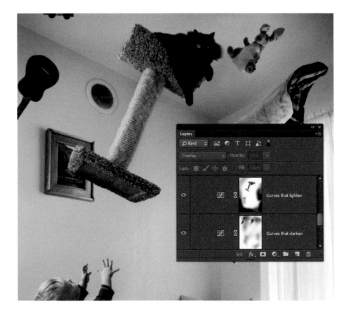

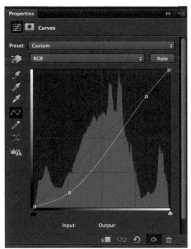

darkening the image corners with stronger vignettes (**FIGURE 7.22**). This will dramatically shift color in a bad way at times, so it needs to be follow up with some form of color control.

4. Control color with a Black & White adjustment layer ▣ placed above the previous effects layer. This unconventional use of the adjustment knocks out most of the offending blotches created from the lighting changes and simultaneously helps create greater continuity throughout the piece by dropping the adjustment's opacity to under 20%. This is just enough to mute the scene, yet still retain enough color for the viewer to buy into it. The coloring will be mostly made up for in step 6 as you add vibrant warmth to the scene.

   Sometimes you may also have to do some manual color control after heavily adjusting the lights and darks of an area (saturation can increase even in areas that were fairly neutral). One way to control color is by using the Color blending mode on a new layer, as it will let you paint in the exact color you want applied to the composite (again, the next chapter goes into more detail). So in short, you can choose a color that is more appropriate (such as the plain wall) with the eyedropper, and paint this in those places that are still color deviants or unruly.

5. Lastly add a customized warm filter (**FIGURE 7.23**) via another new layer set to an Overlay blending mode with a warm yellow-orange spilt across it with the Bucket 🪣 tool. Change this layer's opacity to 15% and you have the effect you see in the final image. I find this to be a much more successful filter than the built-in Photo filters as it handles colors and the highlights specifically in ways that enhance and it doesn't muddy in any way.

FIGURE 7.22 Use an Overlay layer for nondestructive dodge and burn with painting white and black.

The only thing that remains at this point is a nice and controlled cropping to compliment the placement and arrangement of the objects. This is the final touch to getting a balanced composition, so be sure to include and exclude what feels right. The scene was shot on a fairly wide-angle lens, so there was definitely room to play with here as far as cropping. In **FIGURES 7.24A** and **B** you can see how I decided to crop the image for the best composition, including the subjects, while still cutting off a floating object to allude to the idea of a larger scene outside of the framing. This is called an *open* composition and allows for the viewer to infer what's beyond the viewable scene.

Conclusion

The core components to any believable composite come from taking control of as many variables as possible, from color to lighting to the splicing together of layers with varied masking techniques suitable for the situation. It all makes a difference—especially in a composite that we want to believe is real! In this first tutorial, you've learned a solid core of skills: how to successfully match source elements using clipping masks, adjustment layers, selections, and mask painting, as well as how to control lighting. These features are not limited to enhancing the secret life of toddlers by any means, as you will see in the next two tutorials and Section III's project walkthroughs! Practicing and expanding these techniques can lead to all kinds of new possibilities, such as playing with fire (trust me, just keep reading).

FIGURE 7.23 I like to create a custom warm filter with a low-opacity Overlay layer covered with a warm and gooey yellow-orange.

(A)

FIGURES 7.24A and **B** The complete image (a) shows what I cropped out in black, as compared to the final composition (b).

(B)

CHAPTER 8

Blending Fire

COVERED IN THIS CHAPTER

- Blending mode techniques for layering and texturing
- Combining clipping masks and blending modes
- Nondestructive dodge and burn with Overlay mode
- Fire sculpture with Screen mode
- Color control layers with Color mode
- Duplication and variation
- Color range masking
- Shaping with Puppet Warp

Everyone has a little bit of pyromania in them, so what better way to learn about blending modes than by playing with fire? Sculpting Photoshop flames is certainly easier than working with the real thing, just as using blending modes to control transparency and layer interaction can be a quick and effective alternative to using masks. In this exercise you'll create some magical fire play using blending modes to control certain kinds of opacity. As an alternative to masks, this technique can save you the time and frustration of trying to perfect selections or refining a mask to perfectly outline a flame or object that may not *have* perfect outlines. Wispy smoke, for instance, is nearly impossible to mask in all its detail, blur, and subtle contrast. Instead, you can pull out a choice blending mode, such as Screen, and turn the dark background transparent.

Fire and smoke are particularly helpful examples for this technique because their light against dark contrast and intricate nature make using traditional masks difficult. Images like *Fire Play* in **FIGURE 8.1** make us reach for creative solutions to visual challenges. As you work through the steps to re-create the image, you may even discover some innovations of your own.

▸ **FIGURE 8.1** *Fire Play* gives you hands-on experience with fire, smoke, and blending modes—the only way to learn!

Prep for the Composite

Projects such as the *Fire Play* composite use many small selections of different images and are much easier to manage when separated into two files: a main composite document to work in and a second file to draw image elements from, like a palette of photographs with which to paint. Remember creating the photo palette (*Fire_Play_Photo_Palette.psd*, *Figure 8.2*) and composite document (*Fire_Play.psd*, **FIGURE 8.3**) in Chapter 6? Now's the time to put all that great prep work to good use; open these two documents in Photoshop and get ready to composite.

If you did not complete the prep work in Chapter 6, take a few moments to do so now. You'll find instructions for downloading the source files, as well as an in-depth description on how best to prepare files for a composite like this in the section "Creating a Photo Palette." Alternately, you can jump start your project file with *Fire_Play.psd*, a composite file complete with group folders and labels that's included in the chapter's folder of resource files (Chapter8_Resources).

> **NOTE** To access the resource files and videos, just log in or join peachpit.com, and enter the book's ISBN. After you register the book, links to the files will be listed on your Account page under Registered Products.

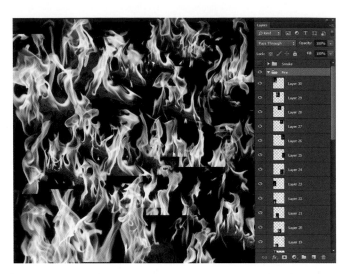

FIGURE 8.2 A photo palette, like *Fire_Play_Photo_Palette.psd* shown here, gathers your source images together into group folders for easy searching

FIGURE 8.3 Group the layers of your main composite document into folders with clearly identifiable names and color coding.

Handle the Hands

Before you can put blending modes to work, you need some elements in your main composite document. The best place to start is by bringing the hands into the *Fire_Play.psd* document, as their placement dictates where everything else will go in the composition. As you begin, try to visualize how you might want to use the smoke and fire. For example, I wanted to play with depth so I knew I needed to have some room for blurring some of the smoke as well as a place to grow a little fire demon between the hands. Don't worry if you're still undecided. Because this composite will be built nondestructively, you will be able to adjust as needed while you work.

1. If you haven't already, open *Fire_Play.psd* in Photoshop now.

2. From Adobe Bridge, browse to each hand file and open *Hand1.jpg* and *Hand2.jpg* as separate document tabs within Photoshop (**FIGURE 8.4**).

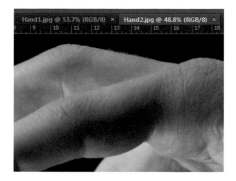

FIGURE 8.4 Bring both hands into Photoshop as tabs before moving them into the composite document.

> **TIP** As an alternative to steps 2 and 3, you can bring the hands straight into the active Photoshop file (in this case *Fire_Play*.psd) by right-clicking each image separately within Bridge and selecting Place > Photoshop. Doing this opens each image as Smart Object layers within the active Photoshop project. Jump to step 4 if you try this method.

SHOOTING SMOKE AND FIRE

Taking your own pictures is a huge step in having complete control and authorship over your work. If you are up to the challenge, here are some tips for shooting fire and smoke:

- Be sure that you have a dark background so that the flames or smoke show up well with good contrast.

- Use as fast a shutter speed and as small an aperture as you can while still getting a usable exposure. The fast shutter speed will reduce the risk of motion blur, and the small aperture (remember, this means a large f-stop number) will enable you to capture greater depth. If your scene is too dark to do both, always put more priority on the fast shutter speed.

- Shoot the fire and smoke separately. For smoke, use a clamp-light, a lamp, or even controlled natural sunlight to illuminate the smoke, but avoid lighting the

background at all costs. Shoot the fire from a side angle into darkness for good results. Nighttime works well for this.

- Incense works well for shooting clean and visible smoke trails, plus you can wave it around to generate the shapes you desire.

- Use a tripod for shooting the smoke.

Remember, you will need to get as many clear images as possible for a good composite. For this composite, in addition to fire and smoke on black backgrounds, you'll need:

- Hands occupied with sorcery on a black background

- Rusty metal or something equivalent

- Shallow moving water in sunlight

- Cracking bark

3. To bring the hands into the *Fire Play* composite document, press V to switch to the Move tool; drag either hand image up to the *Fire Play* tab to open the composite's window, then, without letting go, drag the hand back downwards to drop it in the newly opened window. Repeat for the second hand. I find this method more efficient than having multiple documents open side by side, plus keeping a limited number of documents open as tabs really does help everything stay organized and easy to locate as you work.

> **TIP** To view the document windows side by side or in different configurations, choose Window>Arrange and select a layout from the examples. You can choose from a number of arrangements that might work better for your own workflow and monitor configuration.

4. After bringing each hand into the composite, file their layers away into the Hands folder in the Layers panel.

Remove Backgrounds with Blending Modes

The hands are in position, but their blocky backgrounds are in the way of the new background you'll add to the composite. Instead of using traditional masking to remove them, you can simply change the blending mode settings for the hand layers. Not only does this method save the time and effort of masking, it can provide better fidelity of edge detail, such as hair, shadows, and other elements that are tricky to get right. Because the background of the hands is nearly black and the planned background won't be lighter than the hands themselves, you can apply a Lighten blending mode to the hands as a shortcut around making a mask for each hand.

1. In the Layers panel, click the Hand1 layer to activate it, then choose Lighten from the drop-down menu of blending modes near the top of the panel (**FIGURE 8.5**). Repeat for the Hand2 layer to change its blending mode from the default of Normal to Lighten, as well.

2. From the Other_Textures folder of the resource files, bring *Dark_Rusty_Metal.jpg* into the main composite to add a background texture of rusty metal. Place it towards the very bottom of the layers stack, just above the black background layer. Rename the new layer Background Texture. The background rusted metal texture is a good, very dark base that provides interest and a little contrast against the fire, smoke, and hands (**FIGURE 8.6**).

Using a blending mode can be a great timesaver, especially for dark background situations like this project in which the value point that determines if content is visible or not is set so low. With this method you bypass making

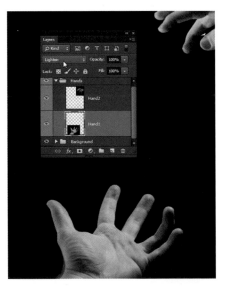

FIGURE 8.5
Changing the blending mode to Lighten will remove a layer's dark background by blending it with the composite's overall dark background underneath.

FIGURE 8.6
Lighten lets the
hands contrast
nicely against
the dark rusty
background.

FIGURE 8.7 A quick sketch with an outer glow as
a fire simulation effect will help you visualize your
ideas and get the composite started.

a selection and refining its edge until it's just right for
masking. Take note though that this only works for some
layers with dark enough backgrounds and light enough
content to show through above the other layers, but when
it does work, it looks great!

> **TIP** If you notice parts of the background show-
> ing over the image, change the blending mode back
> to Normal, and use a standard mask on your image
> instead.

Rough Sketch the Fire

The stage is set with a base background and the hands
are ready, now they need some fire to sculpt. Before they
can sculpt, however, you need to sketch. A visual guide,
even a rough one, can be especially helpful when the creative possibilities are as overwhelmingly limitless as they
are here. Using the Brush tool and a gradient Outer Glow
layer style to mimic fire's glow, you can sketch your ideas
into the composite (**FIGURE 8.7**). Sketching with a flame-
like effect can help establish a better mood for visualizing
your ideas. Then, you can find and fit together the flame's

elements with your sketch as a guide—much easier than
sculpting fire from scratch.

Take a few moments to draw inspiration from your photo
palette before you click the Brush tool, though. For my
sketch, I saw shapes within the photo palette that could
be interesting to use as a creature, one in particular
looked like a demon skull of some kind. In general, I
wanted my fire to begin as a fairly amorphous but cool-
looking blob then to take shape, like it was being pulled
into existence by the hovering hand. Your idea may differ,
but the sketching process is the same.

1. Start your sketch by making a blank new layer and
    dragging it to the top of the layers stack to be sure
    Photoshop sees it as a reference above everything
    else. Name this layer Sketch.

2. Pick up the Brush tool (B), and set the primary color to white.

3. To roughly simulate fire's glow, add a layer style effect. Double-click the Sketch layer's thumbnail to open the Layer Style dialog box, and from there click the Outer Glow check box in the list of Styles list (left).

4. Click the name Outer Glow in the Styles list to display style's property settings at right (**FIGURE 8.8**).

In the Structure section, notice that the Screen blending mode is set by default to emphasize the lights in the glow effect. You'll use the same mode to blend the flames.

5. A custom gradient that transitions from yellow-orange to red as it disappears in opacity will produce a more flame-like glow. In the Elements section, set Spread to 8% and Size to 76px, then click the gradient graphic in the Structure section to open the Gradient Editor (**FIGURE 8.9**).

6. In the Gradient Editor, click the bottom-left color swatch box and adjust the color to a fiery yellow. Click the bottom-right swatch and adjust it to red. You can match my fire gradient in Figure 8.9 or adjust to taste. Click OK to close the Gradient Editor, then OK again to close the Layer Style dialog box.

7. Try a few white paint strokes; the gradient Outer Glow effect gives your strokes the same general look as fire without the heat. My strategy for the sketch is to try some general variations, but not to get too detailed. You want to leave the details up to what you might find within the fire itself.

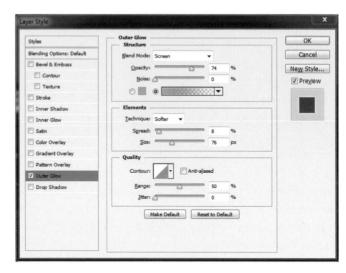

FIGURE 8.8 The Outer Glow check box must be checked and the name selected to access the Outer Glow effect's properties.

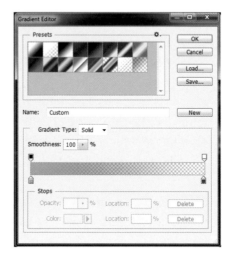

FIGURE 8.9 Create a custom gradient by changing the two color swatches below the gradient bar.

Browse and Position Your Flames

Meanwhile, back at the photo palette, a number of perfect starter flames are just burning to be used. When looking for pieces to patchwork into a semblance of your fire demon sketch, focus on the small elements that could work or that interact in interesting ways: two entwined flames twisting together or a rogue wisp that has a nice curl and wave. These unique pieces can be used in many different ways (sometimes repeatedly if layered well), so try them out by placing them around the composition, flipping, scaling, warping, puppet warping, and rotating until something looks right or just plain cool. Playing with the images and how they fit is a lot like building with Legos; it's not always about how the individual piece fits, but also how they all fit together. Because you'll be pulling samples from an unaltered and separately saved photo palette, the process is all nondestructive, so you can make as many attempts and alterations as you need.

Solo for Better Viewing

Recognizing what fits is sometimes easier when you can see all your layers at once, and at other times it's easier when you can view each piece individually. Called *soloing*, the process of isolating a layer for individual viewing is a handy technique for any composite. Give it a try as you select your first flames.

1. Open the photo palette file, *Fire_Play_Photo_Palette.psd*, if it isn't already. By default, the visibility of each layer is the same as when you last saved it, but that most likely includes many layers, all visible at once. Don't worry, you don't have to manually turn off the visibility for each layer one at a time (a combination of crazy and tedious) to view interesting layers in isolation.

2. To solo an individual layer, such as Layer 25, Alt/Opt-click the Visibility icon (the eye icon) for the layer you want to see by itself. That layer will remain visible while the others disappear. You can bring back the visibility of all other layers by again Alt/Opt-clicking the same layer's eye icon.

   If you change the individual visibility of additional layers after you solo a layer, however, be warned that the Alt/Opt-click toggle will no longer work. You will have to toggle the visibility for each layer separately to bring them all back. So, when you solo, remember to bring everything back the same way before working with other layers.

3. Once you spot a piece of flame that looks use-able, make your first selection with the rectangular Marquee tool (M) on the layer containing the flame you intend to capture. For example, try to capture the piece of Layer 25 shown in **FIGURE 8.10**; it looks vaguely like a skull of some kind, a good base to build on. (Of course, if you have a different fiery vision, choose another layer that better fits it.)

   Always select a generous amount more than what you intend to use to leave yourself extra room for masking seamlessly. In addition to using Screen mode, masking with flame is usually done with a soft brush to avoid obviously fake edges, so you'll need room to feather the edges. I go by the gentleness of the fire's gradient as a guide for how to mimic this transition, so take a look at the softness of the fire's edges and make sure you grab enough room in the selection to mimic the feathering.

4. Before copying, make sure the correct layer is selected and visible (we all miss this from time to time). Copy the selection (Ctrl/Cmd+C), then shift back over to the composite image tab and paste (Ctrl/Cmd+V).

5. Drag the pasted layer (in this case the skull shape) into the Fire group folder, then move your fire image into a good position in the composite with the Move tool (V) (**FIGURE 8.11**).

> **TIP** Lower the opacity of the sketch so you can see multiple layers at once as you place the various fire shapes to make matching the sketch easier.

FIGURE 8.10
Here's a piece that is soloed for possibly working as part of the fire demon/dragon head.

FIGURE 8.11
With the Move tool, position your first fire piece over the sketch.

Mask and Blend

Once a flame is in position, the next stage is to seamlessly fit it into the composite. You can do this in two steps: Change the blending mode, and create a mask.

1. In the drop-down menu at the top of the Layer's panel, change the blending mode of the first fire layer (and all subsequent fire layers as well) from the default Normal blending mode to Screen.

   As you may remember from Chapter 3, Screen lets the lights of a layer show through, while progressively darker areas (like the background) become increasingly transparent. Screen mode is a good choice for the fire, because we want only the light from the flames to be visible, while the rest becomes more transparent as the pixels get darker (**FIGURE 8.12**).

FIGURE 8.12
Screen mode allows the lights to glow through while leaving out the darkness by making it transparent.

SCREEN, LIGHTEN, MULTIPLY, OR OVERLAY: WHICH TO USE WHEN?

Blending modes are a lot like a box of chocolates—seriously. You really *don't* know exactly what you're going to get. You can, however, get pretty good at guessing once you know the shape and look of them. The effect of some blending modes may not be easy to predict when combined with other layers, but you can make a fairly close educated guess by keeping some things in mind.

Use Lighten for an element's layer when:

- The content you want visible is lighter than the background you are placing it above and the background is very dark.

- You want a very dark background to be *invisible* and lighter content to stay completely visible

- Dark content is challenging to mask out, or you don't have the time to get it right.

Use Screen when:

- You need a *gradient* rather than an on-or-off threshold of opacity for content as it gets darker, as is the case with the fire.

- You want to blend lighter content on top of other light content.

Use Multiply when:

- You want to darken content with a texture, much like a deep stain.

- You want to see both layers at once, but just the darker elements such as scrapes, grease, shadows, or other dark texture pieces.

Use Overlay when:

- You want some of the best of both Multiply and Screen, with the darks of a layer darkening the content and the lights of a layer lightening the content.

- You want to dodge and burn nondestructively with white and black painting.

- You want to colorize or make a custom photo filter controlled by layer opacity.

COPIED AND
ROTATED FLAME

FIGURE 8.13 Cloning fire is always a blast, but is also dangerous as it can get out of control and entirely too fake looking. Use variation and masking to help with this.

2. To remove the unwanted portions of the fire, click the Add Mask icon ▣ and paint with black directly on the mask in all the areas you want the fire to disappear. For me, this means using a soft (Hardness set to 0), default round brush that can mimic the smooth gradient of the fire itself; anything sharper will stand out as an edit. Let the fire be your guide for this. Change your brush size to match the gradient width rather than controlling hardness.

Be sure to paint with 100% opacity black; half measures always fall short of removing what you want and instead leave you with a greasy mess by the end of the composite. Suppose you set the opacity to only 90% as you paint. It may look like you masked out portions of the flame you didn't want, but really a slight 10% may be left behind here and there. Although the fraction sounds insignificant, it can build into a thick layer of digital grease when added to strays left behind by other layers. Don't trap yourself into tracking those pixels through the layers to remove them; simply paint at full opacity and flow and bypass the problem.

Duplicate and Vary

When you find a particularly useful flame, you can duplicate it to use in two places at once. Press and hold the Alt/Opt key while using the Move tool (V) to drag the fire element you want duplicated. Wherever you drop the fire piece, Photoshop duplicates it on a new, separate layer. This can be extremely helpful for filling in more flame areas and shapes, but don't get carried away (**FIGURE 8.13**). Duplicating instances works best usually when in combination with other layers that can hide and add variety to the duplicate to help it look less like a cookie cutter copy. Again, think of Legos: All pieces look very similar, but their combination then becomes original. Adding varying rotation, scale, and changes to the masked out areas goes a *long* way to obscure conformity.

For example, if you copy a previously used flame, make sure to add your own variation to it for the seamless effect. Add better variety by transforming it with the Move tool (V); try scaling, rotating, and flipping the image to get the best results and control of the fire. Some parts of the flame may be more identifiable than others, so use the Brush (B) tool to mask these out in the duplicate or even bury it in another flame. The more you add on top of these layers, the less obvious the duplicate is to spot.

> **TIP** To access the hidden Move tool features, be sure that the Show Transform Controls check box is checked in the options bar. Refer to Chapter 2 for all the hidden things you can pull from the Move tool as you work.

Try to avoid drastic differences in scale, however. Drastic size changes to fire are especially noticeable and can look like a miniature or artificially large fire, if you're not careful. Keep enough consistency to look like the flames are of the same scale, but enough variety to not distract the eye with tell-tale conformity.

Puppet Warp the Flames

Editing a layer with the Puppet Warp tool has the potential for *complete* control over a flame and is a technique well worth learning. Puppet Warp can be incredibly helpful for shaping something very specific and refined as it enables you to move every little bend in the flame to perfection.

To understand Puppet Warp, think less about puppets and more about spandex. When you select the Puppet Warp tool, it covers the visible portion of your layer with a mesh that reacts like a pliable, stretchy, spandex-like material. In the mesh, you then place pins from which you can pull, twist, and move the mesh-covered layer, giving you absolute control. Puppet Warp's primary function is also its major drawback, however: It bends and warps *connected* pixels (including the background); to manipulate an object only, you need to separate it from its background so that the background does not also have a mesh and changes applied to it. To better understand how you can use Puppet Warp, try creating a more controlled variety of flame.

1. Copy a long flame, such as *Fire007.jpg*, from the palette and change its blending mode to Screen. Place this flame in the Fire group folder and to the side so that you can practice with it by itself (**FIGURE 8.14**).

   The choice is yours, but I temporarily turned off visibility for the other fire layers.

FIGURE 8.14 Choose a long flame, such as Fire007.jpg, to practice warping.

2. Make a copy of the layer (Ctrl/Cmd+J), so you can always return to the initial state, and click the eye icon of the original layer to turn off its visibility.

3. For Puppet Warp to work best, you need to remove the flame's background so that the tool's mesh is isolated to just the flame. To do this, create a mask (using the Add Mask icon 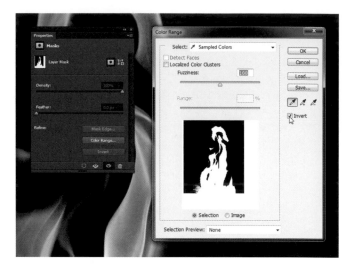) then double-click on the mask to open the Mask Properties panel.

4. Click the Color Range button (**FIGURE 8.15**), and in the resulting dialog box toggle on the Invert check box. Click the black background to the side of the flame, and set the Fuzziness slider to 100. This includes all those pieces that are *nearly* black in the initial mask of the background. Any remaining bits will create small islands of puppet warp mesh, so get rid of as much of the extra pieces as possible. Click OK when finished with your color range selection.

FIGURE 8.15 Color range enables you to mask based on color selections from the layer; in this case, all the black background.

PUPPET WARP TIPS

The Puppet Warp feature is like warping and the Liquefy effect on steroids. It goes further than working with just one kind of spandex as well; there's a range of hidden features packed into this tool. To improve your results, keep these tips in mind:

- When using Puppet Warp with objects that need to keep smooth edges, make sure to add pins in the middle areas only. Adding pins towards the outside will pull the edges outward rather than simply bending the main content in a more general and cohesive way.

- Selecting a pin and pressing the Delete key removes the pin, which makes things nice and simple if you get one too many going on. Think puppet, not pincushion.

- Holding down Alt/Opt enables you either to cut the selected pin (like the Delete key) or rotate (instead of move) it when you click just outside of the pin. Notice that the curser changes to a rotate symbol.

- The options bar holds powerful adjustments for your mesh. Here you can increase the mesh density (helps with precision), change the mode of the mesh and the way that the mesh reacts to pin movement (like switching from spandex to a water balloon), and expand or subtract the edge of the mesh (with the Expansion slider).

5. Mask out any remaining bits of fire you don't want to warp; I masked out everything but that long side stretch and the top flare (**FIGURE 8.16**).

6. To apply Puppet Warp as a Smart Object filter and warp nondestructively, you need to convert the flame layer to a Smart Object. Choose Filter > Convert to do so. Now you can return again and again to the warping mesh without being locked to one version.

7. Choose Edit > Puppet Warp to apply the control mesh to your flame (**FIGURE 8.17**). If you do not see a mesh appear over the flame, make sure that Show Mesh is toggled on the options bar.

   The mesh connects everything in a tension framework that controls how the pixels are stretched and moved; pulling the mesh exerts the most tension at a pin and progressively lessens further away from that pin.

8. Add pins along the inside of the mesh by clicking in various evenly spread locations throughout the flame. These are the points where the puppet strings attach and give you control.

9. Click and drag the pins to manipulate the flame (**FIGURE 8.18**). As with most things in Photoshop though, less is usually more. Don't do anything too extreme; instead, work on mild adjustments for the best effect.

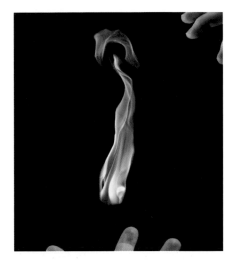

FIGURE 8.16 Mask out the extra pieces you are not interested in warping.

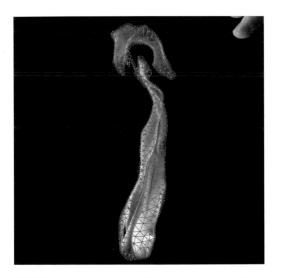

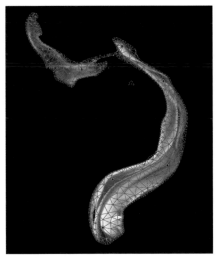

FIGURE 8.18 Puppet pins are the control points that allow you to manipulate the mesh into a new configuration.

FIGURE 8.17 The Puppet Warp mesh shows the framework for how tension is distributed throughout the layer.

Shape the Fire

Continue to bring in additional fire layers piece by piece, and much like carving, use the natural tendencies of the object to accentuate your creation. Fire has a grain of sorts, a flow, and it moves and twists in intricate and beautiful ways, which you can use for a more convincing look. Forcing something too much to your own can break its illusion and beauty, however, so be flexible and willing to change your plans based on the natural direction that the flames want to move. For example, I imagined the dragon/demon head differently in my original sketch, but a piece of fire twisted into an interesting jaw line, so I went with it, then suggestions of teeth formed from another flame, then some mane-like fire tufts seemed to fit into place after dragging a piece towards the neck (**FIGURE 8.19**). All in all, work intuitively and don't over-do it!

This may sound daunting and complicated, but once you bring some flames together, you'll be pleasantly surprised at the actual simplicity. Keep these tips in mind as you sculpt:

- Be mindful of the general shape you sketched and look for pieces that complement that outer edge. The inner filler doesn't need the same amount of concentration; let the flames themselves do most of the work (**FIGURE 8.20**).

- If the fire flow is going in one direction, see if you can continue where one flame left off with the edge of another. This way you can seamlessly guide exactly where your flames are flickering without it looking too choppy.

- Adding more flame layers on top of one another adds to the density and illusion of a 3D form (versus a flat shape), and can be used to simulate better dimensionality.

FIGURE 8.19 Pulling fire from abstract shapes is mostly about looking at the flame's natural tendencies and embracing them (or at least pieces of them).

FIGURE 8.20 Pay attention to your edges as you work, but let the flames generate the inside material and texture.

- Flames don't just vanish from bright yellow to straight black, as this ends up making the yellow a bit muddy-looking, especially when done digitally. So try to avoid masking right up to the brighter yellow portions of the flame—our eyes can notice the difference. Instead, stay closer to the reds and orange colors with the mask whenever possible (otherwise you may have to do some fancy color control for those edges).

- Duplicate the exact layer for a stronger effect. To add intensity to a layer that has a great shape but not enough strength to really glow through, duplicate the layer with Ctrl/Cmd+J. With Screen as the blending mode (which will be the default if the layer is copied from layer with this blending mode), the lights add to the lights and simply make it much more noticeable without making the color or gradients look bad.

In my own version, I worked quickly and didn't over think it. There's something to be said for keeping your image more suggestive and elegant. Too many details may be harder to get right in the end.

Blend Smoke and Hands

With your fire well in hand, it's time for some smoke from the hands. The smoke in *Fire Play* rises from the hands and fingers rather than the fire—it's magic, remember. Working with the smoke images is very similar to working with the flames, only a little simpler as they don't need to look as controlled. In addition, because the smoke was shot with a dark background, you can again use Screen mode to remove backgrounds and aid with masking as you did for the fire (**FIGURE 8.21**).

1. Open the photo palette file, *Fire_Play_Photo_Palette. psd*, if it isn't already. Click the Eye icon of the Fire folder if flames are visible and make the Smoke group

folder visible instead. Follow the instructions in the "Soloing for Better Viewing" section to isolate interesting smoke layers for inspection, if you need to.

2. Find some smoke you like, use the Marquee tool (M) to select pieces of it, then cut (Ctrl/Cmd+C) it from the photo palette. Paste (Ctrl/Cmd+V) it into your composite, and use the Move tool (V) to position it, as you did with the fire. (Don't forget to store the layer in the Layer panel's Smoke folder to stay organized.)

For the original *Fire Play*, I wanted the smoke to be rising from the forearm and top hand to add a little more mystery to the image and subject. I found some that looked like they were curling in a way that worked nicely with the composition and hand placement, specifically *Smoke011.jpg* and *Smoke013.jpg* for the bottom hand and left edge smoke.

3. As you did for the fire layers in the "Mask and Blend" section, change the new smoke layer's blending mode to Screen from the drop-down menu at the top of the Layers panel to remove its background.

FIGURE 8.21 The smoke layers use the same Screen blending mode as the fire but also need some extra scaling and blur filtering to create more depth to the overall image.

4. Again as for the fire, mask out any unwanted portions of the smoke that don't quite work as you planned. Mask with a textured brush and stroke in the direction of the smoke for more seamless masking results (**FIGURE 8.22**). This is especially important for composites like this one that use quite a lot of semi-transparent elements that need to blend on top of one another.

If you brush against the direction of the smoke, the result may look unnaturally faded where it shouldn't be. The smoke has more stringy elements than the fire, and you need to work carefully with them to be convincing.

Add Depth with Smoke

With just the hands and flames, the image appears a bit flat overall, which creates a more passive and objective viewing (**FIGURE 8.23**). By comparison, an image with full dimension makes us feel like we're actually there in first person (known as the *subjective point of view*). As you arrange your smoke, you can also use it to create just a little more depth to the composite. You can emphasize depth with scaling to simulate perspective (closer the object, larger it appears) and by creating an intentional depth blur to mimic something that's close and out of focus because of a shallow depth of field. By now, scaling with the Move tool's Transform controls should be quite familiar. To practice blurring to mimic depth, try your hand at applying a few filters:

1. Find a couple long strings of smoke and scale them way up so that they look close to the viewer's vantage point. (I used the layer from *Smoke011.jpg* for this part.) This gives the illusion that the smoke continues out of the frame for a more open composition, as if we're getting just a window glimpse into a larger

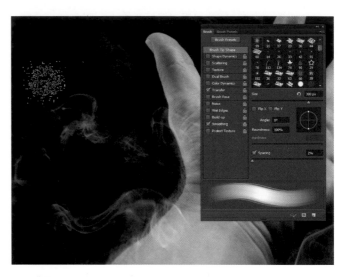

FIGURE 8.22 Use a texture brush for masking the smoke and be sure to paint with the flow direction starting from the outside.

FIGURE 8.23 Before adding smoke, the image appears very flat and dimension-less; adding an extreme close foreground such as blurry smoke can help with this.

scene (**FIGURE 8.24**). Pick up the Move tool and make sure that Show Transform Controls is toggled in the options bar. Shift-drag a corner transform handle to constrain the proportions while transforming.

TIP To use most filters nondestructively, turn your layer into a Smart Object before blurring. Right-click a layer's name and choose Convert to Smart Object from the context menu. This will let you apply Smart Filters that can be turned on and off as you work. This method also severely limits the kinds of blur available. Lens Blur, for example, won't work.

2. While scaling helps, the secret is in the Lens Blur filter. With the same long wispy smoke layer active, choose Filter > Blur > Lens Blur from the menu bar. This blur adds a special twist that nicely resembles the natural shallow depth of field blur made by a camera lens and large aperture opening.

3. Play with the settings that are brought up until you're satisfied with the look of the blur. Moving the Blur Radius slider to the left will decrease the amount of blur, while pushing it to the right increases the amount of blur. For Figure 8.21, a radius of 72px looked right for keeping the smoke identifiable while obviously out of focus (**FIGURE 8.25**). Be patient, waiting for the results; your computer may need some time to crunch the required calculations for this filter.

TIP To run the same filter and settings on another smoke layer, simply choose the new layer and press Ctrl/Cmd+F. In addition to saving time, it also ensures you apply the same settings as for the previous filter for better consistency.

FIGURE 8.24 Enlarging a couple smoke layers can add more depth as if they are closer to our vantage, and not just limited to one plane.

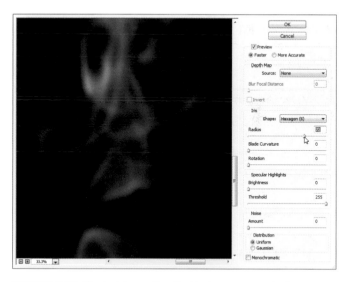

FIGURE 8.25 Find a blur radius that helps create a shallower depth of field for close smoke.

Blend Textures to Enhance

My first version of *Fire Play* felt unfinished somehow, sterile and not gritty enough. The reason, I decided, was the lack of other textures in the hands. Textures applied in combination with blending modes can add another level of finish that really makes a composite shine, or in this case, crack and peel. Specifically, I found that applying a bark texture with Multiply mode added gritty darks and made the smoke feel like it was coming from burnt crags in the bottom hand and forearm (**FIGURE 8.26**). To find a combination that works best for your own images, I encourage you to try several textures and modes; watch the changes in mood and look for one you like. For now, you can practice the process with the *Fire Play* composite:

1. Copy and paste into the composite a nice bark texture from the Other_Textures folder in the chapter's resource files. I chose *Bark.jpg* for my version.

2. In the Layers panel, change the bark layer's Layer Opacity to 50%, and position the texture over the lower forearm (**FIGURE 8.27**). Temporarily lowering the bark's opacity will enable you to see both the layer and where it's going, making alignment easier. Make sure to return Layer Opacity to 100% once you are done moving it around.

3. From the drop-down menu at the top of the Layers panel, change the blending mode from the default Normal to Multiply to mimic the look I chose for Figure 8.26.

   I liked this result, but some of the other blending modes had different, but equally awesome effects on the hand. Next, take a look at all your other options.

FIGURE 8.26 Bark from a tree created a surprisingly cracked forearm when applied with Multiply mode.

FIGURE 8.27 Change the layer's opacity to 50% to better see where exactly you're placing it.

4. Choose Color Burn (the blending mode after Multiply) in the drop-down menu and notice how it changes the look of the forearm. To move to the next blending mode (Linear Burn), press the Down Arrow key. Your image will change to reflect the new mode's effect.

   You can continue to cycle through each blending mode with the Down Arrow key to compare how they look in your image (**FIGURE 8.28**), or work your way back up the menu by pressing the Up Arrow key. I usually go through all of them quickly a couple of times to narrow it down.

5. Repeat steps 1 and 2 to apply the water layers to the top hand. (The water files are located in this same Other_Textures folder.) Change the water's blending mode to Overlay to add in lighter elements while simultaneously darkening the darks; essentially use the layer as a dodge and burn template. This effect brings more attention to the idea of elemental magic and fits in nicely as a contrast to the bark texture of the other hand (**FIGURE 8.29**).

> **TIP** Don't forget to always mask out portions of the texture that aren't necessary. Nothing ruins a composite faster than a texture extending past the boundaries of the layer you want it to affect. And, of course, be sure to clean up any digital grease that occurs along the way.

FIGURE 8.28 Cycling through the blend modes is an easy way to test out effects for the optimal look. Select one to begin with, then move through the menu with the Up and Down Arrow keys.

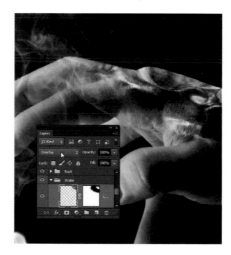

FIGURE 8.29 Applying a water texture with a blending mode set to Overlay gives the top hand a distinctive look.

Play with Color

With all the elements and textures in place, it's time to balance the image with appropriate warm and cool colors. You may have noticed that aside from the fire, everything is lacking in strong color up to this point, especially the gray smoke. Looks kind of weird, doesn't it (**FIGURE 8.30**)?

FIGURE 8.30 The image lacks cohesion, but it's nothing that Color blending mode layers and painting with warm and cool colors can't fix.

When a source, such as the fire, emanates a warm light, the particles around it, such as the smoke, hands, and other reflective surfaces, need to reflect the warmer light as well. This reflection can help create a sense of continuity and stronger cohesion to the parts of the image; without that reflected light the image elements still feel very separate.

In addition to adding warmth to various parts of the image, accentuating areas of the image with contrasts helps, in this case accentuating cool colors against the warm. This warm and cool effect can help create greater dimension, because visually, warms tend to pop out at us and cools tend to recede. (Fine artist Hans Hofmann may not care for the subject matter here, but he'd definitely like the theory behind it!) You can balance the colors in a few steps:

1. In the main composite, add a blank new layer and place it inside the Effects group folder. You'll use it to control the warm colors, so label it Warm by double-clicking its default title.

2. From the drop-down menu in the Layers panel, change Warm layer's blending mode to Color. Now, any color that you paint with on this layer will be applied as the dominant colorant of the entire composite.

3. With the Eyedropper tool (I), pick out a warm hue from the fire itself, some yellow-orange combination should do well for this (**FIGURE 8.31**).

4. Now paint away! But don't get too heavy with this. Instead, paint with a low opacity (under 10% to start) and a soft brush with a radius of about 800px (yes, this large to begin with for general coloring). The idea is about subtlety and making it feel "right," so avoid going too much the other way with getting color happy. In mine, you can see I painted some of the closer smoke and some more on the hands and forearm (**FIGURE 8.32**).

FIGURE 8.31 The Eyedropper can be especially handy for matching an established color palette like the flames.

TIP Sometimes opacity gets away from us as we paint. If your color control layer gets too strong, you can always drop down the entire layer's opacity. Sometimes I do this intentionally to find the right balance. I paint fairly intensely, then drop it back down with the Layer Opacity setting until I am happy with the results.

5. Create a second new layer, label it Cool, and again, change the blending mode to Color. In the Layers panel, drag the Cool layer above your Warm layer so that it supersedes it. If you want the cools to be seen at all, then they must be above the warm layers as any layer with the blend mode set to Color will supersede all other colors below it. I generally start with warm because that's the main color family needing to be represented. Cools are more of a contrast effect for subtly making the warms a little more dramatic without actually increasing their saturation.

6. Begin painting with a rich blue from the Color Palette panel (pull one open using the Window menu if you can't find yours). Try to be even more subtle with your painting, adding just enough to contrast against the warms from the fire. I focused on the area behind the top hand and other places more or less out of direct reach of the fire's glow.

FIGURE 8.32 Be strategic in where you paint warms and cools so it makes sense with what we are seeing as the source of warmth.

Curve the Mood

The final couple stages are mainly about finessing the whole picture, and in this case, taking control of the darks and lights a little more. These adjustments also help set the mood of the composite. One of the best ways to control the mood and contrast is with a curves adjustment layer. The strategy behind this is that when you make the darks a bit darker or the lights a bit lighter, Photoshop adjusts the rest of the values proportionally along a curve, which takes some of the worry out of getting each value just right. At the same time, it also allows for greater control and customizing compared to the simplified contrast adjustment layer.

For the original *Fire Play*, I wanted a mysterious, gritty, and darker mood. Although the hands looked less sterile, much of the scene still felt a bit too light and the hands still lacked much of the intensity and contrast of the rest of the image. Adding a curves adjustment is just the ticket for a dramatic effect, as you'll see.

1. Create a new curves adjustment layer using the Adjustments panel, and place it directly above one of the hands (**FIGURE 8.33**).

FIGURE 8.33 Curves are perfect for fine-tuning lights and darks in the image as long as the curve shape isn't too dramatic from the diagonal baseline.

2. As a default, the adjustment layer affects everything below it, so turn the curves adjustment into a clipping mask for the hand by pressing Ctrl/Cmd+Shift+G. Alternatively, you can Alt/Opt-click the line below the layer or click the small clipping icon at the bottom of the Adjustment Properties panel.

3. Increase the contrast within the adjustment properties window by making two new points along the diagonal curves line (click along the line to add a point).

4. Select the bottom curves point (it will turn solid black), and use the Down Arrow key to nudge it further down just a little bit. Select the upper point, and nudge it a bit higher with the Up Arrow key.

    Making the darks darker and the lights lighter is a good use for curves, but they also have quite a bit of control for a lot of subtlety compared to a related adjustment like levels. Refer to Chapter 4 on Adjustment layers for more on how curves works and why it's an awesome choice for just about all scenarios of light adjustment.

5. When you find an appealing contrast and finish adjusting the curve shape, copy the adjustment (Ctrl/Cmd+J) layer, place it above the other hand layer, and then clip it to the other hand as you did in step 2. Now both hand layers have the same effect applied.

6. Add a final global adjustment layer to the entire composite by placing a new curve adjustment layer at the top of the Effects folder, name it Global Curves. Use this layer for a final adjustment of contrast to either lighten everything up uniformly or darken things down even more. In the original *Fire Play*, I lightened things up very slightly. In general, I use a final curves adjustment above everything to add just a little bit more overall lightness, darkness, or general contrast to the composite depending on what I'm going for in the end. The same methods are still used as stated in step 3, but on a *much* more subtle level with this adjustment—to the point where it may not even be noticeable for most people, yet still has striking effect.

WARNING Never shape a curves line into an extreme S that doubles back on itself. Always keep the curve moving uphill in some fashion. A curve that doubles back tells Photoshop to invert certain values, saying, in effect, that some lights should be darker than some darks—not a good idea.

Dodge and Burn with Overlay

Curves does an excellent job enhancing the composite's lighting, but to add that final polish, you need a blending mode. Specifically, a new layer set to Overlay mode allows for complete dodge and burn control, for lightening and darkening, respectively. It's happily nondestructive too, making it a wise and fun choice for final lighting alterations and adjustments to eye-flow.

Sometimes even after the curves adjustments, a few pieces will fall a bit flat, so I used an Overlay layer to compensate for these trouble spots. Be mindful, however, that less is usually more with this effect. If you start to notice halos or something just looking "wrong," back it up and try again, perhaps on a new layer with the old layer disabled for later comparison (**FIGURE 8.34**). To find that balance, I like to go slightly overboard intentionally before reducing the layer's opacity to something more subtle. Because the dodge and burn changes are on their own layer you can always return and increase or decrease the effect through the layer's opacity. You can practice with your fire composite.

FIGURE 8.34 Dodge and burn nondestructively with an Overlay blending mode, but always remember to keep the effect subtle. Use a low opacity as you work for best results.

> **TIP** Do not make these last adjustments until you are completely satisfied with the placement of elements within the composition as these edits are not clipped to individual layers as before. Because they are placed in the top folder, above all the other groups, they are working on a global level.

1. Create a new layer, name it Dodge and Burn, and add it to the Layer panel's Effects folder above the Global Curves layer to make your final global adjustments.

2. Set the new layer's blending mode to Overlay by choosing it from the Layer panel's drop-down menu.

3. Thicken up all those parts of the flame demon that seem a little weak and too transparent by painting with white at just 6% opacity on the Dodge and Burn layer. For my version of *Fire Play* this was especially important in the neck and around the head; lightening these areas helped me better define exactly what I wanted to show up.

4. Bring out a few more highlights in the fingers and palms as well with the same technique. If fire were really that close, these parts would definitely be fairly bright. Plus, lightening these areas gives a little better eye flow and emphasis towards the flames and forming creature.

5. In the same way you lightened (dodged) the flames and fingers, you can darken down (burn) the shadowy wrists to perfection. In the Dodge and Burn layer, paint with black at a low opacity to darken areas and white to dodge (**FIGURE 8.35**).

    Alternately, you can create a second layer specifically for burning if you prefer to separate the two types of changes, as you did the warm and cool colors. Just remember to set the new layer's blending mode to Overlay.

Conclusion

The blending modes used in this exercise—Lighten, Screen, Multiply, Color, and Overlay—are all incredibly powerful tools for any number of composite challenges, even those not dealing with creative pyromania! Whether you need to drop out a dark background, alter the color of a sky, enhance the lighting on a subject, darken and age an object with texture, or any number of possibilities, these techniques are truly invaluable. So when you come up against a creative wall, try to pinpoint the kind of effect you need to happen and see how a blending mode changes the situation. For further demonstrations of creative uses for blending modes, check out Chapters 9, 10, and 12. Meanwhile, if you'd like to share your own final version of *Fire Play*, head on over to the book's flickr page: www.flickr.com/groups/ amc_compositing_photoshop

FIGURE 8.35 Edits on the Dodge and Burn layer work on a global level as they are within the Effects group folder, which is above the rest of the groups.

CHAPTER 9

Atmosphere, Grit, and Demolition

COVERED IN THIS CHAPTER

- Removing distortion with the Adaptive Wide Angle filter
- Atmospheric perspective
- Refining edges on subjects and hair selection
- Color and light alteration
- Texturing for mud, dirt, and decay
- Building demolition
- Depth separation
- Creating sun-rays

Let's face it, life is messy, and sometimes your composites need to be too, especially scenes of catastrophic survival. Immaculately clean photos of models and cities can be transformed into a gritty scene of decay and sword-filled drama with the judicious use of a few filters, textures, atmospherics, and, of course, hair selections. In this, the deepest chapter in the book, you'll not only learn to salvage a clean but distorted background with the Adaptive Wide Angle filter, but also how to age and weather a scene while working with textures, scenery, atmosphere, color, lighting, and building demolition. As you re-create *Nature Rules* (**FIGURE 9.1**), this project will take you through the steps of shooting in the studio to planting flowers in streets of a new era.

Gather Your Resources

A complex-looking composite doesn't always need a vast number of source images. As you remember from Chapter 6, *Nature Rules* is composed of only six main groups of layers. Open the *Nature_Rules.psd* composite document you created in that chapter to reacquaint yourself with its folders. If you did not complete the prep work in the "Using Tabs: Few Pieces, Big Payoff" section of Chapter 6, take a few moments to do so now. Alternatively you can use the jump-start file *Nature_Rules_Jump-Start_File.psd*, which is included in the Chapter9_Resources folder. Either way, get ready to dig in some digital dirt.

▶ **FIGURE 9.1** You may never jump into a post-apocalyptic scenario like *Nature Rules*, but a sword helps—as do good hair selections. This composite is primarily comprised of five central images: a meadow, model, city, mountain, and some clouds.

NOTE To access the resource files and videos, just log in or join peachpit.com, and enter the book's ISBN. After you register the book, links to the files will be listed on your Account page under Registered Products.

Straighten Up with the Adaptive Wide Angle Filter

We've all been there: You find the perfect background location for your composite puzzle, take a nice wide-angle picture, sit down to edit, and—wait, did the camera do some editing of its own while you were busy looking at the actual scene? Perspective distortion, such as in **FIGURE 9.2**, is as common as it is insidious, but it is correctable with the help of the Adaptive Wide Angle filter. With version CS6, Adobe revamped the filter capabilities of Photoshop and introduced the Adaptive Wide Angle filter for a number of fixes. Found in the Filter menu, the Adaptive Wide Angle filter enables you to correct a fair amount of distortion from angular perspective shots. Before you move forward with any kind of masking, it is important to first get the main shots looking the way you need them to be for detailed compositing, meaning distortion free and easy to match with a range of other shots. For example, I shot **FIGURE 9.2**, a cityscape of Montreal, Canada, with an 18mm lens, and it suffers from that bend and distortion shooting on a wide angle (short) lens naturally imparts to the edge of a building. Because the photo of the model doesn't have this kind of distortion, the city can definitely use some adjustment before being composited with her and the flowering meadow—the perfect chance to practice with the Adaptive Wide Angle filter!

FIGURE 9.2 Shot with a wide-angle lens, this Montreal cityscape shows a good deal of distortion and exaggerated perspective; it needs to be altered to lessen the effect and better match some of the other key shots.

TIP If you have an earlier version of Photoshop that lacks the Adaptive Wide Angle filter, try some alternative methods such as warping to approximate the filter's effect, or use the Lens Correction filter, previously buried in the Filter > Distort menu.

1. Using your favorite method, browse to the Chapter9_Resources folder, then the City folder to find the *City.jpg* file and bring it into the *Nature_rules.psd* composite document within Photoshop. Be sure to place it into the group folder named Main City, which will house all the city layers and the city adjustments for the rest of the composite.

2. Select the City layer, and make a copy (Ctrl/Cmd+J). This gives you clean copy to jump back to if things go wrong (and they often do) and you need to eventually rasterize the layer for pixel edits.

3. To ensure a nondestructive workflow, you'll apply the Adaptive Wide Angle filter as a Smart Filter, which you can be readjust at any time. First, choose Filter > Convert for Smart Filters to convert the City layer into a Smart Object (**FIGURE 9.3**), then choose Filter > Adaptive Wide Angle to open the filter's editing window. Here you'll find some neat tools to help correct for the wide angle and perspective distortion (**FIGURE 9.4**).

4. To mimic the same effect that I have, leave the Correction setting on the default of Fisheye. Your adjustments for the City layer need not match mine exactly, but try changing Focal Length to 80.6 and Crop Factor to 0.67 (Keeping Focal Length at 18mm and changing Crop Factor to 3.11 has a very similar effect.) Even though the image was shot with a wide-angle lens, I found these settings produced the most

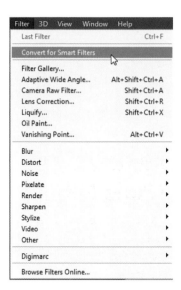

FIGURE 9.3 Smart Objects and their Smart Filters enable you to keep resizing and adjusting a layer until you are satisfied with its filter, scaling, and position, without degrading the quality with each resize.

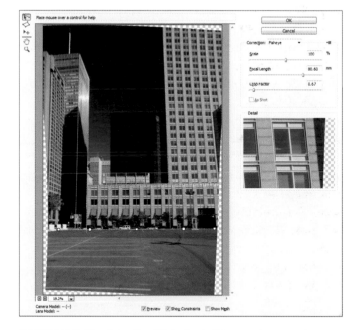

FIGURE 9.4 The Adaptive Wide Angle filter can be a great way to manually adjust the straightening and angle degree of any edge you want.

FIGURE 9.5
To straighten edges, click two distant points along each edge.

desirable results as they didn't try to pinch or overly compensate for the distortion, leaving most of the adjusting to my eye and manual control. These settings will change with each shot, so a good strategy for manual adjusting is to play with the settings until they get you close to the original shot and leave it up to the next steps for fixing those angles and edge curves.

> **NOTE** If your image hasn't been edited before, Photoshop will supply helpful information in the lower left that details the camera and lens you used when using the Adaptive Wide Angle filter. Many times you can find a good match and auto correction.

5. To straighten and align the image's edges, first click the Constraint tool (top left icon). In the large image area, you'll use the Constraint tool to draw lines along edges that you want to be straight. As you add a line, you may notice that it bends with the slight curve of the building edges (how cool is that?), and each line adjusts the image immediately. To try this out, click once for a starting point, drag the cursor, then click again to set an end point (**FIGURE 9.5**) Using Figure 9.4 as a *general* guide, add seven lines at the building edges.

   I started with the outer edges, as adjusting these will set the overall rotation and stretching of the entire image. Anchoring each line with an adjustment to the rotations (demonstrated in step 6) helps set up a good distortion correction base to work from. Adding the additional five lines throughout, covering both horizontal and vertical edges, I altered the remaining bits to taste.

6. Alter and rotate a line by clicking a line to select it; notice the small circles that appear. By dragging these rotation anchor points (similar to rotating with the Move tool), you can change the *angle* of the straightened edge, rotating everything that was on that line to precisely match the angle you choose (**FIGURES 9.6A** and **B**). For the example, I shifted the angles from leaning inwards to a little more straight up and down.

Click and drag the rotation anchor points to adjust all seven lines roughly as I did. I corrected a good amount, but left a little bit of perspective as I still wanted the buildings to feel dramatic and large—and even possibly a little tipsy for added effect. This is generally a subjective choice, so rotate these until you see something that works for you. For the example, I kept rotations fairly small and controlled to not overly distort the image too far the other way.

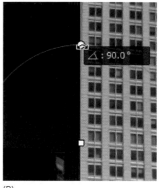

(A)   (B)

FIGURES 9.6A and **B** To begin, the building clearly needed straightening (a). When you adjust the angle of a line, Photoshop provides the exact angle degree as you rotate it (b).

> **TIP** Hold down Shift while dragging a rotation anchor point to rotate at exact 15-degree increments or to jump the rotation to a nice 90-degree alignment. This can really help for those moments that you know you want something straight up and down, but just can't eye-ball it the way you want.

7. When you're satisfied, click OK to exit the dialog box. In the Layers panel, notice that the City layer, which you converted to a Smart Object, now has an associated Smart Filter (and separate mask) that you can enable and disable to see a quick before-and-after view (**FIGURE 9.7**).

FIGURE 9.7 Smart Objects can have Smart Filters applied to them enabling better nondestructive editing. You can apply, change, or remove the Smart Filter at any time.

Mask Montreal

For the *Nature Rules* composite, you need only the newly straightened buildings from the City layer. To make the initial mask of the city, start with the quick selection of the sky; because it's a nice gradient of blue, it's easier to select. Then, you can invert the selection to apply to the buildings instead—much simpler than selecting the buildings by hand, eh? Finally, Refine Edge will help you fine-tune the selection even further before you create the mask.

1. Grab the Quick Selection tool (W) and begin painting a selection of the sky starting at the top. Work your way down and around until the sky is surrounded in an army of marching ants.

2. Invert the selection to apply to the buildings by pressing Ctrl+Shift+I or by right-clicking it and choosing Invert Selection from the context menu. Now when you apply a mask, only the buildings will remain.

3. Subtract the dark, shorter skyscraper from the middle of the selection: Hold down Alt/Opt to turn the Quick Selection tool into subtraction mode and paint over the building, including the top by the sky to be sure no edges remain. If the tool selects the shadows of the tall right building as well, release Alt/Opt to return to addition mode and paint to return the shadows. Work a little at a time, toggling between adding and subtracting from the selection to get exactly what you need selected.

4. Notice that the city's edges have a slight blur. Any alterations and lens corrections will slightly blur the image as well, and you need to simulate this slight blur to make the selection seem more natural (and less like a fake cut-out collage with sharp edges). To do so, click the Refine Edge button in the options bar. In the resulting dialog, shift the Feather slider to 1px. To avoid slight halos from the selections, set Shift Edge to about –40% (**FIGURE 9.8**). Click OK when you're satisfied with the refinements.

5. Click the Add Mask icon in the Layers panel to add the mask to the selection. Although you can do this straight from the Refine Edge dialog box (click on the Refine Edge icon in the options bar), I prefer the manual way so that there is never any confusion as to what is being masked.

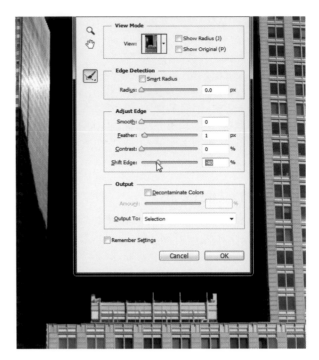

FIGURE 9.8 Refine the edge of a selection for a more seamless effect; adjusting Feather helps match natural edge blue, while lowering the Shift Edge sliders can prevent selection halos.

TIP When refining the edge of a selection, always make sure to zoom all the way in (Alt/Opt+scroll up with the mouse over the area you want to zoom, or press Ctrl/Cmd+ or Ctrl/Cmd-) so that you can actually see what you are refining. What may look just fine from afar is actually quite bad when you edit close up.

TIP To paint on a mask in straight lines (which is handy for buildings), click one end of the edge then Shift-click the other end; Photoshop will paint everything in between in a perfectly straight line at the current Opacity setting. If while using a tablet you notice that the opacity is attenuated even when pressing at full pressure, try turning off pressure sensitivity.

Preliminary Demolition

Although many atmospheric enhancements are finishing touches on a piece, some are easier to put in place if you do a bit of preparation early in the composite. In this case, the decaying look of the buildings will be easier to accomplish if you do some demolition to the mask now. Plus, removing the top section of the building on the right will help you situate the clouds when you're ready to add in the new sky. To make room for the mountain, you also need to change the depth of the small background building as well. A little advanced planning like this can eliminate frustrations and reworking later.

Just remember that your demolition does not need to be well crafted at this moment as you can (and will) refine exactly what the destruction looks like later in the project. For now, crudely smash off the top of the building and figure out your general shape for the remaining composition. For mine, I wanted a general sloped angle to the tall building at the right to help bring the eye flow downwards toward where the mountain, meadow, and subject were going to be placed. The more subtle hints you point in the conceptual direction you want, the better control of the composite and eye flow you will have. A line here, a light spot there, exaggerated contrast, and use of color are all useful tools.

1. Using the Quick Selection tool (W), select a general area you want demolished from the right skyscraper. Again, this can be very rough as your goal at this moment is to make room to add the clouds to better balance the composition (**FIGURE 9.9**).

2. Paint your selection with full opacity black to remove it from the scene. (Go ahead, make some demolition sounds while you paint. The more you can get into the play of your work, the more fun you'll have and the better the end result!) Alternatively you can use the shortcut of Alt/Opt+Delete to fill the selection with your foreground color (make sure this is black).

FIGURE 9.9 Select the areas you roughly want to demolish, such as the top of the right skyscraper.

FIGURE 9.10 Mask out the areas of the city that you want to demolish for later enhancing with greater decay detail.

3. Rough out any other demolition sections you may want to make and check for any selection edges that didn't quite work as intended. To clean these up, use a small, round, and soft brush to paint the areas you want masked with black and the areas you want visible with white (**FIGURE 9.10**).

4. Check that you fully masked out the dark middle building and the smaller background in the previous exercise section. Zoom in close to be sure there are no lingering pixels, as you don't want digital grease to pile on the mountain you'll composite into this space. Although the little building doesn't need to be demolished like its shinny blue neighbor, you will later move it *behind* the mountain layer to add depth. For now, just make sure it's out of the way.

Mask the Meadow

With the city more or less ready at this point, the next phase is to bring in the meadow and mask out the tree line from its source picture (**FIGURE 9.11**). Adding the pretty meadow flowers and lush green will provide a great contrast and clash of moods to the concept of gritty survival and structural decay. The meadow also provides a neat way to obscure the swordswoman's feet. Feet have a way of being the first thing to look "off" when you try to combine a controlled studio shot with an environment, as you'll learn later in the "Select the Swordswoman" section.

FIGURE 9.11 This shot I took of Bell Meadow in the Sierra Nevada Mountains has similar enough depth, lighting, and POV to fit nicely with the city scene.

1. From the Meadow folder of the Chapter9_Resources folder, open *Meadow.jpg* and place it into composite document's Meadow group folder. Remember to keep the Meadow folder above the City group folder; layer ordering is especially important because it directly corresponds to the stacking depth of each section.

2. In the Layer's panel, change the Meadow layer's opacity to 50% so you can see the city horizon and the meadow simultaneously, then use the Move tool (V) to place and scale the meadow to fit at the bottom of the two side buildings (**FIGURE 9.12**). I got decent results with little effort by matching the tree line with the first prominent building. After the meadow is more or less in position, return the opacity to 100%.

3. Click the Mask icon at the bottom of the Layers panel ▣ to add a mask, then paint out the Meadow layer's sky and trees with black, and a round, soft brush (or if you use a harder brush edge, be sure to return the brush hardness to 0 when finished) at full opacity until just the edges of the tree line are left. In addition, I left in a few bushes and trees to incorporate into the scene for better blending, but the choice is yours.

FIGURE 9.12 Changing the opacity to 50% lets you see both layers just enough to find a good place for the meadow.

TIP Double-check your masking coverage by pressing the \ key to display your masked area in the default red. If you notice spots not covered with red (or covered spots that shouldn't be), fix them. Take the time to check for stray pixels as you work to avoid digital grease build up.

4. Choose a textured brush with some speckling in it, such as Spatter (**FIGURE 9.13**), and paint with black in an up-down motion following the natural contours of the foliage. This better simulate the organic edges of the meadow, trees, and bushes, helping the layers to blend more naturally.

Shrink your brush (press the [key) and zoom way in to get this part just right. If you see part of a bush's light green continue in a certain direction, work with these tendencies and don't just bulldoze through them, it will look bad if you do. The more you can let the pictures do the painting for you, the more it will feel "right" in the end.

TIP Anytime you paint too far, press the X key to flip your paint selection, toggling between painting out (black) and in (white) the mask. If black and white are not your default foreground and background colors, press D to restore them to their rightful place.

FIGURE 9.13 A brush with some splattered texture can greatly assist in painting a more convincing organic edge for the mask.

Move a Mountain

Okay, we've watered the parking lot, which is sprouting quite well; it's time to move mountains. Specifically, you'll add an image of a solid granite mountain from my own stomping grounds in Yosemite National Park between the decaying skyscrapers. Adding the mountain is easy; the trickier bit is making good selections and painting the mask to ensure the new cloudy sky shows behind the mountaintop, as well as the detailed vegetation along the edge.

1. Copy the *Mountain.jpg* (**FIGURE 9.14**) from the Chapter9_Resources folder of source files into the composite document's Mountain and bg City group folder. (Again, see Chapter 6 for how best to search for and bring images into Photoshop and the composite if this is still a challenge.)

2. Use the Move tool to position the mountain between the skyscrapers so that the trees are hidden but room remains to bring back that smaller building you masked out along with the shiny one (**FIGURE 9.15**).

FIGURE 9.14 This mountain eventually will replace that shiny skyscraper; for now, put it in the Mountain group folder.

3. Select the bulk of the mountain with the Quick Selection tool (**FIGURE 9.16**). If you grab some of the sky by accident, press Alt/Opt to subtract from the selection (or click the icon in the options bar). In the next steps, you will refine the selection to properly include the trees and shrubs.

4. Click the Refine Edge button in the options bar. In the resulting dialog, add a slight feather (1px or less) and set Shifted Edge to –30%.

5. Next, move the floating Refine Edge dialog box to the side so that you can see both the menu as well as the entire mountain perimeter. By default the Refine Radius painting tool is selected. With it, paint around the mountain perimeter to select those unruly shrubby areas in detail (**FIGURE 9.17**). When satisfied with the selection, click OK.

6. Click the Create Mask icon in the Layers panel to turn the selection into a mask.

7. Tidy up the edges of the mountain by again painting with a textured brush as you did with the meadow shrubbery. Work from the outside in to simulate organic edges and be sure to be zoomed in completely.

FIGURE 9.15 Move the mountain into position covering up the unwanted parts and leaving a place to return the background city to the left of it.

FIGURE 9.16 Make a rough selection of the mountain first.

USE THE REFINE RADIUS TOOL ALONG THE EDGE

FIGURE 9.17 Use the Refine Radius tool when you have bits of edge detail that require special selection.

FIGURE 9.18 Mask the small background building and move it below the mountain in the layer stack to add depth.

TIP To sharpen a mask selectively, change your brush to Overlay mode in the options bar. This will simultaneously sharpen and shift the mask inward wherever you paint along the edge. This can be very useful for getting rid of those last halos that were missed in the selection edge refining.

8. Remember that small building you masked out? It's time to bring it back. Sandwiching the mountain between the near and distant buildings will give the illusion of depth. In the Main City folder, disable the City layer's mask by Shift-clicking the mask to the right of the layer thumbnail in the Layers panel.

9. Now that you can see the background building, make a Marque (M) selection of the light colored background city leaving some room for a mask as shown in **FIGURE 9.18**. Copy this selection (Ctrl/Cmd+C), and use Paste in Place (Ctrl/Cmd+Shift+V) to paste (so that it doesn't get placed somewhere else in the composition) the city piece beneath the actual mountain layer in the Mountain and bg City group folder. Does that long folder name make a little more sense now? Always try to think ahead so that you don't have to pull out the duct tape to patch problems later.

10. Mask out the sky and other buildings of this wee layer using the same methods used on the first steps of masking as you did for the main city image.

Practice Cloud Control

Adding dramatic clouds can change the entire atmosphere of an image. As a cloud photography addict, I can attest to the importance of developing your own database of images so you have a good array of choices—from dramatic foreboding to shining optimism. When searching your options, carefully consider the lighting. If lighting in the cloud image doesn't fit your scene, viewers will notice. They may not be able pinpoint the problem to the clouds, but they'll notice something's "off." You may not have to match *exactly*, but pay close attention to the direction of the highlights and shadows if you want it to be believable. Remember, the shadow changes direction on an object only when we see something at a different angle in relation to our own POV (or obviously if time passes). So if the sun is to the east of one object, it's to the east of all the objects!

For *Nature Rules*, adding clouds will be dramatically simpler because of the previous masking work you did to the city and mountain. The only task that remains is matching the contrast and other pieces that can help make the cloud layer visually fit into place.

1. From the Clouds subfolder of the Chapter9_Resources folder, bring *Cloud1.jpg* into Photoshop as a tab, then move it over to the composite with the Move tool (V). Alternatively, you can use Adobe Bridge and the Place feature (right-click an image thumbnail, then choose Place > Photoshop from the context menu) to bring the entire image over as a Smart Object. If you want a piece rather than the whole object, however, you still need to use the tab method.

2. Scale the clouds down using the Move tool (V) and drag the layer into the last group folder, Sky (**FIGURE 9.19**). See Chapter 2 for a refresher on scaling and other Move tool hidden features.

3. Add a Curves adjustment layer to bring a bit more contrast to the drama: Click the Curves Adjustment icon in the Adjustments panel ![icon], then create a bit more contrast by dropping down the darks and raising the lights as shown in **FIGURE 9.20**.

FIGURE 9.19 Move the clouds to the correct depth, the bottom of the layers stack.

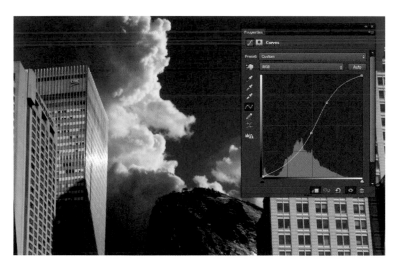

FIGURE 9.20 Curves control clouds very nicely as they are so full of tonal range; this adjustment allows for pinpoint accuracy on the final cloud mood.

4. To clip the Curves to that sky layer, Alt/Opt-click between the Curves and the Clouds1 layer in the Layers panel (**FIGURE 9.21**). Alternatively click the Clipping icon ![clip] in the Layer Properties panel. Either way, this will tie the adjustment to this Clouds1 layer, in case you want to apply a mask in the future and have only the clouds affected by the adjustment layer.

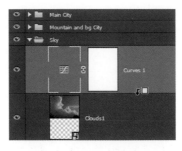

FIGURE 9.21 Clip the curves adjustment to the Clouds1 layer; if you decide to mask the layer later, the adjustments will show on the cloud layer only.

5. At the moment the composition is too left-side dominant and looks off balance. Adding more clouds will balance it out, filling the emptiness in the right sky. Bring in the *Clouds2.jpg* file and place it in the Sky group folder above the Cloud1 layer and adjustment.

6. Cloud2 features a little more back lighting and works better placed closer to the sun's direction; it just needs to be masked to match. Click the Create Mask icon, and choose a large, soft, and round brush. With a low opacity setting, work around the edges until you come to the highlights. Make sure to mask out everything but that one small backlit element. The transition of the sky to highlights can be synced best with another curves adjustment, so for now leave the mask alone when you reach the highlights (**FIGURE 9.22**).

FIGURE 9.22 Mask out everything right up to the cloud's highlights.

7. Create another adjustment layer, place it above Cloud2, and clip it to this layer (Ctrl+Alt/Cmd+Opt+G on the adjustment).

8. Click the adjustment to bring up the Adjustment Properties panel, add another two control points along the Curve's default diagonal as you did in step 3. Shift the darks downward and bring the lights up ever so slightly. Look for that sweet spot where the cloud matches the background sky and other clouds nearly perfectly—no need for detailed and fancy brushing (**FIGURE 9.23**).

FIGURE 9.23 Control the cloud tones with a Curves adjustment layer to match the larger cloud and sky.

Cheer and Color Control

The elements of the scene are coming together quite well; however, overall it just looks too happy and cheerful—not good for a scene supposed to depict decay crushing all the cheer from the world (yes, aside from the pretty flowers). The composite's color palette needs to reflect this melancholy. Doing a global adjustment at this point will help seamlessly add textures and other dramatic adjustments later on without accidentally making the colors too garish.

1. Click the Effect group folder to open it, and add a new Black & White adjustment layer from the Adjustments panel ▣. This instantly makes everything completely black and white, which may seem a little extreme but makes a necessary starting point.

2. Reduce Layer Opacity to about 63%. This will help control the color intensity for the remainder of the project and instantly creates greater continuity as you work (**FIGURE 9.24**).

Combine the Studio and the Outdoors

Seamlessly adding a studio-photographed model into an outdoor scene provides some interesting lighting, texture, and atmospheric challenges. This is really a three-part operation: selecting the model (and especially her hair) correctly, refining the mask to make her look as if she is standing in the scene (for *Nature Rules*, a field of flowers), and adding clipped textured layers so that the studio model blends into an outdoor scene without standing out horribly. Often it is imperative to have multiple pose options to better match the mood and direction you plan for your composite.

Selections

For *Nature Rules*, I've provided three different poses of model and ex-Marine Miranda Jaynes that I photographed in the studio with the help of lighting-Jedi Jayesunn Krump (**FIGURE 9.25**). For the example, I chose the side-draw (*Pose1.jpg*), because it drew the viewer's eye in the direction I wanted. All of the options have their own intimidating flare, however, so you can work with any of these poses just as well.

FIGURE 9.24 Desaturating the composite with a Black & White adjustment layer set to 63% opacity does quite a bit toward creating a more cohesive and wonderfully cheerless look.

FIGURE 9.25 Photographing several poses of your subject gives you more compositing flexibility. Choose one that best matches the idea and composition you are going for.

1. First, choose the pose you'd like to use from the Subject folder in the Chapter9_Resources folder, bring it into the composite document (either with Place or the tab method), and put it in the Layer panel's Subject folder. Don't forget to label as you build up your layers; this one should be called Subject.

2. Turn the layer into a Smart Object (right-click the layer thumbnail, then choose Convert to Smart Object from the context menu), and scale it down until Miranda fits your vision of the composition.

   For the example, I scaled Miranda to just under half the height of the scene from head to feet. This way she is close enough to identify with as viewers, but far enough away to make her feel especially isolated.

3. For selecting Miranda and separating her from the studio background, choose the Magic Wand tool (W). Toggle off Contiguous in the options bar, set Tolerance to 50%, and click in the center of the background behind Miranda—nearly a full selection automatically (**FIGURE 9.26**). For

parts and pieces that weren't included the first time, Shift-click on the remaining tone. The Magic Wand tool works well in this case because of the blessed uniformity of the background; if there was clutter or other what-not, you would need a different set of selection tools.

4. Press Q to enter the Quick Mask mode, choose a large, solid brush in white, and finish off what needs to be included in the selection with a few strokes. (Likewise, if part of Miranda's skin was selected by accident with the Magic Wand, take this time to deselect it by painting with black). Press Q again to exit Quick Mask mode, then press Ctrl/Cmd+Shift+I to invert the selection to encompass Miranda instead of the background.

5. For best results, you'll refine the edge selections in *two* stages: feather and shift the edge of the selection, then in the next step you can do the hair selections. Click the Refine Edges button, then adjust the Feather slider to 0.5px so give the edge a slight blur, matching the sharpness of the image itself. Set Shift Edge to –40% to fully eliminate any halo (**FIGURE 9.27**). Click OK when the edge looks like it fits with the selection (ignoring the hair).

FIGURE 9.26 The Magic Wand selected most of the background in the entire scene with Contiguous off and Tolerance set to 50%.

FIGURE 9.27 To feather the hard selections edges and yet avoid feathering the hair, break the refining into two steps. First, feather the edge of the entire selection and click OK, then refine the edge once again, this time using the Refine Radius tool to select the hair—this takes out the feathering done earlier on the hair, like rinsing out shampoo!

FIGURE 9.28 Use the Refine Radius tool for selecting complex hair with amazing simplicity.

TIP Change the background of the selection back and forth between white (W) and black (B) to better see any white or black halos that remain in the selection while in the Refine Edge dialog box.

6. To refine the hair selection, click Refine Edge again. Just as you collected the mountain's shrub details, brush the Refine Radius tool across the hair to capture the small flowing strands, turning the rather chunky and awkward selections of hair into a fairly precise selection (**FIGURE 9.28**).

7. After all the hair strands are selected, click the Add Mask icon ◙ at the bottom of the Layers panel to see how the selection turned out within the composite and its new background.

8. To eliminate any stray halos that are still lingering, pick up the brush, select Overlay mode from the options bar, and paint with black. This will tighten the selection inwards a little and also sharpen it as well, so use this technique only in moderation.

   Alternatively, you can paint using the default Normal mode with a small and soft brush along the edge. This is my preferred method, but brushing accuracy counts heavily. Also make sure to paint in any holes that came from the original Magic Wand selection; these typically occur in lighter areas such as the sword, hands, or pants.

Standing in the Thick

How do you keep your subject's feet on the ground? Although well-rooted to the studio floor, once in the composite document, Miranda stands on top of the grass with her feet visible. This common problem looks just totally wrong and can ruin the effect of an image. My solution for the example was to take her legs off just below the knee, creating the illusion her legs vanish into the meadow grass and flowers. If this seems too daunting, you could scale your subject large enough so that her feet continue off the bottom of the composite, as if she is standing very close to your own POV (see Figure 2.23). To help you decide, here's how the vanishing into the meadow version works:

1. Painting directly on the subject's mask, grab a textured bristle brush from the Brush panel; paint with full-opacity black to mask out the feet and legs. Stroke from the ground up, mimicking the blades of grass and the

flowers. Don't get too detailed until you know exactly where you want to place the subject in the meadow, however. Each time you shift the subject around, the meadow will look different by the legs and will need adjusting on this mask. You may need to touch up this mask towards the end of the project when you settle on final placement (**FIGURE 9.29**).

2. Adding shadows to better match the scene's lighting and transition, the two layers will add depth and greater realism. Click the New Layer icon  at the bottom of the Layers panel to create a blank layer to hold the shadows, change its blending mode to Overlay and its name to Shadows. Create a group folder above the Subject folder, label the folder Shadows, and move the Shadows layer to it.

3. Switch to a soft brush once again, lower its opacity to 10%, and gently paint in some shadows to the left of the subject and around the lower legs. The low opacity setting enables you to work incrementally (**FIGURE 9.30**).

Again, the shadows need not be too perfect at this stage; you'll need to return to this layer and readjust them depending on where you shift the subject and how you finesse the image.

FIGURE 9.29 Mask out the feet and legs to get a better idea of placement.

FIGURE 9.30 Shadows help dramatically when you first bring a studio subject into the natural world.

Muddy the Model

Nothing adds atmosphere and gritty reality to an image like a little dirt and texture. The studio Miranda is simply too clean to match the post-apocalyptic mood of this composite. Surviving in the wild roughs up a subject. Adding in some textures goes a long way to change the entire feeling of the image, and with surprisingly little effort.

1. From the Chapter9_Resources folder, grab *Cookie_Sheet.jpg* (**FIGURE 9.31**) from the Textures folder and place it directly above the subject both in the composite and Layers panel. Label this layer as Muddy. Metal textures are amazing for a number of uses, and scratched and stained cookie sheets, such as this one, are excellent source material.

2. Change the Muddy layer's blending mode to Multiply so that it will darken the subject with all of the textured elements.

3. Press Ctrl+Alt/Cmd+Opt+G to clip the Muddy layer to the visible pixels of the subject only (or Alt/Opt-clicking between the two layers in the Layers panel).

4. Move, scale, and rotate the texture with the Move tool (V) until you align the blotches and stains to places that look fitting to you. For the example, I wanted to pull out some obvious scuffs and scrapes on the arm, so I found an area that looked promising and shifted it until it had good coverage (**FIGURE 9.32**).

FIGURE 9.31 A metal texture from a used cookie sheet has so much potential for texturing—always be on the lookout for things like this!

FIGURE 9.32 Move the metal texture around until you get some marks in places like her arms and face.

5. The scratches help, but Miranda is still far too clean and part of what stands out is her lighter pants. To darken these and add some additional wrinkles and stains, bring in *Falls1.jpg* (also in the Textures folder). Find a good spot for this granite texture that matches the crease direction, but avoids the water. I found the rocks just to the right of upper Yosemite Falls ended up working well (**FIGURE 9.33**). Label this layer as Dark Pants.

6. Change the Dark Pants layer's blending mode to Multiply and clip it to the subject (Ctrl+Alt/Cmd+Opt+G).

> **NOTE** Avoid too many textures overlapping with each other as this turns mere mud flecks into a swamp! You don't want to drown the subject, just add some texture in selective places, so use a mask on the texture when appropriate to avoid too much texture overlap (this mostly goes for the skin).

7. Although the pants definitely darkened down in my version, so did half her arms and torso. If you run into the same problem, add a mask and paint out everything except where you want darker pants (**FIGURE 9.34**).

Color and Lighting

One of the main things that currently feels ill-fitting is the exact source of the lighting on the subject (not to mention how dark and muddy she is compared to the rest of the image. Although Miranda was shot in fairly neutral lighting with a definite direction that was appropriate, to look natural in the composite, the Subject layer needs greater emphasis and more warmth from the sun, as well as cool colors lurking in the shadows. The specific

FIGURE 9.33 Find a spot of granite to use to darken the pants with the Multiply blending mode.

FIGURE 9.34 With a pinch of granite and a little masking in the mix, the pants are dark and muddy!

color and lighting adjustments your image will need depend on several placement variables, so replicating the exact effects in *Nature_Rules.psd* may be difficult. You can, however, use the following steps as a guide to get you started.

1. Create a blank new layer, and place it above the last texture used just on the pants. Clip this new layer to the one below, change its blending mode to Overlay, and label it as Highlights. Now you're ready to dodge and burn the lighting and shadows nondestructively (**FIGURE 9.35**), similar to the fire and smoke in Chapter 8.

2. Choose a soft, round brush and a low-opacity white. Paint along the pants where the sun would be hitting on her right side (Figure 9.35). Called this layer Highlights, because that's what your painting provides.

   Don't go too crazy with painting in lighting, because it can quickly look painterly and fake. Keep it basic and as natural looking as possible. Think of the sun's location, and use what little lighting direction is still left on the subject as an indicator of what to emphasize.

3. Create a second new layer, this time above Highlights, and repeat steps 1 and 2 naming it Warm Highlights and using a warm yellow-orange to simulate more of the warmth of direct sunlight that studio flashes just don't replicate in the same way.

4. Also on the Warm Highlights layer, add a little more dimension and contrast to the shadows by painting in some faint blue in most of the shadows. In natural sunlight, this is the typical occurrence that Monet and others studied endlessly—what they wouldn't have given for an Overlay blending mode with colors (**FIGURE 9.36**)!

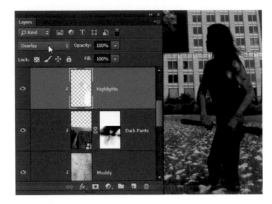

FIGURE 9.35 With an Overlay mode layer clipped to the subject, you can paint exactly the kind of lighting you want.

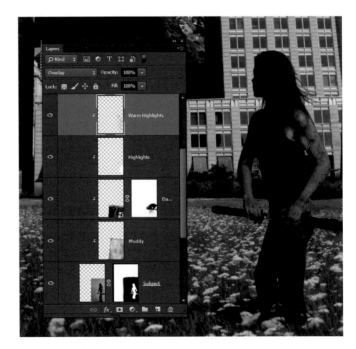

FIGURE 9.36 Warm highlights and cool shadows add subtle dimension with a big final impact.

At closer look the layers of the original *Nature Rules* will reveal I also added a little more texture to muddy the hair and a curves adjustment to darken just the hands and create a more convincing shadow for them. Both of these decisions used the same texturing and lighting methods already covered, just in smaller detail (**FIGURE 9.37**). Try your own combinations of these various techniques while you piece together what enhances your composite and what does not.

> **TIP** Don't underestimate the power of taking a break. Nothing is more important than getting some separation and returning with a fresh perspective, especially when you're trying to get something to look "right."

FIGURE 9.37 Work in small and controlled layers. They can add up to dramatic changes by the end.

Complete the Demolition and Decay

In "Preliminary Destruction" you began taking jagged chunks and pieces out of buildings with the intent of finishing later. It's later. Not only will you return to the original mask to paint out additional pieces, you can add slight shadows to the destruction by painting black on a layer directly underneath the city. To complete the effect, broken buildings need broken windows, which you can supply with the Magic Wand tool and a bit of painting. Some gritty textures like granite and rust can make a dramatic difference, as well. There is no exact science to this; you can make your scene as damaged or clean as you like. The more texture and demolition, the more age the structures seem to accumulate.

1. Just as you did with texturing the subject, bring in a layer of rusty metal (*Rust1.jpg*) from the Textures resources folder, and drop it directly above the City layer within the City group folder (**FIGURE 9.38**).

2. Change the new layer's blending mode to Multiply for nice, dense corrosion. You'll lighten this up in a little bit, but for now just need to get things blending nastily.

3. Clip the rust layer to the city's mask by Alt/Opt-clicking between the two layers in the Layers panel (**FIGURE 9.39**).

4. Also from the Textures resource folder, bring in *Half_Dome.tif* to add some variation to the corrosion, destruction, and general weathering of the right side building. I liked this piece of Yosemite's Half Dome because it has good highlights, dark stains, and downward streaks. Again, clip the new layer to the mask of the city and change its blending mode to Multiply.

FIGURE 9.38 Rusty metal has a great way of texturing and aging just about anything.

FIGURE 9.39 Clip the rust layer to only affect the visible pixels of the city.

5. The textures also make the building look dramatically darker, so lighten it by adding a curves adjustment: Click the Curves icon ▦ in the Adjustments panel. Clip this new layer to the city's mask by clicking small clipping icon ▣ at the bottom of the Adjustment Properties panel.

6. Add two curve control points to the default diagonal curve line by clicking high then low along the line. Move the upper control point fairly dramatically to lighten the building enough to feel like it's still in the sun. As you can see in **FIGURE 9.40**, my version maxed out the lights just after that mid-range histogram peak. The lower control point simply keeps the darks anchored while you lighten the midtones in the next step.

7. Create a *second* Curves adjustment layer for a more subtle adjustment to the midtones. Add one control point and gently bring up the entire mid range as shown in **FIGURE 9.41**. Sometimes one layer is just not enough to adjust subtle emphasis at specific tones, multiple Curves adjustment layers can give you multiple levels of control.

8. Repeat steps 1 through 7 to apply a similar corrosion process to the last glowing beacon of shinny civilization: the small background building.

Smashing Windows

Broken windows impart a haunting, mysterious, not to mention menacing, aura to any building, leading viewers to wonder who might be watching from all those hidden places. Magic Wand selections and a bit of black paint are all you need for this effect. Again, the severity of destruction is up to you. For the original *Nature Rules*, I wanted a vast majority to be missing or have just small fractured

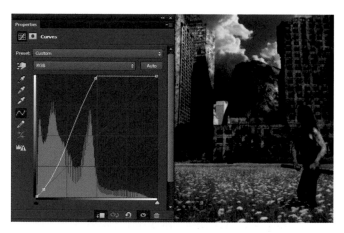

FIGURE 9.40 This Curves adjustment layer is a dramatic shift, but effective in lightening up the buildings.

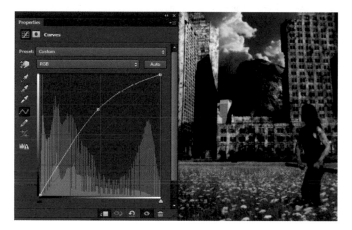

FIGURE 9.41 The second Curves adjustment layer gently lightens all the midtones to balance out the darkness that textures brought to the buildings.

pieces remaining. If I wanted to have complete control, I might paint these exactly right, pixel by pixel, but there's a much quicker way that does a half decent job and it uses Magic Wand selections.

1. Make sure that you have the original city layer selected (not the mask, not an adjustment), then pick up the Magic Wand tool (W).

2. Set Tolerance to 20 in the options bar, and be sure that Contiguous is unchecked.

3. Click an average window. Because the Contiguous toggle was off, portions of all the windows are now selected. Zoom in close to be sure (**FIGURE 9.42**). This obviously saves a great deal of time compared to carefully painting window by window.

4. Create a blank new layer, and make sure it is placed directly above the last adjustment done to the city—name this layer Window before moving on.

5. Grab a black paint brush at full opacity and paint in all the selected window areas. Repeat steps 3 and 5 until you demolish the windows to your satisfaction. Rather than filling all the selections with black, painting allows for greater control over the amount and location of the black.

6. Deselect (Ctrl/Cmd+D) so you can work outside of the selection, and zoom in close with some of the windows for final touch ups and custom painting on the Window layer. While the Magic Wand technique did a great job overall, you also can use what was painted as a base for more fine-tuned and precision window shattering (**FIGURE 9.43**).

FIGURE 9.42 As long as Contiguous is unchecked in the options bar, selecting one window will select similar portions of all windows.

FIGURE 9.43 Painting black in all the window selections instantly makes the building feel more ominous and believable.

Shadows of Destruction

Masking chunks out of a building is a good start, but proper shadows really sell the illusion of believability. For a final convincing appearance, try these steps.

1. With the City layer active, zoom in close to the top of the large building on the right so you can more accurately cause some mayhem.

2. Shrink your brush down to 6 pixels (press the [key), and paint with 100% opacity black on the mask to bring sharp and messy edges to your previous roof demolition. Take a look at **FIGURE 9.44** for some visual aid.

3. Add dimension to the roughed up edges by bringing in some shadows. Create a new blank layer, place it directly beneath the City layer, and label the layer Shadows.

4. Paint with the same 6-pixel brush along the edges that feel like they need greater depth using **FIGURE 9.45** as a guide. If it looks as fake as a paper-thin B-movie set, add some thickness along the edges. From the ground perspective, you would see this thicker part of the wall on the underside or left side, but adding in parts here and there enhance the impression of things not breaking clean, making parts look like an angled smash, is definitely good too.

FIGURE 9.44 Compare this finely tuned destruction to the quickly roughed-out building demolition in Figure 9.9.

FIGURE 9.45 Add in a bit of shadow and mass behind the masked city and it goes a long way for a more convincing effect.

Add Atmospheric Perspective

Some debris in the air further heightens a scene's reality, especially a dirty and destructive scene like *Nature Rules*. A thickness of dust and atmospheric perspective adds depth and separation of the subject and background, as well. With the subject staring off into the distance, adding more obscurity and atmosphere can help foster an ominous and foreboding feeling that also works well with this piece. The idea is to have viewers wondering what exactly she's looking at in the distance and wonder why she may be drawing her sword. The more you can leave details to the imagination of the viewer, the more immersed they'll feel in your scene and contribute to the narrative themselves. For this section you'll create the base atmosphere that you'll enhance further in the final effects and finessing phase.

1. Create a new blank layer (click ), name it Dust, and place it in the Meadow group folder.

2. You're essentially going to paint a smoggy haze into the scene, so pick a pale and fairly neutral yellow from the Color panel (**FIGURE 9.46**). While white has a washed out look, a pale yellow fits into the scene adding both color and the feel of reflective particles. Choose a very soft brush, change your brush Opacity to 5% in the options bar, and adjust the brush size to between 400px to 600px.

FIGURE 9.47 Adding atmosphere by painting can bring a lot more depth and mystery to the composition.

FIGURE 9.46 Use the Color panel to choose a custom atmosphere color to paint into the scene.

3. Everything you want to obscure near the horizon, paint with multiple strokes. Keep your painting more dense closer to the ground, then slowly pile it higher and higher as if it is rising into the rest of the city (**FIGURE 9.47**). Be sure to add enough variety to make it feel natural, such as gentle plumes of haze here and there. Keep in mind that the further away something is, the more atmosphere that accumulates between it and the viewer, so make your painting thicker in those areas you want to have greater depth.

Finesse the Final Effects

Despite this chapter's fairly methodical steps, projects never quite go that smoothly. I find myself working on an area, moving on to another, then returning to readjust something earlier on to harmonize with or enhance later changes. That's largely what this last stage is about: those adjustments and final layers that help make the entire composite fit neatly together with a better overall balance and cohesion.

Here we have the three areas that still need attention: color, shadows, and lighting. You'll first be working in the Effects folder at the top of the layers stack, so your adjustment layers and effects will affect the overall composite.

Color Continuity

Although you muted the color dramatically with the Black & White adjustment layer you added at the end of the "Practice Cloud Control" section, it didn't go quite far enough with creating a continuity and general mood. As a personal preference, I enjoy warmer tones in a final image. In this project, adding a bit more warmth emphasizes the feeling of dusty air and drab greens and blues, making the viewer look for patches of sunlight. A new layer will help you quickly warm up the composite:

1. Create a blank new layer and place it into the Effects group folder. I usually call this layer Warm to help me remember what it does.

2. Choose the Bucket tool (G), and pick out a warm yellow-orange from the Color panel.

3. Spill the bucket across the layer with a single click—you can't miss! Change the blending mode to Overlay and lower the layer's opacity to 11%. You want just enough yellow-orange to add a subtle flavor of warmth to the piece, without looking like the photographer failed to set the white balance correctly (**FIGURE 9.48**).

FIGURE 9.48 Adding a warm color spill on an Overlay layer brings greater continuity and color control to the composite.

Shadows and Meadows

With all your elements in their final places, you can return to adjust the shadows needed to get the subject looking like she actually belongs in the meadow. Some of these shadows involve adjustments to the entire meadow to help create continuity for where the subject is standing. What's nice about working within a group folder such as the Subject folder, is if the folder gets moved, so too will the shadows you paint across the entire meadow.

1. Open the Shadows group folder you created *within* the Subject group folder back while working on the subject's shadow.

   Because Overlay mode darkens the darks when painting with black, but mostly leaves very light parts alone (as they don't contain much to darken), some of the light flowers at Miranda's feet weren't shaded when you first added shadows with an Overlay blending mode.

2. To fix this, create a new blank layer above the first shadow layer (name it Dark Flowers for easy reference), leave the blending mode as the default Normal, and paint with a low opacity black (press 1 for the shortcut of 10% opacity) directly on this new layer. Aim for the light bundles of flowers that the first shadow layer at Miranda's feet missed. Again, use the example file included to see the extent of my flower shading (**FIGURE 9.49**).

3. Create another blank layer above Dark Flowers (each shadow layer will be placed above the next from here on out), name it Shadow Field, and change its blending mode to Overlay. You'll use this layer as the main darkening component for the entire meadow as well as to better blend the subject's legs with the grass.

FIGURE 9.49 If light flowers are in the shade, they need to look like it; painting with a low-opacity black on a Normal blending mode layer is a simple and effective solution.

4. Paint with the same low opacity black brush, this time at about 400px in size; you want gentle, but large changes. This brush size specifically helps with creating an effect of the meadow being partially under a cloud, with full sunlight only at the edges where Miranda is looking. **FIGURE 9.50** illustrates how painting in this way changes the coherence and mood of the image.

▸ **FIGURE 9.50** Play with the shadows and contrast of the meadow to create a more dramatic mood and create a slight vignetting effect to give the bottom of the image more closure.

(A)

(B)

FIGURE 9.51 Paint a spot with a speckled brush (a), then blur it using the Motion Blur filter to simulate sun-rays (b).

Glare and Global Lighting

To continue the effect you created by adding atmosphere and dust to the scene, you can bring in additional glare and even sun-rays. Unlike the layers sitting within the Meadow folder, however, these layers will be global effects. If you're not done remodeling yet, keep working on that and come back to these steps when you're all finished.

1. For the first of the final lighting effects, create a new blank layer, name it Glare, and place it above the Warm layer in the Effects folder.

2. Using the Color panel, choose a light cream color in the yellow family, and change the size of the default round and soft brush to 175px.

3. Paint some final touches of atmosphere, a little thicker this time compared to the first round (start with a 5% or less opacity). Add it to the same places as where you first created some dust and atmosphere, but also spread outwards onto the other buildings as well. This will help ensure that the depth looks right. Notice that the buildings at the edges of the meadow need to be lightened as well. Even just a slight haze painted on top of the black windows will make the building feel more distant and convincing overall. In a landscape photograph, shadows are true black only when they are very close to the viewer's point of view; get this wrong and viewers will notice!

4. Slight hints of sun-rays can help give a more tangible feeling to the scene and enhance its atmosphere. To add some, first create a new layer in the Effects folder, and name it Rays. Choose a nearly white cream color and a large (400px) speckled brush. On the Rays layer, paint one single speckle instance (just one click somewhere in the middle of the scene).

5. Choose the Motion Blur filter (Filter > Motion Blur) to give the painted area a nice smear (**FIGURE 9.51**). Switch to the Move tool, and stretch the blurred paint stroke into a long shaft of sunlight (Show Transform Controls must be toggled for this). You can move and copy this layer where you need it and blend it in appropriately with masking like the rest of the layers. To flare the rays outward, hold Ctrl/Cmd while you drag a transform point outward (**FIGURE 9.52**).

6. A pair of Curves adjustment layers will add the final lighting effects. The first will lighten the buildings and make the places with atmosphere and glare glow a bit more. Add a new Curves adjustment layer, name it Glare Curves, and alter the curve line to gently boost just the highs. Keep the darks anchored as shown in **FIGURE 9.53**. Invert the mask with Ctrl/Cmd+I so that you can then subtly paint in just where you want these glare spots emphasized with a white, large, and soft brush. (See the mask of Glare Curves in **FIGURE 9.55** for a guide to where and how much white I pointed on my version.)

7. Create a second Curves adjustment layer to lighten everything up as a whole while still keeping the clouds from blowing out by getting *too* light. Name the layer Final Curves and place it above Glare Curves in the layer stack. Adjust its curve line to raise the midtones and darks as shown in **FIGURE 9.54**.

The strategy of including separate Glare Curves and Final Curves layers is to control exactly which darks and which lights are highlighted with two separate masks and two variations of curve adjustments. Final Curves is also gently boosting, but boosting everything together without painting on the mask.

FIGURE 9.52 Flare the rays outward by holding down Ctrl/Cmd and dragging one of the corners outward before moving the rays into exact placement.

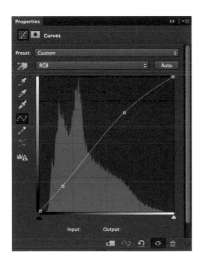

FIGURE 9.53 Glare curves should focus on boosting some of the lighter elements a little bit more, while anchoring the darks to make sure they are not touched in this heavily masked layer. Mask out everything except the few areas of glare, such as the buildings and atmosphere.

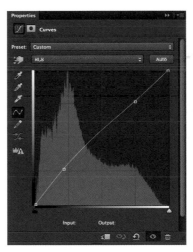

FIGURE 9.54 As one last touch, the darks across the entire image needed to be lifted just enough to get across daylight, yet still staying gritty and contrasting to work with the dire theme—you can't have it too light and nice looking!

In both adjustments layers, be sure to paint with black on the Curves mask in the areas you don't want the Curves to affect, such as the already lighter cloud spots if that is still a problem area at risk of getting blown in your own composition. Take a look at the provided Photoshop file to see how I used these last curves within the composite (**FIGURE 9.55**). The general strategy for final lighting adjustment is about a combination of overall balance (getting things light and dark enough as a whole) and subtlety helping with eye-flow. In the *Nature_Rules.psd* example file, notice that I lightened the entire area around the subject to draw just enough attention and emphasis to this part of the composite.

Conclusion

If your final image didn't exactly turn out like the example, that's okay! The goal of these tutorials is to help you improve your eye, as well as your technique. As it is, there could be a bit more work done on lighting and the rest, but part of good projects that stay fun is knowing when to say enough is enough. *Nature Rules* is a challenging project to get looking perfectly "right," but with enough breaks and adjustment revisions to each section, a seamless and foreboding composite is all but guaranteed. Regardless of the direction you took the project, you should definitely have a better understanding of how to create greater depth with atmosphere, how to make good hair selections, the power behind clipped adjustments, and even how to alter the perspective and distortion of a wide angle lens. I'd say that those alone are some powerful tools with which to face the daunting compositing world.

FIGURE 9.55 Paint with black on a final lightening curves adjustment so that areas such as bright clouds do not get blown out and overly distracting.

INSPIRATION

CHAPTER 10

Mastering Elemental Textures

COVERED IN THIS CHAPTER

- Using source images as inspiration
- Composition considerations for better balance
- Water manipulation with warping
- Blending modes for water and fire effects
- Layer styles to add glow
- Dynamic and scattered brush properties
- Color control and painting color layers

Being able to bend and alter textures and colorful elemental forces is just one of the fascinating and addicting aspects of working with Photoshop—and the genesis to *Control*. In this project I mixed my wife's face with water, added fire to a piranha I photographed while in Peru, and borrowed the eye from a frog hopping around the Erie Canal (**FIGURE 10.1**). Although this may sound like a Frankenstein-esque composite, color control and textures helped me blend everything to create a surreal play on humankind controlling and manipulating the rest of the natural world.

This project is also a good study in being inspired by source images rather than working to some initial plan. Sometimes in compositing you can go out and shoot what is needed (as I did for the face), and sometimes, you can work around imagery that you already have that inspires you and begs your Photoshop sensibilities for additional creativity (as the piranha did). In this project you will see how I worked from both directions to come up with a fun experience and satisfying end result.

▶ **FIGURE 10.1** *Control* combines a piranha, frog, fire, rust, water, and my wife Erin. Adding some textures, blending modes, and layer styles I transformed them to raw elemental powers.

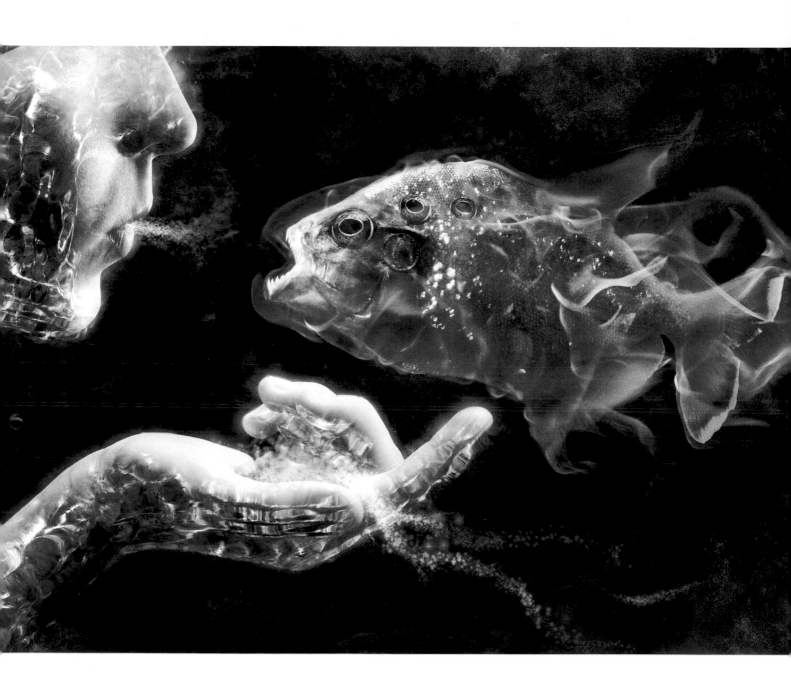

Step 1: Fish for Inspiration

It can be a great idea to look through your photos and get inspired to create something new! My inspiration for this image began with the shot of the stunning gold piranha (**FIGURE 10.2**)

Once I began looking at the fish for a potential scene, I sketched out an idea of a face close up, but it really didn't come together until after looking at my source imagery for other ideas and textures, such as old pictures I took of shallow river water over granite during a camping trip (**FIGURE 10.3**). Looking at these two shots I could see how I might mold the water into various shapes around a close up face and hand. After that idea, the composite just needed a good balancing element, which of course led to my images of fire. A bit more searching of the archive yielded a frog that would add to the surreal theme (**FIGURE 10.4**) and some metal with a long and rusty history to serve as a backdrop (**FIGURE 10.5**).

To supplement the composite material found within my archive, I still needed to shoot original content for the face and hand. I planned the lighting based on the sketch and brainstorm of surreal light more or less coming from the glowing fish. For the shots shown in **FIGURE 10.6**, however, I wanted the key light to be generally coming from the direction of the fiery fish to add to the effect of the fish glowing as well as provide a good amount of contrast between the hand and background. So, armed with a meager clamp light and CF bulb, I put up a dark sheet behind my wife Erin and fired off a few shots with her face and hand fairly close to the light.

FIGURE 10.2 This shot of a gold piranha caught in the head-waters of the Amazon was the central inspiration for a surreal creation.

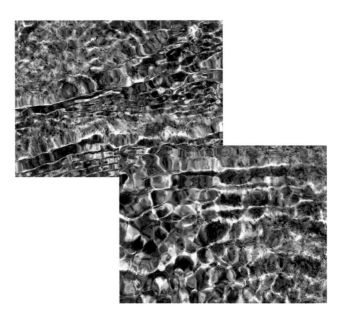

FIGURE 10.3 Shallow water running over sunny granite or other rocks can create a multitude of interesting shapes and forms for this kind of project.

FIGURE 10.4 This fellow was quick, but my shutter speed was quicker. Nature shots also often require immediate action, so don't hesitate when you have the opportunity.

FIGURE 10.5 Metal textures can have a plethora of uses; an abstract and dynamic background is definitely one of them.

FIGURE 10.6 These shots only had to follow the imaged lighting scenario of a glowing fire fish without worrying about the same kinds of seamless issues of other composites.

TIP For close up images like these that aren't showing how they are connected, shoot them separately as you have more control and better mental focus on what needs to be changed or adjusted for each. Get the hand just right, for example, then concentrate on the face.

Step 2: Get Organized

Because this composite's source images hailed from vastly different sources, I wanted to see the workable images together for better comparison and pre-visualizing. Following the same procedures discussed in Chapter 6 and 8, I first compiled individual photo palettes for the fire and water images (**FIGURE 10.7**). I also created black-and-white copies of the of the water images for better discerning of shapes and obscuring the original tinted content. Having grayscale copies of the water let me look for natural forms more objectively as the patterns are easier to pre-visualize and connect. For the remaining elements, such as the background texture and subject, I picked the best shots in Bridge and brought them into Photoshop individually.

> **TIP** Pull the photo palette's tab down and to the side if you have the workspace. For example, I keep my photo palette document open on one of my monitors and piece things together in the composite document on my second monitor.

Also covered in Chapter 6, I made a group folder for each section of the composite, as shown in **FIGURE 10.8**. Finally, I brought in the main elements of the composite by copying and pasting them from their own documents, then moving each image layer into its proper place within the composite image (**FIGURE 10.9**).

> **TIP** Create group folders within folders you already made for those times that you need an extra level of grouping and separation. This would work for subcategories within a larger category, like drops of water within the water category of images.

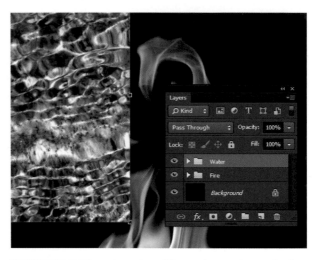

FIGURE 10.7 The categories of fire and water let me look at the textures separately, keeping my workspace clutter free and tab free as well.

FIGURE 10.8 In prepping your composite file, make sure to include both group folders and subfolder when necessary.

FIGURE 10.9 Once you start a group folder scheme, make sure to stay with it and don't leave any important layers in the wrong group.

Step 3: Convert to Smart Objects

To work with the main images as nondestructively as possible while scaling and doing other transforms, I decided to convert them to Smart Objects. This way I could later finesse the composition and scale based on the actual source objects to see how they looked next to one another. As discussed in Chapter 3, when you use Smart Objects, most edits like transforms and filters have better quality control and flexibility as you can return to the edit and keep adjusting it right where you left off—and simply there's no quality loss. Converting to Smart Objects *before* masking is important, because during conversion Photoshop will unfortunately apply any mask you made before the layer became a Smart Object and in effect erase the masked out content (not very nondestructive, eh?). The best approach is to convert your main layers to Smart Objects as soon as they are brought into the composite. With this in mind, I converted the hand, face, and fish to Smart Objects by right-clicking on the layer title in the Layers panel, and then selecting Convert to Smart Object in the context menu (**FIGURE 10.10**).

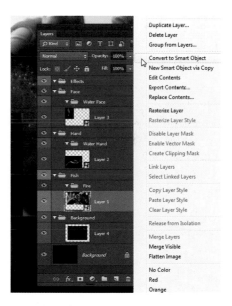

FIGURE 10.10 Smart Objects are a great way to transform a layer and apply filters nondestructively.

> **TIP** If you need to rasterize your Smart Object for any reason (such as small edits or some specific filter use) right-click the layer's title within the Layers panel and choose Rasterize Layer from the context window. You can do this at any time, and the layer will still keep whatever mask you made for it while it was a Smart Object. This will, however, make filters and other edits permanent to that layer. Rasterize wisely!

Step 4: Mask the Fish

All the extra backgrounds of the source elements needed to be masked out to give me a better idea of the layout—and a good place to start was by making a good selection. I used the Quick Selection tool for the fish because it had good clean edges for the tool to cling to as I selected around the scales (**FIGURE 10.11**). I then refined my selection edge using the Refine Edge button in the options bar. From there I made some adjustments (seen in **FIGURE 10.12**) to feather the edge ever so slightly and shift it inwards to avoid any extra halo that might show up.

FIGURE 10.11 Quick Selection does wonders selecting images with a reasonably clean edge on the subjects, such as this fish.

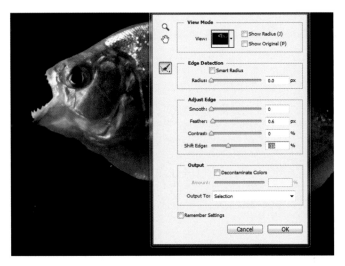

FIGURE 10.12 Using Refine Edge on a selection allows for edge feathering and biting a little amount into the selection to avoid any halos by accident.

TIP If the Quick Selection tool mistakes vaguely similar pixels and includes far too much in a selection, hold down Alt/Opt and notice the cursor gains a small minus inside the brush area. Now you can deselect areas you do not wish to retain.

Next, I added the mask by clicking the small Add Mask icon at the bottom of the Layers panel ▣. As you can see in **FIGURE 10.13**, the mask worked pretty well, but the fish definitely needed some scale reconstruction around where the fingers were holding it, but we'll get into that in step 6.

The rest of the images required similar selecting, refining, and masking.

NOTE The more times you go over an area adding and subtracting, the more discerning and particular the tool becomes as it can tell you are trying to select something specific.

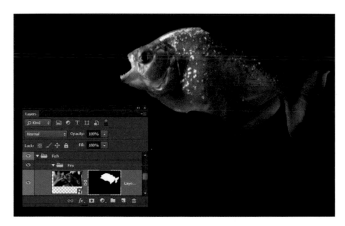

FIGURE 10.13 Once a mask is applied from a selection you can always adjust it by painting with black and white.

Step 5: Scale the Smart Objects

Working with something as a pre-visualized and loose concept is vastly different than seeing the actual images together and adjusting them to fit better, so its a good idea to always stay flexible in your planning and execution—that's why I turned these layers into Smart Objects back in step 3.

As mentioned earlier, converting the main layers to Smart Objects can greatly help with nondestructive insurance. As Smart Objects, a composite's layers can then be altered repeatedly in all kinds of ways without destructively editing the original content. They are superficially limited (only because it adds an extra step) if you want to start touching up the actual raster pixels of the layer (never a preferred edit as it is destructive), but short of that they can be scaled, warped, stretched, have their blending modes changed, and even have most filters applied to them (in the latest versions of Photoshop), plus you can always go back to re-adjust your edits. In short, they are *amazing* for composite work. This feature is especially handy for a nondestructive workflow and staying flexible with the project and image sources.

NOTE In older versions of Photoshop, Smart Objects are more limited and may not have the same abilities as shown in Photoshop CC. So test out your own version to make sure it's working in the ways that you need it to, especially with masks. You can always revert them to a useful raster layer. Seriously, there are many professionals out there that can live without Smart Objects and still do great work, so don't feel left out! But if you can use them, definitely do so to keep edits even more nondestructive.

To make room for the hand and face I shrunk down the fish a little and also played with the scaling, positioning, and rotation of the hand and face until the composite felt right and had a good compositional balance (**FIGURE 10.14**). Finding that sweet spot is a very subjective process but there were a few things I was specifically looking for within the composition: Eye-flow, creating a sense of motion, and imbuing a sense of balance to an image are all part of the process and key for thoughtful consideration. Such extra finessing will definitely be noticed in the final result!

Step 6: Give the Fish a Froggy Glare

The real fish eye from the gold piranha was intense looking, but not as wicked and menacing as the frog's eyes from the Erie Canal, so the fish definitely needed an eye-job to look this disapproving. Plus, it needed to be moved over a little. In fact, he needed more eyes altogether. I decided to swap out the fish's own eye for three copies of the frog's eye in decreasing sizes.

To ensure the original would be unharmed if my surgery went wrong, I made a copy of the fish layer and deactivated the original's visibility by clicking the Visibility icon next to its thumbnail 👁; this is akin to storing away a digital negative of the layer that we can always return to if things get too experimental even for a mutant three-eyed fish covered in flames (**FIGURE 10.15**).

Because the fish had been converted to a Smart Object, I double-clicked the fish thumbnail in the Layers panel and clicked OK in the resulting prompt, which told me that I could edit the layer in a separate document. Photoshop then opened a new document just for the Smart Object where I began my eye operation. Each time I saved this

FIGURE 10.14 Scaling objects as Smart Objects lets you keep adjusting throughout the entire project history without diminishing the original quality of the layers.

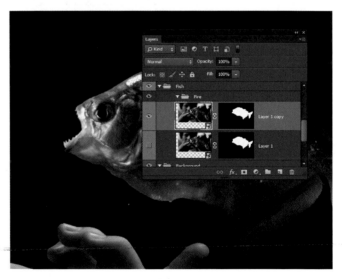

FIGURE 10.15 Duplicate the operational layer; keep one to edit and one to save as an invisible backup.

new document (Ctrl/Cmd+S, not the Save-As function, just Save), Photoshop updated my composite with the new changes. This ability can definitely take the complexity of projects up another notch as you could even have Smart Objects within other Smart Objects—pure genius. Sometimes called *dynamic linking*, this is a workflow godsend for certain projects. Back to the one at hand, I drew a selection around the original fish eye using the Lasso tool. A right-click brought me the context menu (**FIGURE 10.16**), where I selected the Fill command. (Alternatively, pressing Shift+Backspace/Delete will do the same.)

In the dialog box that opened, I chose Content Aware and clicked OK; the selection filled in quite nicely and was all prepped for adding on some frog eyes (**FIGURE 10.17**). Afterwards I saved then closed the document. Back within the main composite I could see that my newly copied fish layer had been updated accordingly.

> **TIP** You can also use adjustment layers while editing Smart Objects in a new document, and Photoshop will save these layers as part of the Smart Object. When you go back to your main composite, you will see the adjusted layer as a single Smart Object. Return to editing it once more by right-clicking the layer's name in the Layers panel and choosing Edit Contents from the context menu. The adjustment layer will be hanging out with the rest of the Smart Object layers.

With the fish now eyeless, I needed to obtain a donor eye from the frog image. Quickly masking out everything but the bulging eye itself, I made two copies of the layer by selecting the Move tool (M) and Alt/Opt-dragging the image within the canvas workspace. Rather than just moving each eye as the Move tool typically does, Photoshop

FIGURE 10.16 Fill-Content Aware is great for those instances of needing to replace an object that stands out with a nearly seamless background based on the selection's surroundings.

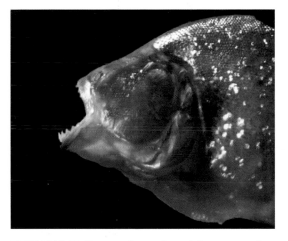

FIGURE 10.17 Content Aware found the surrounding scales and blended them in nicely (for a mutant fish about to be set on fire).

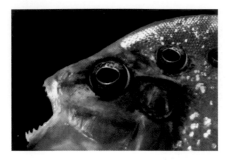

FIGURE 10.18 Copy multiple instances of a layer by holding down Alt/Opt and dragging the image to a new location.

TIP The more you can use clipping masks in clever ways the more time you will have for spending on other work. Your use of them steadily increases as you realize their potential.

instead created clones that could immediately be transformed to create a bit more variation (**FIGURE 10.18**).

Because Photoshop CC can apply clipping masks to folders, I was able to place all the new eye layers into a group folder. To do this I selected the layers then pressed Ctrl/Cmd+G, then created a Curves adjustment layer clipped to the folder (select the Curves adjustment then press Ctrl/Cmd+Alt/Opt+G). Doing adjustments to multiple layers this way is much more efficient as opposed to making three new curves, each doing the same adjustment. In the Curves adjustment layer I lightened the lights and darkened the darks, moving the two control points on the Curves line until each eye popped with the same contrast as the fish.

Other fishy operations included adding some copied scales to where the fingers were pressing against it. This worked in much the same way as the eyes: I masked and copied material from other parts along the edge of the fish to keep a decent continuity. Knowing also that the fish would soon be covered with fire, I didn't spend a great deal of time striving for seamlessness by limiting the appearance of duplicated scale patterns.

Step 7: Harness Fire and Water

Fire and water are mesmerizing in their own right, but control their shapes and color by morphing them into something impossible (and just a hint wicked), and you have the ingredients for purely riveting visuals that can be applied to any scenario. When using fire and water as textures, forget what you know about physics. Try to see the images for what they are: a fascinating mix of light and dark shapes, gradients, patterns, and random variations. Look beyond the obvious and concentrate on what you *see* in the images not what you know about fire and water to find and harness pieces that match the main composite elements, meaning the curve of a face, hand, and shimmering scales of a fish for *Control*.

Starting with the fish, I wondered how glowing scales might look wreathed in fire, so I studied the fire photo palette and singled out shapes that seemed to match the contours and flow of the fish (**FIGURES 10.19A** and **B**).

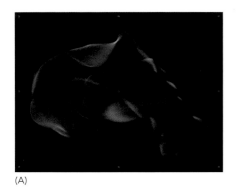

(A)

(B)

FIGURES 10.19A and **B**
Fishing through the fire photo palette, I found a piece (a) that seemed to fit perfectly around the fish head as a glowing exterior element (b).

HOT TIPS SETTING SUBJECTS ON FIRE

As you look for fire pieces to combine with parts of another object, keep these strategies in mind:

- Match shapes by ignoring the angles at which they were shot—very much like a jigsaw puzzle, keeping a piece oriented exactly as you picked it up doesn't help fit it in place. The Rotate tool (R) is your ally in this task; it's very helpful for working at different angles without having to transform and rotate the actual layer. Press R, then simply click and drag the curser as if you are rotating a puzzle piece by hand. Double-click the Rotate tool icon 🖐 to return to the default orientation.

- Get with the flow and movement. Fire acts much like water, and water, like skin, conforms and covers any shape. When we see a subject and perceive forward motion, however, matching the flames to this expectation can have a positive result. In this case I found the edges and tips of some of the flames and matched them to flow behind the fish.

- Try flames as filler, but don't over plan where they fall. Part of the illusion is it not looking too perfect so that viewers will buy into the randomized quality of natural fire.

- Experiment with limited scaling, making sure the flames feel consistent and not so varied that the result is collage-like. When some flames are larger, the edges may be noticeably softer compared to flames that have been scaled down and have sharp edges to them. Our eyes pick this up and the illusion gets disrupted.

- Be absolutely sure to mask out all flames not associated with the subject you are covering (in this case the fish). You can help control this by placing all the layers associated with the subject into a group folder and add a mask to the entire group to find those stray bits of hot digital grease. See Chapter 12 for more on masking and group folders.

For more advice on playing with fire, take another look at Chapter 8.

Scooping up the water sources and moving them into place was much the same as working with the fire. When searching out the water, I again concentrated on the form of the pieces and matching shapes to the ripple. Sometimes I would see a section that could work as an underlit fingertip with the right warping or the glowing curve of a knuckle. The process was definitely a squint-athon that needed heavy-duty imagination processing power, but again, I only had to find water approximately close to what was needed to match up as I would later warp these images to perfection. In the end I found a few pieces with ripples that alluded to a three-dimensional form, which I could easily mask and warp to match the subjects' forms (**FIGURE 10.20**).

> **TIP** Take your time looking for matching textures and work on a small scale, piecing the composite together like a 1000-piece jigsaw rather than a 100-piece puzzle!

To ensure the water or fire pieces shined rather than obscured, I changed the blending mode for each fire and water layer to Screen. As for the *Fire Play* project in Chapter 8, everything in the layer that was darker than the composite disappeared and everything lighter came through brilliantly (**FIGURE 10.21**). This technique is especially helpful with any image in which the background is truly dark and the lights are nice and bright.

Step 8: Transform with Warp

Photoshop shines at bending reality, and offers the Warp tool for just this purpose. With the pieces scaled and positioned roughly into place already with the Move tool (V), I repeatedly used Warp to transform selections of water and fire to become perfect curves in the wrist, chin, thumb, and elsewhere.

FIGURE 10.20 Finding the ripples that looked like they curved around a form took some careful searching, but had great results once pieced together.

FIGURE 10.21 Changing the blending mode to Screen makes fire flash and water glitter by visually removing their darker portions.

Warp enables you to stretch and bend pixels based on a three-by-three grid and Bézier curve handles (**FIGURE 10.22**). To access this feature, I selected the Move tool and a layer intended for warping, then clicked on the edge of the bounding box to activate the transform mode. I then right-clicked the image to bring up the Move tool's transform options (**FIGURE 10.23**). From this context menu, I selected Warp and began warping each layer as needed by pushing or pulling the Bézier curve handles as well as dragging across the grid to squash or stretch the image as necessary.

> **NOTE** Show Transform Controls must be toggled on in the options bar for you to access Warp and the other transform features of the Move tool.

For better results using the Warp tool, especially for such textures as water, keep a few tips in mind:

- Think of dragging the parts you want pushed and pulled like smearing bits of clay. The parts under your finger (or in this case the cursor) move the most dramatically while the rest move less so but are still clearly connected.

- Control the outer edges and the general shape of the layer by moving the warp handles that adjust the curve strength and direction of the *outer* edges. To bend a layer like this to fit a finger's curve, for example, I move the outer handles toward the direction I want the edge to bend, which gives me a great element of control.

- Don't overdo it! Warping something that already has dimension to it, such as the water texture, can cause the layer to start looking a little flat and you'll loose what you originally found interesting about its texture.

FIGURE 10.22 Warp is a good tool for bending pixels to fit exactly how you want.

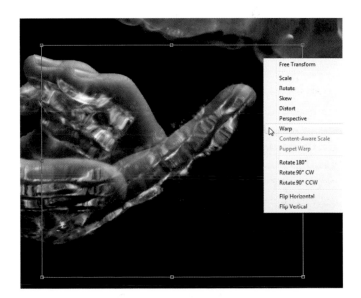

FIGURE 10.23 Left-click an edge of a layer with the Move tool, then immediately right-click to bring up the context menu containing the Warp option.

Step 9: Cool the Fiery Fish

Although enveloping a fish, the fire still looked normal at this stage and was not pushing far enough into the surreal and mysterious for my taste. To defy viewers' expectations (and physics) a bit more, I decided to swap the fiery warm colors for their polar opposites: the cooler blue-violet tone of deep, icy water. A Hue/Saturation adjustment layer was just the tool I needed for color-changing magic. For me, keeping the scene more monochromatic lent itself to a more dream-like setting and has a nice continuity effect—plus it's always mesmerizing and visually fascinating as warm colors suddenly become cool.

For further continuity, I decided to adjust color for the group folders containing the fish and fire shots altogether rather than working on the elements piecemeal. I selected the Fish group folder, which contained everything fish related, and created a new Hue/Saturation adjustment layer (click the 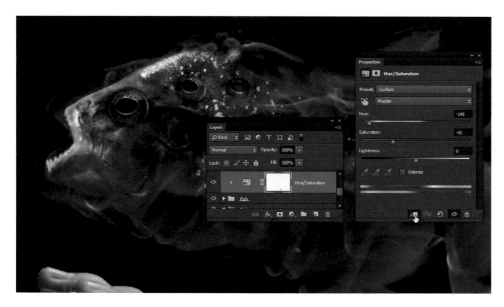 icon in the Adjustment panel) just above the folder. I shifted the Hue slider far left until all the fire and fish became the same cool blue-violet. To make sure the change affected only the Fish folder I then clipped the adjustment layer to the folder below it by clicking the small Clipping icon within the Adjustment Properties panel (**FIGURE 10.24**).

> **NOTE** As you are working with many new layers and groups, remember that new layers always appear above the layer you currently have selected—unless the folder is the top-most layer, then it falls into it.

FIGURE 10.24 Adjusting the hue can be fun to watch, but the secret is in clipping the adjustment to only affect the layer or folder directly underneath the adjustment.

Step 10: Control Color but Retain Depth

After adapting the fiery fish to the cool end of the spectrum, I needed to fine-tune the entire composition's look and feel with some global edits. These are the kinds of edits that, for the most part, are best to perform once the arrangement, positioning, and specific edits of the individual elements are more or less locked down. Part of this global editing process is getting a good idea of continuity as it can seriously help a composite. With this in mind I decided to create a layer that turned the rest of the composite into rich blues and violets to match the flaming fish.

Why not just turn everything blue-violet all at once? Although it may seem like an extra step, the best practice is to get the colors of each section close to your final intent before doing a global color adjustment and masking. This way the color alterations don't have to be shifted quite so dramatically at the very end of the project causing it to look flat and less rich with subtle varieties. In that case of the fire, it's best to use the natural color gradient of the flames and scales, shifted to a range of cool colors, rather than making it a flat global color adjustment.

To control the composite colors as a whole and match the fish's cool colors while also giving them additional accents and richness, I created a blank new layer and dropped it into the Effects group folder. I then filled the entire layer with royal blue by clicking once with the Bucket tool (G)—a bit dramatic and shocking. The first time you do this is a bit unnerving, as it feels like you knocked over a can of paint across the canvas. Luckily, a simple change of blending mode finishes the effect. Specifically, I set the blending mode of the new wall-of-blue layer to Color; instantly my other images came back, only bluer (**FIGURE 10.25**). Changing a blending mode to Color like this adds the layer's colors to the composite even where there was no color or very little to begin,

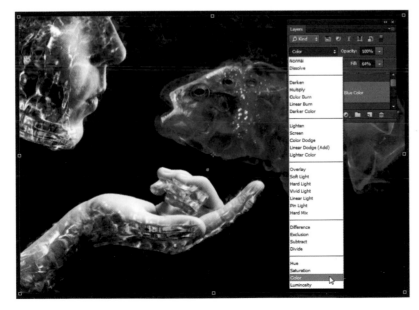

FIGURE 10.25 The Color blending mode is wonderful for infusing your own custom color, but can come off a little strong, so it's always a good idea to back off the layer's opacity a little.

such as desaturated areas with more gray tones like the desaturated water. Initially the color always comes off too strong and needs adjusting in either opacity or masking (as in this case) to sit better within the composite, so always bring it back below 75% to start with. For *Control*, I attenuated the fill to a pleasing 64%.

Because the fish already had its own cool alteration with subtle variations created by shifting the hues of the flames and scales, I also needed to add a mask to this Color layer so it applied to only the background, face, and hand, but not the entire fish. When comparing the variety of hues created from shifting the color versus spilling a flat color with a Color blending mode, the blending mode method feels forced and flat as we expect flames to have a more dynamic and varying look to them—even blue ones!

> **NOTE** At this point in the composite I had settled on the scale and positioning of each main element and could safely do some global effects and masks tailored to fit the entire composite. Alternately, you could always apply one of these layers to the folder of each group and clip it for more isolated control as I did with the fish.

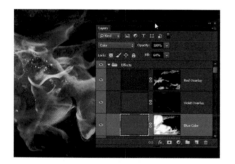

FIGURE 10.26 Three main layers control the composite's overall color. Each had its own mask for better isolation.

Other colors I added in a similarly controlled manner (masking and changing the blending mode) were a vibrant and deep red and a very regal violet each on separate, additional layers (**FIGURE 10.26**). With these two layers, however, I changed the blending mode to Overlay rather than Color to control tones in addition to color and because Overlay is not as aggressive with color changing. (For more on blending mode differences, see Chapter 3.) Having each color layer separated out this way allowed me to paint just on their masks with black and white, flipping back and forth efficiently by pressing the X key (be sure to press D first to reset these black and white defaults). I used masks heavily with these two layers starting with an inverted mask (invert by pressing Ctrl/Cmd+I after creating the layer or by holding down Alt/Opt when clicking the Add Mask icon) so that there would be better control and conservative placements of each color and again not cover the fish.

Step 11: Brush in Magical Lighting

What surreal image is complete without some magic wind-spirits flying about? To brush in these flowing wisps for the mouth and hand, I first created a blank new layer and placed it within the Effects folder, making sure it was directly below the Color layers so that whatever I painted using white would be colored to match the scene. To create the scattered brush effect, I started with the basic soft brush and toggled on Shape Dynamics, Scattering, and Transfer within the Brush Properties panel (**FIGURE 10.27**). Painting with a Wacom tablet (or other tablet with pressure sensitivity), I was able to change my pen pressure to control the shape and opacity of what I was painting, which was perfect for streaking small controlled waves of this brush around the image.

An added small Outer Glow layer style effect also helped complete the look. With it each little scattered burst of white paint from the brush had an added

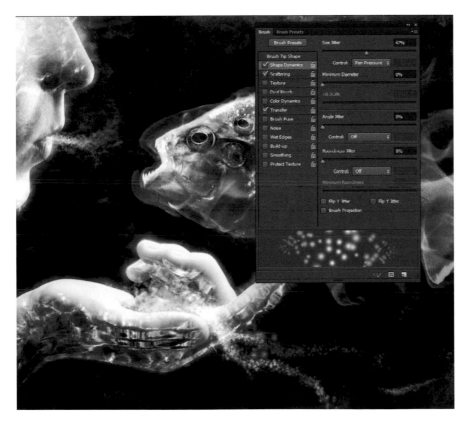

FIGURE 10.27 Even a simple round-and-soft brush can be modified within the Brush Properties panel to become something dynamic and interesting.

TIP If you want to create a dynamically changing brush without the luxury of a tablet, change the Shape Dynamics Control option to Fade with a value of 100 and the Minimum Diameter set to 20%. This won't exactly replicate the look that you can achieve with a tablet, but will create a tapering effect that can be stroked first in one direction, then the other.

glowing effect contributing to the fantastical and surreal nature of the piece, helping the brush stroke feel less flat. I added the layer style by clicking the Add Layer Style icon fx. at the bottom of the Layers panel (**FIGURE 10.28**). When using Outer Glow, don't go too far overboard with the effect; keep the size limited to a gentle coloring and thickening of the brushed dots.

Step 12: Glow

Although it may not be the glowing waterfalls of Tolkien's Rivendell, the composite definitely needed to have some of its sharp edges softened and made to feel as if glowing light was blooming from the lighter elements.

For the final effect of the composite, I again created a new blank layer within the Effects folder and labeled it Glow. Switching brushes back to the simplicity of the soft, round brush, I gently painted (with opacity between 5% and 10%) around the bright and sharp areas that needed an extra glare and softening to them, such as the hand and face and various lighter parts of the water (**FIGURE 10.29**). This helped increase the feeling of bright glowing light, made it more dreamlike, and softened up the edges in a subtle, but pleasing way.

> **TIP** Making the glow slightly uneven can add a subtle effect of shimmering. When a glow is overly even it loses this shimmering quality as everything appears equal all the time.

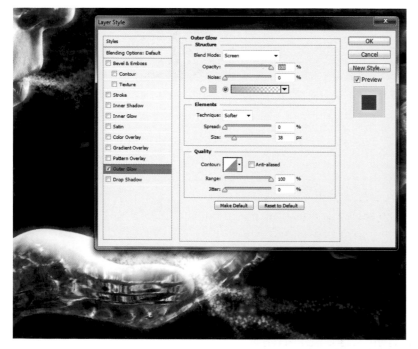

FIGURE 10.28 The final result with an added Outer Glow layer style meant magic in the air!

FIGURE 10.29 Compare the image before and after adding the final Glow layer—a small layer with a big impact!

Conclusion

Working with textures, especially fire and water can be daunting and always meticulous, but so very rewarding in the end. This project is a good example of how regular, everyday photography can be used to inspire a new world of imagination, one where controlling a strange, fiery, frog-eyed fish is as easy as blowing in its face with glowing breath. The main concepts to take away and apply to other projects, however, are the power of color control over textures, such as water and the rest, and the potential of finding inspiration in a strong initial image. What was very much the everyday banal soon became the extraordinary and intriguing in *Control*. Have the digital courage to chase down your surreal dream and bring it to life piece by piece.

MARIO SÁNCHEZ NEVADO

http://aegis-strife.net

Mario Sánchez Nevado is a Spanish freelance illustrator and art director. His studio, Aégis, is focused on bringing digital art to the covers and packaging of music bands and publishing houses all over the world. One of the very few illustrators with the Master Award on illustration in two consecutive editions of Exposé, Mario has had his work exhibited in New York City's Times Square and Creatives Rising. Although Mario's work is surrounded by obscure and surreal environments, his messages often point to ideas of enlightenment and self-conscience.

How do you use color theory in your composites? How does it affect the meaning of your work?
The use of color is a key in my illustrations. I use it to create certain moods, because for me, the emotional impact at first sight on my images is very important. I tend to create harmonic palettes for the surroundings and turn into complementary or contrasting colors for the focal points of the compositions, so they grab attention and establish a starting point to "read" the image in the direction I want. I really like reds for this matter, especially when they are contrasting with blue.

How do you create such great depth from tiny pieces of flat images?
It's important to use photos with neutral and flat lighting as much as possible, with no hard shadows cast, so you can more easily build on it. You can then create something homogeneous by hand painting the lighting over the photos, directing it from the sources you establish and adapting it to the atmospheric conditions if the action is taken into an environment. It's crucial to keep in mind the depth of field.

A DYING WISH, 2007

▶ BETRAYAL, 2012

DELIBERATION, 2012

CHARADE, 2013

INDIFFERENCE, 2011

What does your planning process look like?

It has two variations. The spontaneous one is the most common. I just sit in front of the computer and let my imagination flow. It is like throwing things to the canvas and seeing what happens. Then, when I know what is actually happening, I take total control over it to build a narrative and make of it an effective communicating illustration, changing elements and adding or subtracting new items or atmospheres. The other way is when I plan every single aspect of the image if it's been conceived in a very specific way. So there would be a set of sketches and a list of resources I might need, then the relevant photo shoots and the combination of everything in Photoshop.

What's your secret weapon as far as tools or other Photoshop features?

Well, this might surprise you, but after years I have realized that the Brush tool has almost everything I need. When you need high-end finishes, you better do everything little by little by hand, like painting the lights or the small details like particles on the air and such.

How many layers are typical for one of your composites?

As my illustrations tend to go from very complex, baroque-like compositions, to very simple ideas, it really depends—usually, no less than 40 or 50 layers for very simple artworks. I use many adjustment layers, so for the most complex ones I think I can end up with around 500 layers.

Where do you get your source material?

I try to photo shoot or paint everything by myself. I often plan trips for photo shoots on natural spaces, so I can have images of landscapes, textures, several items, and so on. Also I tend to contact several friends for modeling

NIRVANA, 2012

as well. But it is hard to gather everything you need, so sometimes I end up taking a look on royalty-free stock websites, both free or paid ones, but I really try to use only my own resources.

Do you have any tips or suggestions for others following in your footsteps?

To quote Doris Lessing, "Talent is actually something very common. The rare thing is perseverance" and Charles Bukowski, "Find what you love and let it kill you." I couldn't sum it up in any better way.

What's been your greatest success as an artist?

To be able to make a living out of what I love the most. But also, the chance it brings me to get to know myself and my environment in a deeper way. ■

Put Daddy Down, Please!

Many parents see their children as amazing, but what if a baby really did have super powers?

One night, after putting my own little super-dude to bed, I quickly sketched out what I thought could be a fun idea to try someday. The next morning I made the sketch a reality, almost on a whim. By the way, it is always a good idea to mention any potential plans like this to your housemates. In this case, I really should have warned my wife Erin *before* she came downstairs to find me posing on top of my son Kellen's highchair…which was also on top of the table.

In any case, I soon won Erin over with a batch of coffee and enlisted her involvement with the shoot. By the end of the morning I had all the images I needed, and by the end of the day, I had a finished version of *Put Daddy Down, Please* (**FIGURE 11.1**). On the surface, this project was an exercise in selections and masking, but it also demonstrates the power of good planning and a thoughtful setup. Although I didn't realize it at the time, without my sketches and preparation, the image really would have been impossible.

▶ **FIGURE 11.1** No parents, cats, or babies were harmed in the making of *Put Daddy Down, Please*. One plant did get a little disheveled but is recovering wonderfully.

Preparing for a Composite

Each composite presents its own challenges, however I have found a few things to be absolutely critical to achieving success with subject-object-background composites like *Put Daddy Down, Please*:

- Use a tripod.

- Shoot in camera RAW and use a large memory card.

- Use an intervalometer (a remote trigger with a timer). They're available for most DSLR cameras, and even a simple, inexpensive one like mine will save you hours of time when shooting by yourself (**FIGURE 11.2**).

FIGURE 11.2 An intervalometer can save you time and frustration when doubling as cameraman and subject.

- Set your lighting and exposure controls, then don't change them.

- Get some clean shots of the scene empty of props.

- When you shoot the props, over-shoot a variety of positions and possibilities. You never know which ones will work and which won't until it's too late!

- When working with babies or toddlers, be prepared to make the shoot entertaining and fast. Keep toys or something fun handy to motivate some super interaction. A partner to help can be invaluable, as well.

- Be prepared to do it all over again. Things may not look the way you imagined after the first shoot, so study your shots and ask yourself how things can be improved. Try again if needed; you'll notice huge improvements by the end because you will be able to visualize the scene better after all that practice.

> **NOTE** To watch a short video on the shoot and editing process, just log in or join peachpit.com, and enter the book's ISBN. After you register the book, links to the resource and video files will be listed on your Account page under Registered Products.

Step 1: Sketch the Scene

Never underestimate the power of planning. The rough sketch I jotted down the night before (**FIGURE 11.3**) enabled me to envision lighting conditions, composition, point of view (POV), props, and a slew of little details I might not have been able to think about while shooting.

FIGURE 11.3 Plan everything from angles to lighting. Making changes when it's time to shoot is fine, but go in with a plan so you at least have something to start with. Re-work it from there.

So, sketch out your idea. Whether it's rough like mine or detailed and meticulous, make sure your sketch includes:

- Lighting position and direction
- POV and lens size (if not in millimeters, then an indication of wide or more telephoto)
- General composition and mood

FIGURE 11.4 shows a rough sketch for *On the Edge*, another picture in the Raising a Super Child series (**FIGURE 11.5**).

FIGURE 11.4 Compare this rough, initial sketch to the finished image in Figure 11.5.

FIGURE 11.5 Some things definitely changed from the original concept, but the sketch gave me a solid idea of how to start shooting, where the lights should be, and where to place Kellen.

Step 2: Set Up the Shot

It's always easier to place an object rather than remove it, so start any shoot clutter free. You can use Content-Aware Fill and the Clone Stamp tool to fix up just about anything, but why spend a half hour in post instead of a few seconds in properly setting up a good base shot? Save your photo-mojo for things that you really can't change without Photoshop, like an ill-placed light switch or ugly carpet. For the *Put Daddy Down, Please* base shot, I cleared away all furniture and props (except for the table) from the scene beforehand (**FIGURE 11.6**).

For this project I also took my time in finding just the right POV and wide angle (15mm lens on a APS-C size sensor, not full) to frame the scene properly. I wanted the position to be subtly low to help viewers identify more with the baby as a subject and his perspective of looking up.

Exposure Controls

Finally, check your exposure controls and intervalometer before you begin, and adjust as necessary. Lock everything down (including white balance) in Manual mode so that there are no variations from shot to shot. I gave myself a challenge by shooting into the light, but I wanted the room's windows in the background with their bright and beautiful morning light as the dominant source for this shot. My idea was to play with contrast and a near silhouetting in parts of the scene. I mostly exposed for the brightness of the windows while still trying to keep some detail in the shadows. Shooting in camera RAW files would give me plenty of pixels to fine-tune in post-production. You'll notice that my original shot is severely under-exposed for most of the picture (**FIGURE 11.7**). In retrospect, I should have brought in additional lighting and saved myself work in post. Unfortunately though,

FIGURE 11.6 Make sure you shoot a good blank image or two as a background for layering your other images.

FIGURE 11.7 Trying to find the balance of lights and darks in a high contrast situation is never easy, but when in doubt, don't blow your highlights if they are important.

grabbing my lighting kit would have woken Erin, so I used what was at hand. You'll always encounter unanticipated limitations during a shoot, so be creative and work with them as best as you can.

> **TIP** You can always pull out a bit of noisy detail from shadows—not so from blown highlights! Although RAW can help at least a little with highlights, don't depend on it.

Setting the intervalometer to take a picture every 5 seconds left me just enough time to run around like a madman and hold something in place for each shot. (Kellen thought this was hilarious. I found it less so.) When you're working with children, however, too much can happen in 5 seconds. For Kellen's shots, I shortened the interval to triggering every 2 seconds. Increasing the frequency of shots with the intervalometer increases your chances of getting that great performance moment from the little one.

Step 3: Place the Objects

Placing objects sounds easy: You just run around holding things in the air and freeze before the picture snaps. It's not. Not only must you hit the right mark, the object must be oriented to both look good and be of use for the final composite. Here are some tricks for getting it right:

- Stand out of the way of the background. Just because you *can* use Photoshop to remove yourself from behind the object does not mean you should. Extricating yourself takes time, and the results may still look funny even after investing that precious time. In short, stand aside!

- Hold objects with your hands behind the prop or at the very edges whenever possible. You need to keep your visual involvement with the object to a minimum. If you can grab a prop from its back or edge, do so. The results will be better looking and removal will be easier. Multiple exposures of holding an object from different edges can also potentially help those tricky ones, as well. Once in post-production, you can stitch the best sections together.

- Variety is an absolute must in prop placement. As you walk around the scene holding objects awkwardly in the air, you may think you are varying object placement greatly. In reality, you're probably not. When you're not behind the camera with each shot, it's pretty impossible to know how prop positions—especially *depth* and orientation—will look in the final selection and the overall composition. Easy fix though, just overshoot until you get the hang of it! I've reshot scenes more times than I can count, we all have—or will.

Step 4: Select Your Best Images

After you transfer your images to the computer, launch Adobe Bridge and start combing the shots for composite-worthy candidates. I used the Filmstrip workspace for this step (you can choose this from the options bar). Filmstrip allows for easy thumbing through the shots and good side-by-side comparisons when multiple image thumbnails are selected while holding down Ctrl/Cmd.

Rather than deleting anything at this stage, use the ratings feature of Adobe Bridge to rank them: Select an image and press Ctrl/Cmd+[a number from 1 to 5] to give it a one- through five-star rating (**FIGURE 11.8**). You can later sort by rating; to see all images with four or more stars, for example, press Ctrl+Alt/Cmd+Opt+4 or click the star filtering icon to the right of the workspace name (**FIGURE 11.9**).

TIP If you shoot in both RAW and JPEG, filter by file type RAW before rating your images. This way you'll be comparing only RAW files and won't accidentally rate any JPEGs. You can always put your JPEGs in a separate subfolder if things get too confusing.

The general rules for my rating system are:

- 5 stars: Perfect shots I just *know* will work
- 4 stars: Could be great in the final composite, but I need to see it to be sure
- 3 stars: Might be workable, but only if I can't find better

I never use shots below 3, so I simply just don't bother rating the bottom tiers. I start my final selection by displaying only those 4 stars and above (Ctrl+Alt/Cmd+Opt+4) and only include 3-star shots if I'm desperate for more variety.

FIGURE 11.9 View only the best shots by filtering your images by the star rating.

FIGURE 11.8 Adobe Bridge is ideal for sorting through your shots and rating them.

Step 5: Edit in RAW

Once you're satisfied with your collection of filtered images, it's time to edit. I selected everything (Ctrl/Cmd+A) and then double clicked one of the shots to open the images for editing in Photoshop's Camera RAW Editor (**FIGURE 11.10**).

Once in the Camera Raw Editor, batch processing makes tedious work quicker. For example, these shots were mostly too dark. I selected them all, then lightened some of the shadows with what used to be called *Fill Light* in CS 5, now in CC it is simply called *Shadows* (**FIGURE 11.11**). I found the slider sweet spots for these images by looking at both the shadows and highlights to strike a more even balance for the scene. When balancing your own images, be sure to get as much detail as possible in both lights and darks while still maintaining a good contrast.

TIP If you shot in JPEG and still want to learn about RAW editing, right-click one of the selected images and choose Open With Camera RAW from the context menu. Be aware though that because the JPEG file has already been compressed, the editing sliders are very limited compared to adjusting an actual RAW image, especially in regards to highlights and white balance.

When I'm done editing the images in camera RAW, I click Done rather than Cancel or Open. Clicking Done nondestructively saves the slider positions but does *not* open all the images all at once within Photoshop, instead letting you later choose which to open at a later time. Too many tabs opened in Photoshop can easily become overwhelming and confusing. Keep them controlled whenever possible.

FIGURE 11.10 Using the Camera RAW editor in Photoshop keeps edits nondestructive. Plus, you can batch process them.

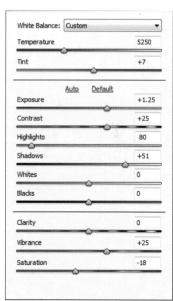

FIGURE 11.11 Camera RAW sliders will adjust all your images once they are selected on the left.

Step 6: Set the Stage with a Clear Base Image

The value of finding a good, clean, and evenly lit first background image cannot be underestimated. This shot has to be clear of extraneous props, people, pets, potatoes, and so on for it to function well as a background stage image. For *Put Daddy Down, Please*, I settled on that 5-star shot of the empty background (**FIGURE 11.12**), opened it with a double-click to bring it into the Camera RAW Editor, and then clicked Open [Open Object] to bring the image all the way into Photoshop for composite editing.

FIGURE 11.12 This is the main stage image empty of most props that had a good five-star rating.

Step 7: Organize from the Beginning

When you move into a new home, you first put your boxes in their designated rooms; leaving the box of kitchen supplies in the master bedroom won't help when you start opening boxes to put things away. Think of your base image as your home. The next step is to bring in the other objects and layers, organized in folders that, like the moving boxes, relate to their designed locations. Although every move is different, there's no budging on this point: Label and organize from the get-go! For this project I immediately made group folders for each part of the composite (**FIGURE 11.13**). An organizational structure like this will help eliminate confusion and enable you to order elements based on depth (foreground, middle, and background). Remember that layers you want to be behind others, such as the background, also need to be stacked towards the bottom. Whatever layer is above another is seen first as visibility is read from top to bottom in the Layers panel.

FIGURE 11.13 The group folders for *Put Daddy Down, Please* helped me stay organized as the project's complexity grew.

Keep these organizational tips in mind as you group your images.

- If there are layers that need to be above others, plan this out in your group folders. Keep in mind that we see top layers first. If some layer's don't touch or conflict with one another, don't worry about which comes first in ordering.

- Your Effects group folder must be above all other groups and layers. This folder will house global adjustments, such as lighting, that affect everything.

- Color code. I don't use this much, but wow is it helpful when I do!

- As mentioned in Chapter 2, label layers as much as possible, or at the very least, label the group folders. Sticking with a default name may seem to save time at first, but it costs a lot more when you're trying to decipher just what's on Adjustment Layer 47.

- Save your Photoshop document in a place you can find and with a name you can search. Just like folders and layers, if you can't find what you're looking for, it's no good.

Step 8: Select from the Chosen

For composites like this one I prefer to view all the potential elements together before I begin picking and placing, like laying out all the pieces face up before working a jigsaw puzzle. This way, I can see what I have to work with and try fitting them in various positions. For this project, I used Adobe Bridge as my composite palette and bounced back and forth from Adobe Bridge to Photoshop ferrying pieces into the composite file (**FIGURE 11.14**). Starting with Kellen and myself as subjects, I found the few potentially usable images of each of

FIGURE 11.14
Choose all the useable shots for each category of image you need. Here I've picked all the best shots of the image's main subjects.

us before opening them all the way into Photoshop and proceeding to step 9. I didn't want to bring *all* composite images into Photoshop, because massive tab trains easily get confusing. Opening a relatively small number of sibling images (images in the same category) can be very beneficial for staying organized and efficient for finding the best of each. After copying and pasting a group of images into the composite file (step 9), I closed their individual tabs in Photoshop and went back into Adobe Bridge for the next family of images (such as the toys) to also bring them into Photoshop and their respective group folder.

> **TIP** You can always bring in more layers than you need and then turn off their visibility once in Photoshop. It's good to still keep them around until you're absolutely sure of their uselessness.

Step 9: Copy and Paste in Place

Shooting all of your images from a matching point of view makes compositing *much* easier. Instead of cutting, pasting, and painstakingly repositioning the image pieces you wish to use, you can use Paste in Place (Ctrl/Cmd+Shift+V) to paste your copied selections into the composite in spots corresponding to where they were taken.

Take a look at how I added Kellen to the background, for example. As you can see in **FIGURE 11.15**, I selected a big rectangle around him (and each subject) with the Marque tool (M). Quick and dirty, this gives me a good chunk of the subject with a fair amount of the surroundings I can use later for seamless blending with masks. Think of it as collecting slack for tying two ropes together.

After copying the rough selection with Ctrl/Cmd+C, I returned to the composite image tab and pressed Ctrl/Cmd+Shift+V to paste Kellen into the background in the exact place he occupied in the image I cut him from (**FIGURE 11.16**).

> **NOTE** Keep your workspace clutter free whenever possible: Close the tabs of the source images as you copy from them.

FIGURE 11.15 I like to use marque selections with plenty of extra room for blending around subjects.

FIGURE 11.16 Use Paste in Place to add a selection, and it goes right where it needs to.

I repeated this sequence for the remaining elements (going back and forth between Adobe Bridge and Photoshop), using Paste in Place to add all the elements I wanted to bring into the composite, then saved. Having everything loaded into one file is great for this kind of composite. Unlike other composites where you may be taking from vastly different imagery, kinds selections, and objects, everything for this project was shot in the same space, with the same lighting and camera position. Because of this uniformity, I could quickly bring everything that was potentially usable on the stage and begin choosing one object variation over another for a drastically stronger overall composition. Masking something out when it might not even get used can eat too much valuable time.

Step 10: Refine Selections

At this point in a composite project, you have a choice: You can continue to refine the edges on an element with the selection tools before applying a mask, or you can simply begin painting on a layer's mask with black and white. Good selection technique goes a long way when it's needed, but painting on a mask gives you absolute control. The drawback is that painting directly can take more time for an image with lots of nooks and crannies around the edges—a *lot* more time if you're not used to it.

How do you decide which technique to use? My general rule is to make a good selection *before* masking if:

- You intend to move the pasted image around a bit from its original location within the shot. For example, you need a rough idea for various compositions before choosing the best.

- There are other layers that need to overlap with the pasted image seamlessly, especially objects that need to go *behind* it.

- You find selecting the object easier and less time consuming than getting a mask just right by painting.

Otherwise, if the pasted image doesn't meet these guidelines, then go straight to step 11.

For images that need a selection first I use a variety of tools depending on the job. For the floating objects here, I used the Quick Selection tool (**FIGURE 11.17**). If this tool fails to grab the selection and some appendages of the image, the Magnetic Lasso tool usually enables me to be a little more specific with my selection as you can see in **FIGURE 11.18**.

> **TIP** Sometimes it is easier to select an object by its background. Select the background, right-click the selection, then choose Select Inverse from the context menu.

To hone in your selections even more (and save a little more time and effort in masking), use the edge refining tools. For example, I selected the bus, then clicked the Refine Edge button (center of the options bar) to open the Refine Edge dialog box (**FIGURE 11.19**).

When refining edges, keep three things in mind.

- Feather your selection. Matching the focus and blur of the image is critical for avoiding the typical collage look. If the image has a little blur about 2 pixels wide, add this to your feathering. If it has a focus blur of 3 pixels, match it in feathering. Zoom in close to be sure it looks right.

- Shift the edge in the negative to bite just a little into the selection to avoid any greasy halo pixels. Halos stand out immediately in bad composites; even if our eyes can't tell exactly what's wrong with an image, they still know that *something* is wrong. Usually that something is a slight pixel halo from not shifting this edge inward.

- It doesn't have to be perfect. My preferred way of making things look "right" is to paint on the mask itself, which you'll see in the next step.

FIGURE 11.17 The Quick Selection tool is great for speed.

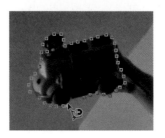

FIGURE 11.18 The Magnetic Lasso tool allows for better definition in a selection.

FIGURE 11.19 Refine Edge does wonders for cleaning up selections.

> **TIP** To avoid halos and digital grease, try changing your refinement background to better see what is part of the selection and what is not before you mask. Press the B key to change to a black background, W for a white, and L for the background layer(s).

Step 11: Add the Mask

For any kind of composite, masking is the magic behind the scenes. To make the magic happen for the bus shot, I added a mask by clicking on the small Add Mask icon in the Layers panel (**FIGURE 11.20**).

In this case, my refined selection of the toy told Photoshop to keep that area visible and make everything else invisible. But this is only the beginning as it almost always takes some hand painting to get things looking just right.

Step 12: Paint the Mask

I have one rule for painting on a mask: I always keep my brushes sable soft. When removing a background, such as with my floating self, for example, I used a small, soft brush (Hardness set to 0) and painted out the unwanted bits (**FIGURE 11.21**).

Using a hard brush while painting on a mask produces an amateurish result, like a collage cut in a rush with dull scissors. Instead, soften up your brush and blend things seamlessly.

When you need more detail and a sharper edge to your brush (because you always will), change the brush *size* instead. This will allow you to be more nimble and articulate with the brush in ways that a big hard brush could never dream to be. The smaller the brush, the sharper the edge and the more painting dexterity.

A few other tips to keep in mind are:

- Press backslash (\) to see your mask highlighted in obnoxious red. Now you can avoid leaving any digital grease behind! You will be able to see exactly where those pesky remaining pixels are that add up over the long haul.

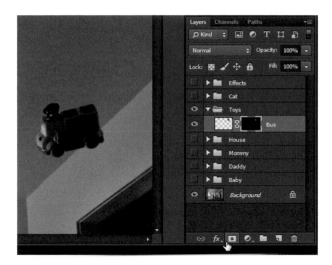

FIGURE 11.20 Add mask to a selected layer by clicking on the Add Mask icon.

FIGURE 11.21 Paint on a mask with a soft brush for better blending.

FIGURE 11.22 Masking myself required a small but soft brush about the same softness radius as the blur of the photograph.

FIGURE 11.23 Kellen's mask needed gentler blending and a much larger (yet still soft) brush to accomplish it.

- Press the X key to switch back and forth from painting with the default black and white paint while you mask. Remember, black erases, white brings it all back.

- Never use a brush radius softer or harder than the blurriness of the original shot; if you do the result will look fake! Again, I keep a soft brush and simply change my brush size to work with an edge that is less fuzzy.

- Adjust your brush size to mask out larger sections. The Right (]) and Left ([) Bracket keys make your brush larger and smaller, respectively.

I painted in the mask for both Kellen and myself (**FIGURES 11.22** and **11.23**) without first making a selection. For the image of Kellen it was more important to paint the shadows in gently with a brush. Besides, because everything else matched the background perfectly, making a tight selection was fairly pointless. Save time where you can!

Step 13: Use Clipping Masks for Isolated Adjustments

Imagine you accidentally left a jigsaw puzzle piece in the sun on your windowsill and it faded. When you fit it into place, it will still look wrong compared to the other pieces. In composite projects, too, sometimes you need to adjust one piece, one layer, *only*, not the layers below it. Clipping masks and clipping layers are designed to affect just that one troubled piece.

Most of the layers for this kind of composite (where you are working from one POV, one scene location, and the same light sources) should match up almost exactly to the original background shot, but natural lighting conditions change over time and depending where you stand (and more importantly, where your shadow falls) in relation to each object, will change even more so. To compensate for this reality we can make a clipping mask and a series of subtle adjustments that will get each layer puzzle-piece to really *sit* into the composite.

For example, I needed to change the lights and darks of the sitting baby layer. The light had shifted from that first establishing shot to something a little darker and slightly bluish (**FIGURE 11.24**) by the time Kellen was on stage. Curves were the first tool I needed for the job.

FIGURE 11.24 Notice the lighting differs from the baby layer to the background shot.

FIGURE 11.25 A slight Curves adjustment light-ened the layer.

For adjustments like these, get the lights and darks looking right first; colors will change *after* you alter the contrast in Curves. To add a Curves adjustment layer, I used the small Curves icon in the Adjustments panel (**FIGURE 11.25**).

FIGURE 11.26 Clipping masks are a genius way of making selective adjustments.

Now here's the secret to fitting just that one puzzle piece: Add a clipping mask! This keeps the adjustment from affecting the layers below as well. By pressing Ctrl+Alt/ Cmd+Opt+G I *clipped* the selected adjustment (the Curves adjustment) to the layer below it (the baby). Unless I tell it otherwise, the Curves adjustment will now use the mask of the layer below it and affect the visible pixels of that layer only (**FIGURE 11.26**). Once you master this technique, you can apply it to just about any scenario of selective adjustments and or effects. It's quite the subtle, yet incredible feature.

As for the actual adjustment, unless you are going for something dramatic or radical, less is more in Curves. The super-child was only a little underexposed compared to the background so the Curves could be very gentle. **FIGURE 11.27** shows the results.

FIGURE 11.27 Compare the shot after the Curves adjustment with Figure 11.24.

Next come color adjustments. After adjusting the lights and darks with Curves, I clipped a Properties panel color adjustment to the layer to take care of the bluish hue from the change in lighting (**FIGURE 11.28**). It wasn't a great deal off, but enough to throw it even with a blended mask applied. As you can see in the figures, I temporarily disabled my mask (Shift-click a mask to disable or enable it) for a larger sample area to make adjustments to and see their effects. Now I am able to see that my color adjustments of slightly more red and less blue again hit the mark for matching the background.

Just from a couple minor adjustments, the baby layer fits in nicely. This adjustment process is what I call sitting a layer into the composite.

As part of the demonstration I disabled the mask for this layer so now that I am finished with my adjustment I can once again enable my disabled mask—and we have ourselves a seamless edit (**FIGURE 11.29**)!

I made similar adjustments across the entire composite for those shots that needed it. Some images, though also needed a little more adjustment triage before they could really sit, typically in Hue and Saturation ▦ or even in some clone stamping such as with some of the remaining hands that could not be simply masked out.

Step 14: Use Clone Stamp to Remove Unwanted Fingerprints

No matter how carefully you hold your props, a few fingers or even a whole hand may end up visible even after careful selection and masking. The Clone Stamp tool (click the 🔲 icon or press S) will help you remove them.

FIGURE 11.28 A second clipped layer to remove the bluish cast will ignore the other clipped layer adjustment below it.

FIGURE 11.29 The seams are now nearly invisible from these two adjustments.

The watchword for success with this tool is "small." Examples of bad cloning are all too easy to find, and many share the same flaw: The cloned sections are too large and when repeated they look just like another part of the image. The key is to construct something new by cloning multiple pieces together for a subtle and seamless result. To improve your results, remember to:

- Use a soft brush.

- Keep your sampling point and brush size relatively small.

- Vary the sampling point location to avoid tell-signs and obvious pixel repetition. Take samples from little bits of multiple areas for a good blend.

- Use small strokes, always small strokes! Again, this will help avoid things looking too cookie-cutter similar as well as helping avoid the clone sample point drifting astray into unwanted areas.

For *Put Daddy Down, Please*, I needed to remove a rogue hand from beneath my chair (**FIGURE 11.30**).

Take a look at Chapter 2 for more tips on cloning, but for this section I kept it fairly simple. I set my sample point to the small area beside the hand by Alt/Opt-clicking once. I began to piece the chair back together with very small and careful strokes. I kept moving my source target around as well to avoid the look of cloning and the obvious pixel repetition (**FIGURE 11.31**). The final results reveal a hands-free dining set (**FIGURE 11.32**).

UNWANTED HAND

FIGURE 11.30
The Clone Stamp tool can help you remove awkward, disembodied hands.

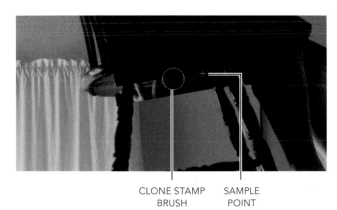

CLONE STAMP   SAMPLE
BRUSH   POINT

FIGURE 11.31 The more source locations you target, the better the results, especially when blending two sides together. Here, two fingers are almost gone already.

FIGURE 11.32 Hands off my chair.

Step 15: Combine Techniques as Needed

Sometimes clone stamping or any one technique just isn't enough. Take the shadow above my head for example (**FIGURE 11.33**).

Originally, I was sitting over the *table* on a high chair and at a very different angle and elevation as well (**FIGURE 11.34**). Once I was relocated over to my floating position, the shadow also needed to be moved and rotated to match, and no amount of clone stamping was going to get me out of that one! I needed a bit of everything.

I made a copy of original me in the high-chair by Alt/Opt-dragging that layer down one level in the Layers panel (or press Ctrl/Cmd+J to the selected layer) (**FIGURE 11.35**). Next, I painted a mask to remove myself and isolate my shadow, then I rotated the shadow with the Move tool (V) to match the correct perspective (**FIGURE 11.36**). To finish it off, I used more clipped curves and color adjustments.

FIGURE 11.33 The shadow above my head needed extra manipulation that couldn't be accomplished just with the Clone Stamp tool alone.

FIGURE 11.34 The original shadow overhead was from a different part of the ceiling with different perspective. This shadow needed to be altered to match the new floating location.

FIGURE 11.35 Make a copy of a layer by holding down Alt/ Opt dragging to a new layer position or by pressing Ctrl/ Cmd+J. In this instance I copied the layer to one position below the original.

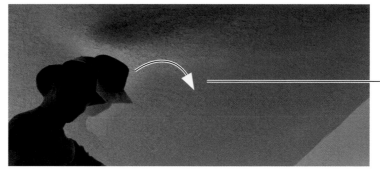

ROTATE THE COPIED LAYER TO MATCH THE CEILING PERSPECTIVE

FIGURE 11.36 Rotate the shadow with the Move tool.

Step 16: Adjust Lighting and Effects

After everything is more or less in place, it's time to begin perfecting the lighting. Here are some post-production lighting tips:

- Direct the viewer's attention. Humans are a lot like moths, we go for the light (and faces too). Add subtle light to those places you want noticed first.

- Add a little more contrast or brightening to draw the viewer's attention to a subject. If there needs to be an emphasis conceptually, make one visually.

- Make changes that can work on a subtle level; use a soft and large brush for slight edge darkening (creating vignettes) or gentle brightening of the center of the composite to draw the eye where you want it. People won't really notice the large visual impact of these changes, but they will definitely experience it! See the video for a look at this final step.

- Work on light and color continuity, usually in the form of low-opacity overlay layers or general adjustments. Make sure they match the scene!

For *Put Daddy Down, Please*, I found the darks horribly distracting while editing, so I painted in my own perfect lighting. I usually do a roughed out job of this early on if lighting is as problematic as in this shoot, then I fine-tune it at the end of the process.

FIGURE 11.37 Choose Overlay as your blending mode to dodge and burn nondestructively with white and black paint.

FIGURE 11.38 The Effects folder contains my final lighting and other layer adjustments such as Curves and dodging and burning with nondestructive Overlay layers.

The secret to master lighting adjustments is to create a brand new layer with the new layer icon ![icon]. Always adding adjustments and effects on their own separate layers helps keep the entire process nondestructive, which is endlessly valuable when compositing. Once there is a new layer, I can change the blending mode to Overlay (**FIGURE 11.37**); I would consider this to be the big-guns of lighting effects.

As mentioned in Chapter 4, the Overlay blending mode is particularly incredible and versatile. In Overlay mode, you can dodge and burn the image nondestructively just by painting with white (dodging) and black (burning), Because I didn't like how dark most of the images came out form this shoot, this Overlay layer truly saved the composite from becoming a well-composed dark mud puddle of pixels.

> **TIP** Bring your brush opacity way down (sometimes well below 10%) when first painting on an Overlay layer. You want to work subtly and avoid painting in accidental halos or severe and obvious lighting alterations. Low opacity will help you better control the force.

Other effects in this final stage include a black and white adjustment layer ![icon] at 46% opacity to control the color. A heavily masked Curves adjustment ![icon] is fantastic for getting things to really pop with strong lighting and contrast. Finally, I painted on another blank overlay layer with black and white for end-of-the-road lighting touchups on faces and detail shadows. This is equivalent to dodging and burning only nondestructively. Overall I lightened the center of the image, my face, Erin's face, and Kellen, as well as emphasized the shadows and highlights around all of us. **FIGURE 11.38** shows the Effects folder containing the final four touchups that I used. Both the Small Adjustments and Overlay Dodge layers were set to Overlay blending mode. The masked Curves adjustment allowed isolated and subtle exposure controls that avoid looking too painted, as can be the case with too much dodging and burning.

> **TIP** Keep your dodge and burn Overlay layers separate for more isolated adjustments with layer opacity to find that sweet spot you are truly satisfied with. If you lighten everything just a little too much, bring down that layer's opacity while maintaining the same painted locations.

Conclusion

Each composite is obviously very different from the next and will present its own challenges and successes, but with enough practice and creativity, really any kind of magic can be accomplished in Photoshop. My son will forever be a super-child now, how cool is that (**FIGURE 11.39**)? *Put Daddy Down, Please* highlights a style of compositing that can easily be completed in a day or two and is so much fun to do. Sketch out a few ideas of your own, and make them happen! The power is truly yours!

FIGURE 11.39 With all the pieces put together and the lighting polished, there's nothing left to say but, *"Put Daddy Down, Please!"*

ZEV AND ALIZA HOOVER

fiddleoak.wordpress.com

Teenagers Zev and Aliza Hoover are a brother-sister team from Natick, Massachusetts, that collaborate to turn Zev's photography and Photoshop projects into an intriguing and tangible world filled with "littlefolk." Zev has been featured internationally for his artwork, which casts himself, friends, and family as tiny people adventuring and living in a very big world. Together the pair creates images that have an elegant simplicity that allows for larger, imaginative narratives to unfold. Aliza adds to the conceptual and visual development of each piece with her critical eye and technical know how with photography, while Zev contributes in front of the camera and behind the computer, working each image to seamlessly composited perfection.

When did you first get the idea to create a window into the world of littlefolk?

Zev: I was 12 when my sister and I came up with the idea of the littlefolks while on a walk in the woods. I think it started sort of as a Photoshop challenge, something to improve my skills. Nowadays, it is inspired by how fun it would be to walk in waist-high moss or fly on a paper plane and by how different the world would be to someone of that size.

What's your experience and familiarity with Photoshop and photography?

Aliza: I have dabbled in photography for a while now, but only recently have I taken my own work seriously. I can't say about photography in general, but I know for a fact that if it weren't for Zev, I would know absolutely nothing about how to use Photoshop. I enjoy Photoshop, but if I have any really editing-skill-intensive ideas, I have him help me.

THE MELODY, 2012

FINLAND, 2013

How well do you two work as collaborators?

Aliza: Zev and I have been working together on our pictures ever since he has been interested in photography. For the most part, we brainstorm and shoot together, but I leave most of the technical parts to him. I encourage him to take photos if he hasn't in a while. We bounce ideas off of each other. I model for him or help him take self portraits. We have separate work, separate websites, and separate styles, but we help each other out a lot and know each other's styles pretty well. Sometimes a shoot will start with his concept and end as a collaboration, or my concept will branch out and grow from his input. We sometimes can't tell which photos are "mine" and which are "his." I tend to lurk behind his back while he's editing and give him opinions over his shoulder. I think with editing it is helpful to have a second pair of eyes, whether he's trying to make a littlefolk look convincing or is just deciding on color correcting.

What are your strategies or techniques for creating a seamless composite?

Zev: Probably the most important part of building a composite like these is matching the lighting between whatever pictures you are putting together. I try whenever possible to take the picture of the person in the exact same location and at as close to the same time as possible to the background to make everything more seamless.

How does a shallow depth of field contribute to your images?

Zev: Our eyes see in 3D; we can tell what is close and what is far. In a picture we don't have that parallax, so I use depth of field to create that same feeling of depth. It also helps to make the world in my pictures feel smaller and more personal. Depth of field is not the only way

BLESS MY SPONGE BATH, 2012

SUMMER TALES, 2012

of adding depth; shooting in fog or smoke also does a fantastic job.

How do you compose one of your background images with future editing in mind?

Zev: Well, I always make sure to clean the plane of focus of any unwanted bits of dirt or leaves or whatever. Also if I can, I try to find something to hide the person's feet behind—a lump of moss or a little stone. If you can't quite see where the feet touch the ground, then it is left up to the imagination. I also make sure that if there is harsh lighting, the shadow will not be going over any semi-transparent or bumpy objects, as these would be difficult to add a shadow to.

What's your favorite tool or technique in Photoshop?

Zev: On the most basic level, masks are probably the most useful and fantastic part of Photoshop. A bit of an unsung hero is the Polygonal Lasso tool. For me, it is faster and easier at cutting out objects than using even a pen tablet. On the other hand, a fantastic, little known technique for adding contrast that I use on nearly all of my photos is to make a Black & White adjustment layer and set its blending mode to Overlay. It creates wonderful, structured contrast like nothing else.

Can you briefly walk through a typical scenario from idea conception to final image?

Zev: Well, the inspiration could come from anywhere, from other photographers to a nice object. For taking the images, I start with the background picture, the scene without any people in it. Sometimes it is just a simple nature macro and others it involves many small things suspended with thread. Most of the time, it is more than one picture (usually two to five) composed in a sort of panorama to make one big picture with a larger field of view. Then I take the picture of the person I want in the

THEY THOUGHT THE RACE, 2012

scene, trying to match the lighting as closely as possible between the person and the background. With both pictures in Photoshop, I cut the background out of the person picture, draw shadows in, and adjust all the colors to match.

What's your favorite part of the entire creative process for the littlefolk images?

Zev: I love every bit, but capturing the background picture is definitely a favorite. I like tinkering with everything to re-create what is in my head and that feeling when you know you got the winner shot.

Aliza: I think the most exciting part is the brainstorming. Putting our heads together helps us think of things neither would have on our own. I can let my imagination go wild and leave the grueling time in front of the screen to Zev! ■

CHAPTER 12

The Hunt

COVERED IN THIS CHAPTER

- DIY lighting and epic selfies
- Group folder masks
- Fur grafting
- Smart sharpening
- Painting shadows and other 3D shading
- Alternative blending mode uses

The Hunt has an interesting and yet highly embarrassing story behind it. The interesting part is the mammoth; it's actually a metal statue textured in Photoshop with patches of kitten fur. The embarrassing part is that the hunter, who's not covered in much of anything is me in my underwear with flowing, digital-hair extensions. While my wife and I were attending graduate school, I took a summer off from classes and used whatever means I could scrape up to make some fun digital art. For *The Hunt*, I used our bedroom lamp to light a nearly naked me doing very stupid and yet epic poses on our bedroom floor. Combine one of these with a mammoth, some kittens, and an image from a trip to Canyonlands National Park, and you get *The Hunt* (**FIGURE 12.1**).

This project proves that whether you have a fancy-pancy photo studio or just a lamp in a tiny apartment, you can create killer results. Just match the lighting angle to your background inspirational shot, and much can be forgiven.

▸ **FIGURE 12.1** *The Hunt* has four main elements to it: the hunting caveman falling to his peril, the background shot of Canyonlands, the mammoth, and the background clouds.

Step 1: Use Photography as Inspiration

Take pictures like crazy! *The Hunt* was possible only because I had so many pictures of Canyonlands National Park from a distant road trip (**FIGURE 12.2**). Location scouting and shooting is a huge part of compositing. The more pictures you take, the more possibilities you have that combinations can fit together and be made to look "right."

The Hunt is made from four or five main images (the Canyonlands, some clouds, the mammoth statue, and me in my underwear), as well as a plethora of smaller shots, including kittens to supply hair for the beast and my wife to supply hair for me.

In browsing for images, I typically look at the point of view and setting while trying to imagine what scene or narrative could potentially unfold within a composite.

FIGURE 12.2 National parks, such as Canyonlands National Park, are a perfect way of getting background images as well as inspiration for future composites.

Step 2: Sketch Alternatives

Really enjoying that epic shot of the cliff to begin with, I wanted to put in a narrative that also accentuated the potentially dangerous landscape. I was mainly interested in having the *wild* kick some humankind butt as my graduate work was about environmentalism and consequences of human impact. So regardless of the historic inaccuracies and using Canyonlands as the backdrop, I sketched a quick commentary on aggressive humankind being dramatically humbled by the wild and it stuck.

When exploring potential narratives, try variations on any idea you think could work well—your first idea may not always be the best. **FIGURE 12.3** shows one of my first sketches, but after further consideration I chose the other instead.

When inspired by your own photographs, keep a few things in mind while sketching:

- The depth, scale, and placement of key elements are important to get right. For example, I had to figure out how large the mammoth and caveman were going to be in relation to each other and to the cliff as well. Clouds and atmosphere also would balance and bring the larger narrative into focus with the rest of the image.

- Pinpointing and roughing out the lighting direction helps tremendously. When you have to shoot extra elements after the fact, you need a solid blueprint to build on.

- Allow for movement and capture the right timing to have the greatest impact emotionally and visually. For this image, the right timing was after the caveman was committed to the fall and possibly throwing the spear but before impact. This leaves viewers to imagine what is going to happen next and to carry forth the narrative that's just a mere snapshot in time. The *time design* factor, or "when" of an image, enhances and changes its meaning and scope.

FIGURE 12.3 The top sketch was the first possibility, but I decided on the bottom sketch so that there would be less hope of survival.

Step 3: Shoot the Subjects

Not having my own time machine to get an authentic picture of a caveman (not to mention one willing to leap off a cliff backwards), I played the part myself while my wife snapped the pictures. Armed only with a crumby house lamp, I set up the shot in the darkness of our small bedroom, paying attention to the direction and harshness of the scene's lighting (**FIGURE 12.4**). I had to make sure that I was fairly evenly lit and fully in the shot and the pose looked like I *could* be falling—if only I wasn't sitting awkwardly on the floor amongst our things.

When posing and photographing a model for a composite, consider these tips:

- Plan ahead by drawing a separate sketch of the lighting scenario you will be matching. A quickly diagramed bird's eye view will often take care of this part as you figure out the camera position, subject position, and lighting angle. Take a close look at the inspiration shot, take note of the angle of shadows and plan from there.

- Make sure that wherever your subject is resting on does not overlap your subject, necessitating cloning or other fixes later on.

- Model a believable pose! Simply sitting on the floor without mimicking a believable action won't look any more dynamic in your composite. You'll still look like you are sitting on the floor, simply in new surroundings.

- Plan to use support props to help your subject balance and hold still for the shot. Motion blur in the source elements needs to match the level of blur appropriate for the scene you're creating. *The Hunt*, for example, is simulating an action shot with no blur whatsoever.

FIGURE 12.4 Even a small college room lamp can work to your advantage to create an effective source image.

- Photograph plenty of poses and a variety of shots. A range of options will be a great help when compositing—and can save you from mistakes. Halfway through the shoot for *The Hunt*, for example, I remembered that my watch was still on. Talk about an awkward moment! I took some new shots of my hand and the end result was much better for it.

- Previsualize where your subject is looking in relation to the shot and other picture elements. Consult the original sketch frequently! Sometimes even very small changes in head tilt or body angle will throw off the direction and orientation, so make sure to plan it out ahead of time.

- If you're acting as the model, as I was, use an intervalometer or recruit someone to photograph you. If no other option is available, the camera timer will work for this, but it makes positioning difficult and may require many takes to get the right look.

Step 4: Piece It Together

Before the detail work, it is important to first get the keystone pieces in place for structural integrity of a composition. To lay *The Hunt*'s foundation, I planned to set the mammoth and caveman in place in relation to the background image. Because the clouds would need a bit more piecing together, I decided to bring them into the composition at a later time, but I needed to make some room for them to balance the composition. To organize this project, I created the basic scaffold of group folders for building of the composite: Effects, Hunter, Mammoth, and Background, which contained the image of Canyonlands and a Sky subfolder (**FIGURE 12.5**).

FIGURE 12.5 To help with layering and overall effects, I set up my group folders by depth. Always stack the folders in the order they would be seen in the composite with the closest object on top.

> **TIP** To enable you to move and edit the background layer more easily, unlock it by double-clicking its thumbnail in the Layers panel, then press Enter to close the harmless pop up dialog box you don't have to change. Unlocking the background will also let you expand the canvas without necessarily creating a solid white addition to your starting layer (in my case, the Canyonlands layer).

Make Room for Clouds

Because the Canyonlands image was oriented as a landscape picture, I needed to create some more headroom for the clouds and billowing volcano ash. Starting with the background image, I expanded the canvas height by another 90% (Image > Canvas Size or Ctrl+Alt/Cmd+Opt+C). You can change your canvas size by various measurement units, but I prefer percentages because they make the change easier to visualize (**FIGURE 12.6**). I set Height to 190%, then set the expansion direction as indicated by the arrows and anchor point to add the

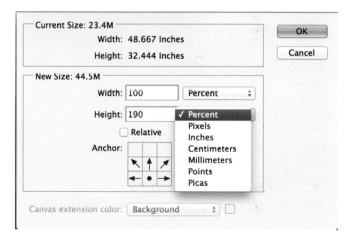

FIGURE 12.6 I prefer to change the canvas size by a percentage rather than a fixed measurement unit, which can be harder to visualize.

extra canvas space to the top of the composition. Be sure to expand your own canvases in the direction you intend (not equally in all directions). With the three-by-three grid in the Canvas Size dialog box, you can customize the point of canvas expansion by clicking within one of the boxes.

Caution, Mammoth Territory

Opening the mammoth picture into its own tab within Photoshop, I selected the bulk of the mammoth with the rectangular Marquee tool (M), copied (Ctrl/Cmd+C) and pasted (Ctrl/Cmd+V) him into the composite, then moved the layer into the Mammoth folder so that the depth ordering would be correct with the rest of the images (**FIGURE 12.7**).

Transforming the mammoth to the proper size was my first priority; I right-clicked the layer in the Layer panel and turned it into a Smart Object for nondestructive transforming. Using the Move tool (V) with Show Transform controls toggled on in the options bar, I scaled the mammoth to mostly match the original sketch. (By pressing the Shift key while scaling from a corner I was able to constrain the height and width proportions.)

FIGURE 12.7 Bringing in the mammoth helped establish a key element and sense of scale before bringing in the hunter.

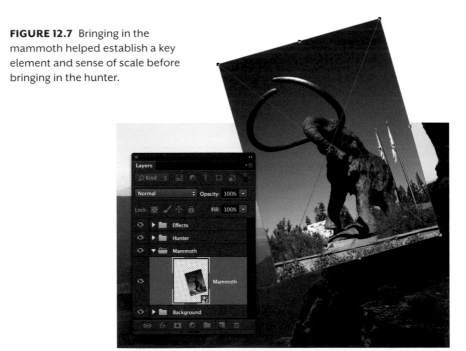

In addition to scaling it, I added a bit of rotation, as well, to make that foot on the left sit flat on the ground instead of hanging in the air after scaling. When your source images are fairly different (like the mammoth image's lighting and perspective versus the canyon's more telephoto look), the more ways you can ground them and make the images sit better together, the more convincing the final payoff. Here, I rotated the mammoth's front left foot until it was level with the cliff top so he was standing *on* rather than above it.

> **TIP** To find the sweet spot while scaling and rotating, change the opacity of the layer being transformed to 50%. Not only will Photoshop let you do this mid-transform, but you won't have a big mammoth blindfold on you as you do.

Using the same method of copying and pasting, I brought the hunter into the composite and scaled the image to roughly match the original sketch that I tucked away within my Effects group folder (**FIGURE 12.8**). Keeping the sketch handy at the very top of your layers stack (such as in my Effects folder) can help keep you on track with the original idea and look. Knowing where this is, I can turn on and off its visibility at any time without having to go hunt it down.

FIGURE 12.8 The caveman was brought in and similarly matched to the original sketch

Step 5: Mask a Group Folder

Using masks on group folders is a bit of a workflow shift from relying solely on clipping, but using group masks has several advantages. For example, by using a mask on an entire group you can clip adjustments to portions within the group while still controlling the group with one overall mask, something not yet possible using clipping even with the latest CS6 and CC releases. In addition, sometimes clipping various layers to a single layer's mask can be more limiting than it is helpful. *The Hunt* centered more on masks created for entire groups and pushing the different and controlled elements that could come of it. This allowed for better controlling of embedded group folders and more complicated ordering.

Mammoth Mask

Although clipping masks are simple and quick to continue adding, they do not have the lateral mobility to enable you to work on areas in different ways, such as with multiple subfolders and between clipping layers. For the mammoth and all its parts (from fur to lighting), I instead decided to place all the elements into a group folder and apply one master mask to the folder and everything within it.

To start with though, a good selection saves mask painting time, so I first selected the mammoth with the Quick Selection tool (W). I made sure to include a little of the surrounding area the feet were standing on as well (**FIGURE 12.9**) to allow for a whittling down of the extra pixels while creating the mask. It's often harder to add to a masked part you cannot see versus simply refining the mask down to its needed shape. As usual, I used the Refine Edge feature to soften the edges with a small (1px) Feather setting and shifted the edge inwards by sliding the Shift Edge slider to about −40%. Biting into the

FIGURE 12.9 Select the mammoth with the Quick Selection tool and include some area around the feet to work with later.

selection edge with Shift Edge helps with some of the blue halo, but it can linger from especially saturated skies like the one behind the mammoth (**FIGURE 12.10**).

With the selections adjusted for a better overall look, I clicked the Mammoth group folder within the Layers panel. I then clicked the Add Mask icon ▣ to add a mask to the entire group and everything I wanted to be masked along with it (meaning anything inside the group has the mask applied to it). This has a similar effect as clipping a lot of layers to the Mammoth layer and then applying an individual mask. The difference is applying a mask to a group folder offers more freedom of structuring sub-group folders and clipping to various layers within the

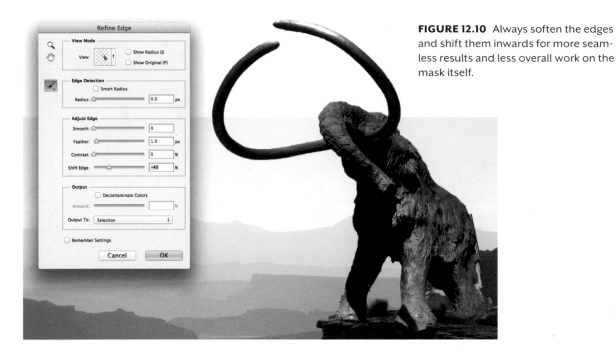

FIGURE 12.10 Always soften the edges and shift them inwards for more seamless results and less overall work on the mask itself.

entire group. For an element as complex as the mammoth, having the entire folder carry the mask worked brilliantly. Unfortunately though, the masking job still needed quite a lot of work all around. Literally.

Paint Around the Edges

Just when you think you've got a good selection happening, the mask comes into play and immediately brings attention to all the spots that need further detail work. I favor using a soft brush with full opacity and a radius matching the softness of the edge focus. For the mammoth group mask, this translated to a 10-pixel radius (**FIGURE 12.11**). Paint around the edge for a more precise and customized mask. With practice, you can be nearly as quick with painting a mask as with using the Quick Selection tool, especially when using a palette.

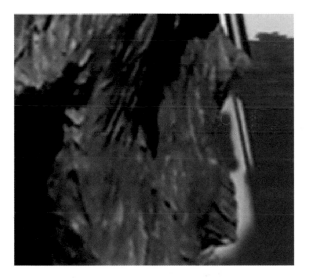

FIGURE 12.11 Paint around the mammoth mask with a small and soft brush to get a smoother and more exact mask area.

The Hunter's Mask

The caveman's mask was even trickier for the Quick Selection tool and is a good example of how painting can be more efficient and better at improvising than most selection attempts. Here's a quick list for when I personally opt for painting an accurate mask versus trying to select one with the selection tools:

- When the edges are dark and blend in with the scene to the point that Photoshop cannot discern where they are, but your knowledge of shape and form can infer, just as in figure painting. In this way it's similar to painting, only you have the added benefit of painting in an actual picture.

> **TIP** If you put a mask on an actual layer rather than the group folder you intended, simply drag the mask onto the folder thumbnail in the Layers panel and—POW!—mask moves without a hitch. Somewhat related, this can also be a good way to copy masks: Hold the Alt/Opt key while doing the same procedure and—KAPOW!—duplicated mask.

- When you will need to make subtle changes by painting even after a selection. Sometimes it is just faster to skip the refining and jump straight to the painting portion.

- If you know you are clever with the paintbrush and selection tools just tend to annoy you. Digital frustration is a real thing and can turn even the best project into a freeway pile up. By all means, take the back road!

In **FIGURE 12.12** you can see the method of going around the edges and meticulously getting the mask precise; I'm using a paintbrush set to the default round at 7 pixels. Notice also that I am painting on the Hunter folder that contains the hunter and not on the hunter layer mask itself. In cases where you have no studio in which to shoot against a background that's easy to select and remove, painting will be (for most occasions) your optimal approach. You can, however, make selection and removal easier by using a solid-color sheet as a background under or behind your model.

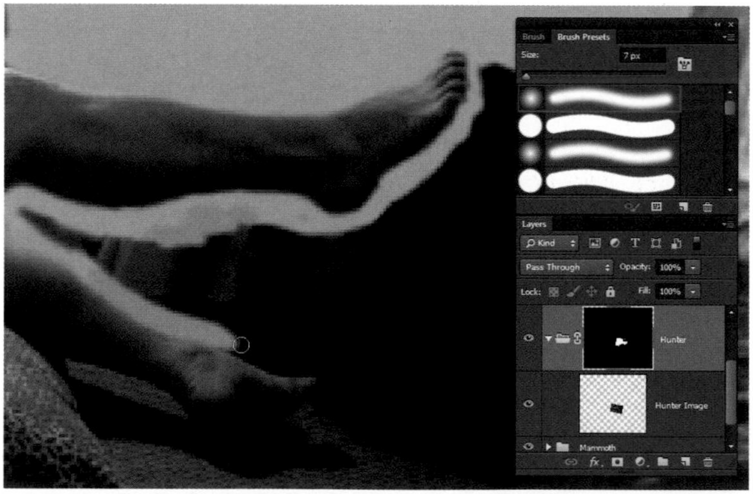

FIGURE 12.12 While tedious and requiring some skill and patience, painting the mask manually is sometimes needed for best results.

Step 6: Put Hair on that Mammoth

In general, the mammoth had two obvious problems with fitting into the composite. The original mammoth picture's bright midday lighting was all wrong for the final scene, and the hair looked metallic—because it was! For a convincing composite, both of these needed to be fixed, and the hair was the best place to start. I planned to order lighting changes above the hair additions in the layer stack to alter the mammoth's overall look.

Because this monumental rebuild has several phases, I broke these down into group folders within the main Mammoth group folder. This arrangement works well for complex projects: All of the subfolders are still contained by the mask paired with the topmost folder (Mammoth, in this case), so you can essentially work on a composite within a composite. **FIGURE 12.13** shows my layer stack and folder arrangement for the mammoth rebuild.

Fur Palette from Fuzzy Kittens

When looking for how to add hair to the very metallic mammoth, I decided a photo palette of kittens was just the trick for proper browsing, picking, and pasting into place. (Chapter 6 details the process of building a photo palette.) I filled the palette with photos of rescued kittens I took at a photo shoot at a local shelter to make sure I had enough variety to work from (**FIGURE 12.14**). Because the photo palette was a Photoshop document, I was able to stay within Photoshop while trying out various sections of hair, which dramatically improved my workflow—no bouncing back and forth from program to program or multiple tabs just to see if a tiny section would or would not snap into place and have hair flow in the right direction and shape.

FIGURE 12.13 Within the mask on the main Mammoth group folder, the sections of the beast are broken down into subfolders for better organization and editing customization.

FIGURE 12.14 Although a bit of a cute overload, this photo palette of kitten pictures was useful for piecing together hair on the mammoth.

Smart Sharpen the Fur

Taken during a photo shoot intended for finding homes for rescued kittens some years back, the pictures had a fairly large variety in lighting and fur coloring, not to mention their soft focus. While useful for over-the-top accentuating of cuteness, soft focus is not preferred for texture sources. I decided to apply the Smart Sharpen filter to the layers within the photo palette.

The Smart Sharpen filter has had some dramatic quality upgrades in Photoshop CC, and the kittens provide good demonstration material. (Be sure to solo the layer in your photo palette you want to work on before you begin.) As before, choose Filter > Sharpen > Smart Sharpen (**FIGURE 12.15**) to open the Smart Sharpen dialog box. Here are a couple handy aspects of the latest version:

- The Smart Sharpen dialog window is scalable. No longer are you limited to a dinky section of the image that you have to zoom in or out repeatedly. Instead, drag a corner of the window outward to expand your work and viewing area.

- Sharpening images used to create fairly dramatic noise as the filter found all contrasting pixels and exaggerated them, including the noisy ones. This phenomena has been substantially reduced in the latest version, thanks to a more intelligent algorithm behind the scenes that looks for edges and detail and not simply all things contrasting. It does a better job at sharpening in general, and not just when dealing with noise.

- You can compare the older version of sharpening by checking the Legacy option hidden within the Settings icon ⚙ in the top-right corner of the dialog box.

For optimal sharpening of the kitten fur I used a radius of 2.3px to stretch that depth a little deeper artificially. The radius needs to be pushed right up to the point before creating noticeable halos (especially if small and close up

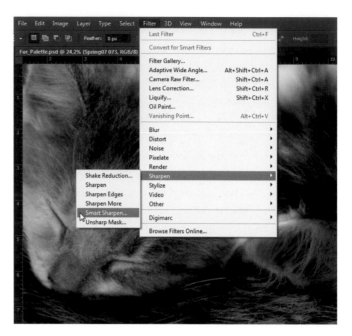

FIGURE 12.15 The Smart Sharpen filter was redesigned for Photoshop CC; its new features are accessible through the Filter menu.

sections of fur are going to be used as texture). It used to be that anything over a 100% on the Amount slider would potentially cause some issues, but this newer version can be pushed a bit further with fairly solid results. Again, when you begin to notice halos or other distortion, ease the Amount slider back down slightly to avoid this effect (**FIGURE 12.16**).

Once this filter is finessed and applied, you can apply it to the remainder of the layers in your photo palette by similarly selecting and soloing each layer, then pressing Ctrl/Cmd+F. This will apply the last-used filter to the selected layer. You still have to apply the filter individually, but with the Ctrl/Cmd+F shortcut, this goes fairly quickly. Be prepared for longer processing times once the filter is applied, however, because it is doing better analysis and final rendering.

Texturing Tips

Finding pieces that fit in the mammoth fur patchwork was ultimately less about the lighting shadows and highlights (I planned to add those later) and more about getting the right direction and form to the fur. Using the statue base as a guide, I found much of the form and hair-flow were provided by the metal, and it then became a game of seeking and matching. There's no quick way of working around this meticulous process short of painting in your own hair strands (no thanks, that can be even more difficult to get looking right), but there is some strategy involved in sewing it all together (**FIGURE 12.17**):

- Find small pieces that have a little shape and direction to them.

- Change the blending mode in some areas; try Screen and Overlay to lighten and darken while retaining the form of your subject beneath. For example, not all of the fur layers needed to be full opacity and Normal mode over the original mammoth. The statue already provided a nice three-dimensional form, which I used as a good under-painting. Changing a small patch of fur to Screen, for instance, can add the lighter parts of the fur while keeping the dark shadows of the statue. Overlay will likewise allow for a place that has existing 3D form while still texturing the metal as hairy and organic feeling. This is where a lot of experiment-as-you-go comes into play, because there often is not a direct way of planning it, so have digital courage and try some variations.

- Rotate and scale the parts that need it. If there is a section that is supposed to be rounded and disappearing around the backside of your subject, having smaller textures near these edges can help enhance this illusion disappearing around a curve.

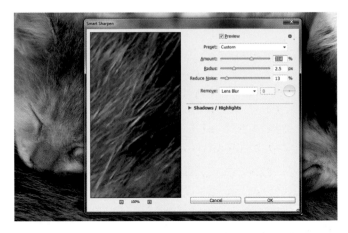

FIGURE 12.16 Push the Smart Sharpen sliders to the point just before causing halos or other less desirable effects.

FIGURE 12.17 Add the fur and don't worry about the lighting, just texture only.

- Duplicate hair that works. I must have duplicated about half of the 24 fur layers from two or three good sections of hair. Ctrl/Cmd+J is definitely your friend for this procedure. Change the orientation, scale, blending mode, and the rest for additional variety. (See the hands-on tutorials in Chapter 8 for more manipulation techniques.)

- Just focus on hiding the metallic qualities (or whatever material you are covering up) first and foremost as that is the largest tale-tell sign when dealing with organic material textures.

With the fur more or less in place, the next stage was to control lighting and color to mimic a scene nearly backlit by the sun.

FIGURE 12.18 Work in lighting stages; this first addition was about a subtle and even darkening of the main shadow areas.

Step 7: Adjust Mammoth Lighting and Color

An important aspect of seamlessly compositing elements is to match their lighting to the scene as closely as possible. To match the scene and stop looking like a weird, wet kitten-mammoth, the mammoth needed some highlights for the backlit sun and deeper shadows to match the rock formation's shadows.

I started with some basic blocking of shadows with a new layer inside the Mammoth Lighting group folder and set its blending mode to Soft Light (**FIGURE 12.18**). This blending mode has the ability to take strong black coloring and apply it more gently than Overlay or Color Burn would. On this layer I painted the first semblance of a shadowed area, mainly on the haunches and body.

Next came a new highlights layer with its blending mode set to Color Dodge to create a dodging (lightening) effect. Soft Light and Color Dodge are a little more

sophisticated and particular than Overlay; paint with these when you need specific lighting and color control (**FIGURE 12.19**). I chose a hair-like textured brush from the Brush Properties panel and selectively stroked in highlighted fur.

Next I added the dramatic shadows, which are the kicker to syncing the mammoth into the scene: I left the blending mode on a new layer as Normal and painted with plain old black. Sometimes you *don't* need to change the blending mode for something you just want darker in all areas like a shadow. You simply need to paint (with low opacity) over the other content on a new layer to darken the entire thing down rather nicely in conjuncture with the other layers (**FIGURE 12.20**). Painting in this fashion also tends to obscure some of the detail of the texture as it is

FIGURE 12.19 To add highlights I used a Color Dodge blending mode and painted white with a textured hair-like brush in selective areas.

FIGURE 12.20 Painted shadows on a new layer with a default Normal blending mode can get the darks looking much more appropriate as they are toned down as well as add a 3D look as the layer name implies.

being painted over, which is an especially good thing in this case as the hair's not quite right in some areas; hide away the obvious faults with no one the wiser!

Mammoth-ish Color

Although its lighting was better, the mammoth still had a fairly metallic color overall and needed more of the reddishness already featured in the landscape palette. To control the color, I added a new layer with its blending mode set to Soft Light then painted on a nice burgundy for the proper effect. This blending mode is able to combine some of the effects from Overlay (such as darkening the darks) mode with Color mode (replacing color and adding saturation) while still being very gentle in its application of both (**FIGURE 12.21**).

FIGURE 12.21 Painting a burgundy red on a new layer with a blending mode of Soft Light gently added a more reddish hue while simultaneously deepening the darks similar to overlay.

Step 8: Make Additional Alterations

To better fit the mammoth into the scene as a whole I hid the back foot with a small shrubbery taken from the original canyon scene and truncated the left sided tusk with a pasted copy of just the end on top of the old tusk (**FIGURE 12.22**). A mask blending from one to the other was easy enough to get looking right as long as the tusk edges lined up together.

Finally, the last pieces that put the cherry on the trunk were some glare from the sun and proper shadows on the rocks beneath the mammoth. I added a clipping layer to the Mammoth folder (by selecting all the mammoth layers and pressing Ctrl/Cmd+G) and did not have to worry about painting on anything but what is currently visible of the mammoth.

To give this clipped glare layer a try, create a blank new layer directly above the main group folder (Master Mammoth in the example), and with the new layer selected, press Ctrl+Alt/Cmd+Opt+G. From then on, wherever you paint, it will apply to everything visible within the group folder including new alterations and additions.

Using a soft white brush set to a fairly large 150px at 10% opacity, I painted around the edges and created a nice glare effect that would match the rest of the scene (**FIGURE 12.23**). The shadows were similarly painted, only on a layer beneath the mammoth and its mask so that it could be seen outside of the hairy border.

FIGURE 12.22 The left tusk was too exaggerated to fit with the more telephoto lens shot of the canyon; the other issue that needed covering was the back leg, so a shrub did the trick for that part.

FIGURE 12.23 I created glare by gently painting around the edges on a clipped layer directly above the Master Mammoth folder containing all of the various pieces; shadows need to be below the main Mammoth folder containing the mask.

Step 9: Accessorize the Caveman

With the hunted in good shape, I turned my attention back to the unfortunate hunter. For the epic eye-candy effects and overall narrative, he needs a few accessories: more muscles, a tan, hair extensions (or perhaps grafting is more apt a description), and a spear.

I started with the muscles. Adding them was exactly like creating the highlights for the mammoth: I created a new layer and placed it in a subfolder (named Hunter Effects) in the Hunter folder above the main image. I then changed the blending mode of this new layer to Color Dodge and once again painted with white in all the places that either needed muscle enhancement injections or

highlights from the sunlight (**FIGURE 12.24**). Painting with white on a layer set to Color Dodge mode lightens things with enough subtlety and control to pull off a convincing look (for something that's just cosmetic).

To give these new muscles an equally new suntan, I created a new Hue/Saturation adjustment layer and cranked the Hue to the left to –12, creating a nicely baked red matching the warmth of some of the rocks and grass (**FIGURE 12.25**).

If you ever need to change the hair length of a subject, simply shoot a hair model with the appropriate matching lighting. For *The Hunt*, I caught my wife drying her hair on the edge of the bed with the same lamp and backdrop I used for the hunter source images. In Photoshop, I moved the hair into place and masked out the pieces I didn't

FIGURE 12.24 Any kind of muscles can be more or less enhanced or airbrushed on once in post-production, but the sunlight is also important to mimic as well; setting the layer's blending mode to Color Dodge lets you do just that.

FIGURE 12.25 Adjust the skin hue with an adjustment layer and the Hue slider.

want or need while also trying to create a more uneven dreadlock look (**FIGURE 12.26**). For this one it was all masking by hand painting.

Oh Spear Me

To create a spear from scratch, I needed a perfectly straight line. Rather than draw it freehand (which can be a huge pain in the butt), I let Photoshop help. To draw your own perfectly straight line using the paintbrush, click at one end of your line (say one end of the spear), press and hold Shift, then click at the other end of your line (or spear); Photoshop will draw a straight line from A to B for you. From there it was a matter of matching the spear's lighting and color to the rest of the scene, so I chose an orange-gold in the Color Picker and painted the highlights (**FIGURE 12.27**).

> **TIP** Zooming way in (Ctrl/Cmd-scroll up) to the pixel level can help you paint things with believable detail and precision—even things that don't exist. Get in close, take your time, then zoom back out for quick referencing (Ctrl/Cmd-scroll down).

On the Other Hand

The mammoth got a tusk job, but the hunter needed some limb replacement (as you may have already noticed). Specifically, I swapped out an arm for one with open fingers as if he'd just thrown the spear—and without a watch attached to the wrist. I matched the same initial position and faded from one to the other by painting on a mask overlaying the arm socket positions. This is in many ways similar to adding in various objects and subjects in *Put Daddy Down, Please* (Chapter 11).

FIGURE 12.26 Take pictures of someone else's hair. With some careful masking and light matching, it will flow just right!

FIGURE 12.27 Draw straight lines for things like the spear by holding down Shift between two single clicks, one at each end of the line.

Step 10: Cue the Volcano

The setting really completes a narrative. While the rest of the scene needed to be subtle and non-distracting, *The Hunt*'s background needed more impact in the form of a volcano and a composition-enhancing cloud of ash. Both of these reside in the Background group folder down at the bottom of the layers stack. When working on backgrounds, it's important to follow the timeline of cause and effect for circumstances like this. *The Hunt* has a distant volcano and needs a hazy plume related to it. So as a line of attack, the volcano itself must be the first thing to get right as the rest depends on its placement and size.

Painting a volcano is actually easier than you might think in this scenario, because of the flattening effect that atmospheric perspective has had on those background mountains. Notice that there's just about no detail at all. To provide a volcano silhouette, I grabbed a piece of the far pale-blue canyon with the Eyedropper. On a separate layer, I began painting with a very fine detail brush with a radius matching the sharp edge of the background. In a very short time, I drew a rough triangular peak that resembled volcanic mountain without adding any variation or detail work (**FIGURE 12.28**).

Dormant volcanoes don't have the same effect. The volcano needed to be active, so I brought in some "lava," which was just the simple cloud picture shown in **FIGURE 12.29**. Well, really, it's an upside down piece from a sunset, so it naturally had some nice vibrant edges that could be interpreted as spewing lava without close inspection. Because the whole thing was going to be faded far in the back, the cloud would work. The sunset provided just a hint of warmth that when faded with the rest of the mountains using a white layer, it appeared to be a burst of lava.

FIGURE 12.28 Painting with a matching flat blue can fool the eye just enough to see a volcano peak.

FIGURE 12.29 Adding a cloud goes even further towards completing the illusion of an active volcano in the background.

I pieced the rest of the clouds together much like the kitten fur patchwork and the fire from Chapter 8. Here are some tools and tips that I use when blending and creating new cloud creations (**FIGURE 12.30**):

- Immediately mask out all edges; if you don't, you'll leave digital grease. Hunting this stuff down is never a fun exercise in patience and willpower testing.

- Create basic adjustment layers clipped to each cloud to get it to match others.

- Always look at lighting direction. It doesn't need to be perfect, but nearly so as our eyes recognize that something looks wrong when the cloud lighting isn't consistent.

- Go small, work piece by piece, and don't worry about finding that perfect cloud that does exactly what you want; those are pretty rare—especially when you may not know what you want until you land on it.

- Add additional atmosphere to cover parts that may not be working the way you want.

Step 11: Turn Up the Temperature

The entire image was far too cool, commonplace, and recent looking. It doesn't feel ancient or perilous. For some reason, when I think of prehistoric times and volcanoes, I think of the ash creating a warm filtered light, much like forest fire smoke creates stunning and brilliant sunsets. To create this warm effect, I added three final layers to the Effects group folder (**FIGURE 12.31**):

- A bucket-spilt (G) yellow-orange layer with the Soft Light blending mode and 33% opacity. Soft Light has a similar effect to Overlay and Color combined, but in this case retains just a hint of the blues in the shadows as it doesn't apply the color so heavily.

- A copied version of the spilt yellow-orange at 33%, but with a Color blending mode instead. You can see the masking done to this layer so that it affects only the background canyon and clouds, reining in those last cool temps and creating a more solid uniformity.

FIGURE 12.30 Blending clouds is much like blending fur or even fire: Always be sure to get very soft layer edges first and foremost.

- A red layer with 40% opacity and Soft Light mode. The entire scene felt far too yellow and green (because of the blending of blue and yellow-orange), so red was a good choice in canceling out these variations. This layer completed the final color range, especially where blue was mixing too much with the previous layers.

Conclusion

Sometimes it's good to get outside of your comfort zone, to push yourself—whether that means trying new blending mode strategies for controlling color and tone or seeing what you can do with that growing collection of cat pictures on your hard drive. Going all-out in effort and experimentation can definitely pay off and be a lot of fun. Pay close attention to details such as lighting and color, and you'll discover that most things can be put together in some fashion. After surviving this project, I learned to always retain a do-it-yourself attitude as you really can make just about anything happen in Photoshop, even if you don't have much more than a lamp, some textures, and your idea. Make your own imaginative narrative a reality!

FIGURE 12.31 These last three layers control the warm palette of the piece in three different but collaborative ways.

HOLLY ANDRES

www.hollyandres.com

Holly Andres uses photography to examine the complexities of childhood, the fleeting nature of memory, and female introspection. She has had solo exhibitions in New York, Los Angeles, San Francisco, Atlanta, Seattle, Istanbul, and Portland, Oregon, where she lives and works. Her work has been featured in The New York Times Magazine, Time, Art in America, Artforum, Exit Magazine, Art News, Modern Painters, Oprah Magazine, Elle Magazine, W, The LA Times, Glamour, Blink, *and* Art Ltd., *which profiled her as one of 15 emerging West Coast artists under the age of 35. Most recently, Andres's first major museum exhibition,* The Homecoming, *premiered at the Hallie Ford Museum in Salem, Oregon.*

What do you look for when you set out to compose a new image? What's your process?

To borrow a distinction coined by Jeff Wall, I'm more of a farmer rather than a hunter. Although I have a really perceptive "internal camera," I'm not a photographer that shoots on a daily basis. I usually embark on a photo project with a prevailing theme in mind for the entire series and then, rather systematically, craft each individual photograph. Typically an idea evolves from a life experience; memory or conversation that elicits a powerful image (or filmstrip) in my mind. Depending on the shoot, I may even create a storyboard for it.

The way that I work requires a lot of pre-production, much like preparing for a film shoot, as well as an extensive post-production phase. Often my work involves the tension between an apparently approachable subject matter and a darker, sometimes disturbing subtext. I'm interested in the cognitive dissonance that can result from employing formal elements such as bright colors, decorative patterns, theatrical lighting and characters that reflect stereotypes of innocence, girlish femininity, and motherhood to address unsettling themes.

BEHIND THE OLD PAINTING, SPARROW LANE SERIES, 2008

Cat Whisperer, 2011

How does Photoshop fit into your workflow?
Photoshop is an integral part of my workflow and allows me to use photography to materialize images that would otherwise stay trapped in my mind. My educational background is in painting and drawing which significantly impacts the way I approach photography. I am fascinated by photography's legacy to be perceived as an agent of "truth," and recognize that Photoshop provides me with a powerful tool, not inherent in the more traditional art forms, to exploit this.

I've welcomed the spontaneity and experimentation that has resulted from transitioning from a large-format film camera to a digital camera. Shooting exclusively with my digital camera provides me with so many more files to consider when I'm creating my final image. I use Adobe Lightroom to peruse all my source files and flag any files that I think may possess some potential. From there, I start to create really rough composites in Photoshop. I experiment with a variety of options, and it's a very creative period in the overall process for me. This is when I set the tone and can get a sense of the most ideal character interaction, formal unity, and the potential to the effectively guide the viewer's eye around the frame.

How do you use lighting to enhance the meaning and narrative potential of each idea?

At the most rudimentary level, of course, photography is about capturing light. Not only do I employ light as a formal device to emphasize my characters, but also as a content carrier. The illumination of light in and of itself often suggests a revelation.

What do you find to be the most challenging part of compositing after a shoot? What's the most rewarding?

Without a doubt the most challenging part is combining all of the assets in such a way that the image actually appears convincing. The most rewarding part is when I start to see the potential of bringing a mental vision to life. It takes a lot of finessing, and in the end, none of my images are flawless. As I continue to grow and learn, I'm also working to embrace the artifice of my process and my limitations with the medium.

THE GLOWING DRAWER, SPARROW LANE SERIES, 2008

GUNFIGHT, 2012

How do you direct the subjects in one of your shoots for getting the results you are looking for?

For the Sparrow Lane series I revisited many of the covers of Nancy Drew books that I read as a child for inspiration. Because they are illustrations they have a vastly different, a more hyper-mannered quality, than we typically see in photographs. I love the melodramatic body language, the way their figures frame the scene, the separation of their fingers, and their startled, but lovely, expressions. While directing I emulated this aesthetic.

Currently I try to embark on my shoots with a consciously prepared vision, still consisting of a constructed environment, theatrical lighting, deliberate costuming, and implied narrative, but with an attempt to capture natural uncertainty. I am finding that the counterbalance of a choreographed structure and the unpredictable response of the subjects' "performance" can create the most compelling results. Shooting digitally certainly allows me to capture more of these "off moments," than I was ever able to when I previously shot exclusively in film.

Do things generally go as planned on a project? How flexible do you have to be with your style of work?

Despite my best efforts, of course things never go as planned! But, I feel like I've been shooting long enough to have faith that if I free myself up to stay flexible, and open, precious moments of serendipity can and will occur. There's a degree of grief that always seems to result from what I've captured and how it departs from the vision that was in my mind. There's an adjustment period, and while it can sometimes be frustrating, surprisingly after a few days, I may realize that what I captured is actually more compelling than what I initially sought out to create.

What is your most favorite composited image or series to date?

The Sparrow Lane series is of course a personal favorite and is probably my most celebrated body of work to date. It was shot on a large-format camera. and because the film is so expensive to shoot and digitize, the compositing work is relatively subtle. I embarked on the project with the intention of concocting a set of identical "twins" out of just one girl. Like most people, I find identical twins mysterious and compelling, and I wanted to explore the idea of them as counterparts, equivalents, or accomplices embarking on these discoveries together.

Additionally, *The Cat Whisperer*, which is far more elaborate in its compositing, is also a personal favorite. It's so tempting to use Photoshop in a rather gratuitous way to multiply entities, but I think this image is a good example of employing this technique to build and reinforce a narrative.

Do you have any advice for future artists combining the worlds of photography and Photoshop?

I think having some sort of foundation in drawing, as well as understanding linear perspective and the logic of light and shadows, can go a long way when you're shooting photos and manipulating them in Photoshop. Otherwise, I think recognizing that you must make an investment. It takes a long time to develop a discerning eye, and even longer to master the techniques of Photoshop so that you can "fix" the problems that you create for yourself. Stay perceptive, continue looking at other artists work, ask questions, and keep practicing. ■

CHAPTER 13

Sculpting with Texture: Growth

COVERED IN THIS CHAPTER

- Using a prop as inspiration
- Roots and bark textured as new skin
- Painting and shaping with textures
- Map making and color control with Luminosity
- Sculpting with light

Textures can truly transform any common object into something entirely new, such as ordinary hands into elemental tree hands. For *Growth* I applied a plethora of textures from jungles and forests I've visited over the years to my hands, mixed in some aerial pictures I shot while flying above the Sierra Nevada Mountains, and blended it all with masking, color correction, and Curves. The result was a somewhat fantastical coopting of a construction and development meeting that featured authoritative and anthropomorphized tree hands deciding where to put a new lake and forest on top of an existing city (**FIGURE 13.1**).

▸ **FIGURE 13.1** *Growth* is composed predominantly of textures and aerial photographs and is the cover image for my series of projects on reversing the nature-versus-human dynamic.

Step 1: Follow Your Props

Sometimes images turn out well because of a certain prop that just takes the entire composite in an enjoyable direction and builds creative momentum. *Growth* was definitely one of those projects for me. As usual I began with a quick sketch of the hands and their blueprints for adding green to a city. I had an earthy and ancient-looking parchment scroll that was a film prop used in a previous production, so brought it to a light table to see what it might offer. The light table added some mystery and a touch of glowing fantasy lighting as well; it also brought out all those wonderfully craggy creases and wrinkles from the textured prop—I had my inspiration.

Next, I photographed my left hand against the parchment, then the right (which is harder than you'd think with a DSLR), all the while keeping in mind the angles and orientation and trying not to deviate from the first shot (**FIGURE 13.2**). I began this first shoot as a test shoot to see if the idea would work, but once I saw how they turned out, I loved the framing and simple gestures so I kept them. This was a good lesson in being mentally prepared to return, but keeping open the possibility to be pleasantly surprised if it worked out the first time.

Step 2: Assemble Nature's Photo Palette

Because this project was another heavily textured composite, I used a photo palette of trees, bark, leaves, and other natural texture images for an efficient workflow. Most of the images sprang from a jungle trip to the Peruvian headwaters of the Amazon, where the forest was rich with both plant life and a cornucopia of phenomenal textures. The jungles and other places with interesting bark typically had softer lighting, because they were shaded by a larger canopy. Because of this softer light, the palette had some continuity and the images lent themselves to customization. In other words, it was the motherload for texturing as I could always paint in my own lighting afterwards (**FIGURE 13.3**).

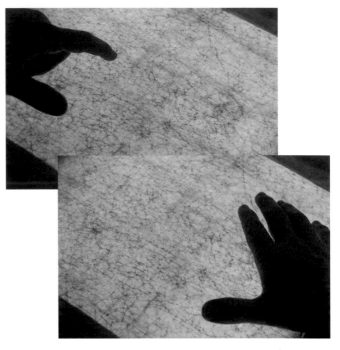

FIGURE 13.2 Each hand was shot against the parchment and light table and ended up being perfect for the final composition.

FIGURE 13.3 The images from the canopy had softer lighting, perfect for grabbing textures and shapes, then painting in my lighting a bit more afterwards.

Step 3: Paint Textures Together

Get ready to squint. This section included a ridiculous amount of looking back and forth between bark and roots of the palette and the shape and form of the hands, while trying to match up the pieces mentally before making a selection and copying it over to the composite. Because this section is really the core of the project's workflow and uses mostly the same editing techniques again and again, I'll focus mostly on the strategies for each portion of the hands and the tips for getting things to look right. A few core strategies for texturing any subject are:

- Closely look at the three-dimensional form that the hands (or whatever you are covering up) create and match this with organic matter that does roughly the same thing, even if it is just for one small moment, one small piece that actually works. Mask out everything else. Simply texturing an image is not enough; creating form is a key part of the detailed illusion (**FIGURE 13.4**).

- The Move tool (with the Show Transform Controls toggled on) is your best friend here—use it. Not only does each piece need to be moved into position, but they must be fluidly rotated and scaled as well (**FIGURE 13.5**).

- Every piece added from the palette needs its own color and Curves corrections using clipped adjustment layers. Some trees are more mossy and green, others more brown or gray—which is all fine and good on their own. When combined into a single entity, however, the result can start to look like you used a hammer to smash mismatched jigsaw pieces together: They clearly don't fit. Going by the feel and direction of the texture is not enough, adjust for color and contrast as you go. (Chapter 4 covers these adjustment layers in good detail, if you need a refresher.)

FIGURE 13.4 Match your texture pieces to the same form beneath it, in this case the hand.

FIGURE 13.5 Use the Move tool to get each piece in position and use all those Swiss army knife transform features you learned in Chapter 2 to get the piece looking just right.

- When masking, flip back and forth between using a round, soft brush and a textured brush (such as one of the Spatter brushes). The soft-and-round default can help mask out the crisp edges of the layer and create very even transitions to a textured brush. Use the textured brushwork to better simulate organic material (**FIGURE 13.6**). This usually has a better effect once there's already a base of covering textures to work with so your base shape doesn't show underneath. For your second or third coat, brushing in the direction of the texture's shapes helps the result appear more seamless.

FIGURE 13.6 Brushes with more uneven and organic edges can help blend organic material when masking.

- Cut the grease! Always mask out all hard edges and areas outside your desired content. Sometimes this means starting with a black mask (invert an active white mask with Ctrl/Cmd+I or Alt/Opt-click the Add Mask icon ◙) so that you can paint in just the parts you want with white. Unless you work with precision, painting mask upon painted mask (and selections are virtually useless in this case) can collect digital grease like a swamp.

- Sharpen each piece when you bring it into the composite, but only after you scale it to fit. Sharpening the texture before scaling will obviously make it sharper, but once this sharpened image gets scaled, it may look too sharp if scaled down or not sharp enough if scaled up after the filter (for Smart Objects this means you have to readjust the sharpness settings after each transform for the best results). Scaling an image larger will make the sharpness feel softer because pixels are being stretched and copied, while scaling an image smaller will appear to make it sharper because pixels condense on each other. So find that sweet spot that works with the shape and form first, then sharpen the piece to match the sharpness of the images around it.

- When you find a useful piece of bark (or other texture) that is easily identifiable as three-dimensional looking with a prominent curve to the texture, make the most of it and use it liberally. Nothing is harder than getting the right curve around an edge to give the feeling that it is three dimensional. In **FIGURE 13.7** you can see that I found a keeper—as well as a repeater! The more obvious repetitive parts can be blended over with additional textures if things start feeling too cookie cutter like.

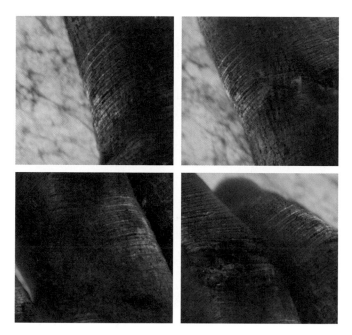

FIGURE 13.7 Find a piece that provides the dimension you are looking for and use it as needed; here are four examples of a single curved texture with white streaks being used repeatedly for different areas of the right hand.

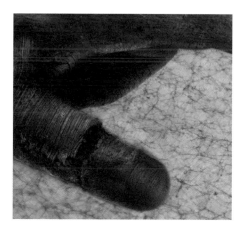

FIGURE 13.8 The thumb's texture successfully deviated from its original edge, but only because so much of the rest of the hand matched the edges exactly. Consistency for the majority enables infrequent variation to lend credibility and interest.

Edges

The edges around the fingers have their own look and feel to them and are important to get right. For this project the hands serve as a frame-like outer boundary of the content, and the edges around the fingers frame the hands. Because they are so prominent and important, the viewer will notice quickly things that are wrong, like cuts or bad masking. Here are a couple things to try out when working on textured edges:

- Know that shapes matter. For edges, matching the outer shapes is just as important, if not more important, than matching form (3D qualities) for texturing a recognizable image. At times you can deviate, such as when a texture lends its own interest (notice the thumb in **FIGURE 13.8**), but for the most part, getting a good amount of similarity between the object edge and texture edge is optimal. Primarily retaining consistency between edges has an unexpected liberating effect: The more consistent you are overall, the more likely viewers will accept deviations and your illusion, perhaps thinking "Oh, that thumb's a bit messed up and barky-looking, but definitely a thumb to the rest of the hand."

- Work on a very small scale. Zoom way in (hold Alt/Opt while scrolling up) and look for those matching edge shapes one small stretch at a time. Once you get it outlined with a base layer, you can always go over it again with another texture or two in order to refine the look.

Tendons

Although I wanted human-shaped hands, I also wanted an abstract look of a nature/human hybrid, something more alien. To achieve this, I used some roots I photographed while in a Peruvian jungle as tendons. These roots had massively webbed and stretched out pieces that felt like tendons that had been exaggerated under tension—but on a huge scale. It was partially this sense of scale that let them function so well as they fit just the way I was hoping for on the back of the hand (**FIGURE 13.9**). The key piece to get right was matching the angle and depth of the root. The wrong angle made it feel like the root wasn't stretching straight out from the hand, and too deep a web-like tendon wouldn't match the depth of the other textures. These things were controlled by both the actual image source (the angle of the roots in relation to myself and the tree's core), as well as masking, not leaving them to stretch too deeply against the other textures. Although the tendon roots had the capability of looking even deeper and more stretched, I felt this just didn't look quite right. Masking a shallower ending helped blend them in with the rest of the flatter surface textures.

Top of the Hands and Flat Filler

Because of the angle of the photographs, the tops of the hands were flatter, so I needed to match that flatter angle with the texture. Finding appropriate pieces of bark proved a challenge, because most trees have an obvious roundness and don't contain large flat spots. The trick for this was in scaling the right parts: only those middle sections! These areas don't have the same obvious bark texture curvature compared to the rounded edges that get scaled smaller and smaller before they disappear around the backside. Unlike fire and water, which physics tells us should appear a certain way, organic matter comes in an infinite variety of scale and variation. What is detailed and small on one tree may be huge and craggy on another; because of this, adhering tree textures to an object allows for greater play in scaling without raising any alarms. **FIGURE 13.10** shows a piece of bark from the center of a tree that was scaled to appear flatter, yet still

FIGURE 13.9 Tree roots shot at a certain angle looked like stretched tendons to me—which was perfect for the tree hands; here you can see the roots in place.

at an angle to match the angle and direction of the hands. Though the original tree was not large compared to the others, taking a longer middle section helped add a line of flat-looking cracks.

Use Water for Fingernails

For the fingernails, I deviated from the bark and tree textures. Here I used water to simulate the contrast of our own skin against shiny nails—not to mention this looked awesome and contributed to the anthropomorphized nature in general (as opposed to Tolkien's Ents and their twiggy hands). The most notable challenges were re-creating a shine and providing a convincing and detailed rounded shape for the edges the nails recess into (**FIGURE 13.11**). By playing with the scale and repetition of a curved texture I was able to not only paint the nails with water, but sink them into the rest of the barky textures.

Step 4: Make a Map

Showing the lay of the city in the process of being transformed into forest was as straightforward as grabbing a small textured brush (between 5 and 15 pixels) and painting—well, nearly that simple. First, I created a new layer and placed it above the background images so that it would still show up but be underneath the textured hands. Then I painted the streets and buildings as I saw fit.

To keep the map consistent with the rest of the paper texture and coloring, I changed the layer's blending mode. I chose Luminosity, because this mode borrows the exact coloring of the layer beneath it. Nothing will have the same continuity as using the exact color of the background parchment and its subtle variations throughout. Using Luminosity mode helps avoid creating any visual rifts or separation between the two layers (**FIGURE 13.12**).

FLAT SECTIONS OF BARK

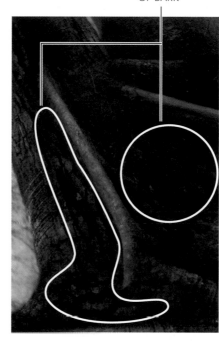

FIGURE 13.10 This craggy piece of bark was scaled to create a flatter look in an area lacking the curve of the edges and tendons.

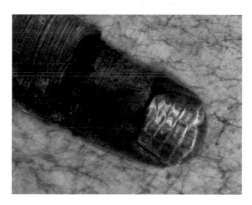

FIGURE 13.11 Fingernails needed to be a contrasting texture and shine as well as to look as if they were recessed into the fingertips.

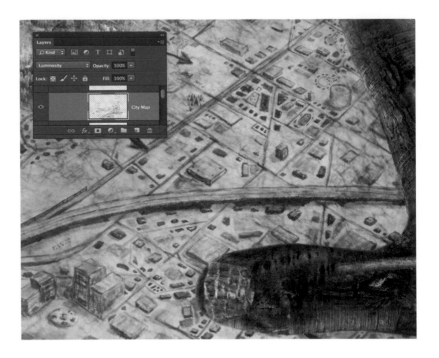

FIGURE 13.12 The map details were painted onto a new layer with the blending mode of Luminosity to keep the map's painted color consistent with the background parchment.

Aerial Photographs Show the Expansion

Although part of the map, the photo-real areas needed a different feel to them. This section benefited from some aerial photographs I took on a flight over the Sierra Nevada Mountains. Dangling your camera and head out the window of a small plane while in midair can be a bit nerve-wracking, but it's well worth the effort (just keep a firm hold and focus on the amazing images). The idea behind using real photographs against the drawn lines of the city was two fold: to help foster an imaginative context (one less grounded in the literal and therefore allowing for the suspension of disbelief) and to create the feeling of forward motion and narrative trajectory. I wanted the message of one-way expansion in the favor of wilderness (**FIGURE 13.13**). I blended the photographs much like other textures, jumping back and forth between a soft (for times of gentle transitions) and textured (for

areas of following organic shapes and edges) brush while painting on the mask.

The aerials were lucky imagery frankly, but still didn't finish the look. To make the trees appear to be part of the map rather than actual trees growing out of the map, I again changed the blending mode of each of the tree layers to Luminosity. Once the colors from the map and parchment beneath the tree layers were applied to their values, the small forest looked like part of the map and the entire project had greater continuity (**FIGURE 13.14**).

TIP To change the blending mode of multiple layers at once, select all the layers together (Ctrl/Cmd-click on the names of layers) within the Layers panel and then change the blending mode. The selected blending mode change will apply to all of them—workflow optimized!

FIGURE 13.13 Using aerial photographs helped create a clearer narrative of sketched out plans actually coming to life in three dimensions.

FIGURE 13.14 Changing the blending mode of the forest aerial shots helped them become a part of the map rather than something just sitting on top of it.

Build a Building

The one tricky part to the project was creating photorealistic buildings, because I didn't have any aerial images of skyscrapers. I did have quite a few photographs of very tall buildings taken from the ground looking upwards. A session with the Rotate View tool proved if you turn the world, or at least these shot-from-below images, upside down, it looks as if you shot the images from way up high looking down. To further sell the simulated appearance of buildings viewed from above, I filled in the original bases to look like the new tops of the structures with some roof-like materials (**FIGURE 13.15**). I used some basic pavement texture that was fairly smooth, yet consisted of just enough variation to appear textured. Masking it to fit, I then painted with straight lines (holding down Shift while clicking one corner, then the other) to simulate the roof's top ledge as well as painting some straight-line shadows

FIGURE 13.15 To simulate a top-down view of a skyscraper (such as the larger building in the middle here), simply rotate a shot taken from the ground looking up and fill in a roof to complete the look (as seen in the buildings to either side).

for added dimension. To blend the "base" of the building with the trees I used careful, up-close masking, following the shapes of the trees as a masking guide. I made sure to leave some trees in front of the building and not just cut it off artificially. Once again I brought in the consistency by changing the layers' blending mode to Luminosity, which completed the look I wanted.

Step 5: Sculpt with Lighting

Lighting does far more than simply change how bright or dark the image is. Lighting can actually sculpt textures like those of the fairly flat-lit hands. The final step in this project included encouraging the forms that had been hinted at (by using the best textures available) to feel more fully three dimensional.

The hands felt a little dull, so I added a group folder called FX and a new (and final) Curves adjustment layer to give them greater dimension. On this new layer I made two control points: one to anchor the darks and keep them rich

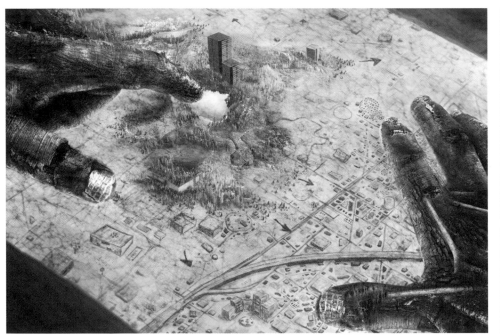
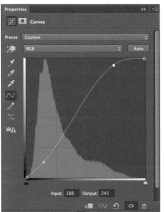

FIGURE 13.16 The last lighting effect combined the use of a Curves adjustment layer and a mask to bring out key highlights on the hands and certain locations on the map.

and not washed out and the second to boost the midtones and highlights to create greater contrast. This adjustment, however, was a global one when first created, because it was above everything in the scene and the layers stack. Some heavy masking was definitely in order.

I decided to mask out the entire adjustment layer, then paint the effect back in just over those key spots that needed it. Inverting the initial mask (Ctrl/Cmd+I), I picked up the ever-useful soft-and-round brush and painted with white just in those areas needing highlights, including the bottom highlights on the hands created from the glowing map and other areas that accentuated the depth (**FIGURE 13.16**). Parts of the map that were a little dull or flat looking I also painted with white at a low opacity until the look felt balanced, meaning the highlights of the hand and highlights of the map seemed to match one another.

Conclusion

Seeking out and matching just the right texture shapes can be time consuming, but well worth the effort as doing so is literally a transformative process. Projects like *Growth* are also incredibly helpful for building up your own blending and mask-painting chops! Repetition does wonders for improving technique and efficiency, and projects such as this one have quite a lot of repetition to them. Each time your eye slightly improves and becomes more discerning, not to mention you become more confident in exactly what to do. So whether you have a deeper concept you want to communicate or simply want to morph a banal object into an organic and raw-bark version, get some good texture material, work carefully piece by piece, and transform, adjust, and mask to perfection!

MARTÍN DE PASQUALE

www.behance.net/martindepasquale

Martín De Pasquale is an Argentinian retouch artist based in Buenos Aires. As senior designer for RDYA and art director for Crossmedia and Selnet, he has been a professional leader in industry photomanipulation and compositing. His personal works often play on self-reflective irony and imaginative scenarios of the impossible come to life.

His artwork often contains humorous critiques designed to provoke amusement, shock, and questions from its viewers. Always exploring unexpected visual strategies to convey his ideas, Martin has worked with many international brands, design studios, and photographers from around the world.

How do you plan and execute one of your ideas? What's your typical process?

The process is always the same: I have an idea and then find the best way to solve it. I always carry a notebook where I write ideas that I would like to make, as well as sketch the best way, the best angles, views, colors, and style. Once I compile the information, I take the pictures, search for elements, and go to post-production.

What advice do you have for creating a seamless and believable composite or retouched image?

Light, light, and light. The lighting is very important if you want it to look credible. If there is a dominant light source, it is important that everything respects that source. The resolution of the image is important; detail makes for an interesting composition. When you see photo retouching work, you always want to see up close in detail, see the trick behind it. For this reason, the details are extremely important.

ABSTRACT SUMMER, 2013

NIGHTFALL, 2013

In what ways do you play with scaling? What helps create a believable look even with a dramatic change in scale?

The same resource: the light. Things that you want to enlarge need to have more definition, so the detail is not lost when it is scaled. Shadows should be altered, and you must operate as if the object were giant or very small. Light works and matters the same if you have a scale of 10 centimeters or 10 meters. You always have to observe objects of similar sizes, and see what happens with them.

What is your favorite feature within Photoshop?

I don't have any particular favorite. I never really use any of the automatic options or filters, or anything like that. For me, it's really about using the basic tools and many, many layers.

What is your strategy for using color within a project?

I see many references wherever I go, and I keep them in mind, trying to copy environments and palettes that I like. I don't like saturated or vibrant colors. I like pictures with harmonious tones, few colors, a desaturated look.

PREY, 2013

KARMA, 2011

How many images do you typically use in one of your creations?

That depends on the project—sometimes one, sometimes two, maybe up to 50. Many times, when I take photos, I take more than ten, all of the same subject but with small variants to angle, light, color, position of objects, so I can pick the best.

What's your biggest challenge, and how do you handle it?

Any project that I cannot visually solve. I may not always understand where I'm going wrong, so I prefer to delete it all instead of fix it; bring it back to the zero starting point in order to make the project better. Projects that require CGI are difficult, because the whole process is very complex, and I typically ask the help of other experts.

Any advice for those looking to jump into the commercial photo retouch world?

Be prepared for a lot of work. Gain lots of experience and practice at every opportunity. It is very important to ask the advice of other professionals as they are the only ones that can enhance your work and give you meaningful feedback. Common sense goes a long way, as do good taste and good choices of light and colors; all are very important to make your work professional looking. It is not something that comes out from one day to the other, but years and years of hard work. Finally, go see many artists, exhibitions, books, and courses; as this all serves to extend your tools. ■

Spaguetti, 2012

CHAPTER 14

Big Store, Big Scenery

COVERED IN THIS CHAPTER

- Shooting and matching backgrounds
- Using the Smart Sharpen filter
- Noise reduction
- Painting vegetation
- Painting clouds and mist with advanced brush settings
- Texturing buildings

With a touch of customization, clouds become mist, plants become anthropomorphized, and you can transform even the most mundane, common space into an entirely new scene and narrative. As part of a series about reversing the relationship between humans and nature, *Forest Construction* visualizes what the landscape might look like if our positions of expansion and progress were reversed. In this project, the forest sprawls to swallow the urban Big Box store, greenery erodes cars, and each element progresses like construction phases. The idea lent itself to some hugely fun compositing, as I brushed in the various elements from actual photographs. In the end, the project was as much a lesson on the relationship of correct depth, color, sharpness, noise, and lighting to seamless compositing as it was a commentary on human progress and nature (**FIGURE 14.1**).

▸ **FIGURE 14.1** For a hypothetical vision into development with nature and human role reversals, *Forest Construction* enabled me to practice a variety of techniques to paint with photographs, using nature images as a palette.

Step 1: Photograph

One of the main mechanisms to compositing is not the work done within Photoshop, but photographing the right shot that you can bring *into* Photoshop. Before you can composite, you need to find a base and inspiration to build on. For the *Forest Construction* concept to work, I needed to find the most typical department store around. Syracuse, New York, supplied a location that fit the bill perfectly (**FIGURE 14.2**). When I shoot a background image, I keep my plans for building on it in mind, along with a few other strategies:

- Scout locations. Find a perspective that gives you what you need to build on or alter at a later time. The parking lot view of the store, for example, grounded the perspective and enabled me to expand the composite into the overcast sky above and behind.

- Shoot for variety. There's nothing like having options. You may *think* you captured that perfect shot in camera, but seeing it larger on the computer screen may expose flaws and reasons why the shot won't work after all. Having several images and a variety of shots is the kicker for success. Each new angle or location can increase your chances for one of them working out.

- Don't just think about the image content. Instead, plan for an interesting point of view and frame the background shot with the potential to add more things to it. Even if you don't know exactly what you will do to the image, plan and allow for growth in an already workable shot. Figure 14.2 was angled upwards purposely so that I could build on top of the store without the image feeling forced. Changing the position of objects in post-production can have a strange effect, like distorted mirrors in a carnival fun house, if you're working with an image not taken with a telephoto lens.

FIGURE 14.2 This shot of a big-box store (which prefers to remain anonymous) makes a perfect background because of its clutter-free surroundings and iconic urban sprawl representation.

- Always use a tripod whenever possible! True, sometimes you can get away without one for bright daylight shots, but tripods offer more than a stable base. Setting up and using a tripod also slows the whole process down a little, forcing you to think about the composition a bit deeper compared to a quick walk and shoot.

You don't usually see waterfalls while walking in downtown Montreal, Quebec, but they came quickly to mind when I spotted the building in **FIGURE 14.3**. The building's very angular forms were perfect for contrasting against the organic bursts of water. Finding this background shot made it easy to composite in nature to start its beautiful demolition process.

FIGURE 14.3 As in *Forest Construction*, the background image here formed a natural base on which to build and integrate into something new. The waterfalls highlight the rigid and immense forms of modern buildings.

FIGURE 14.4 The photo palette for this project was composed of images I shot while on a trip to beautiful locations around Peru.

Step 2: Build a Photo Palette and Scaffolding

As a compositor, I have found that traveling and photographing are invaluable. The number and variety of images I have within my database is really the only thing that enables me to create my unique projects, rather than relying on stock images. For *Forest Construction*, I again gathered potentially useful shots into a photo palette that I could draw from to piece together the final image. Some of the shots that worked best for this project were from a trip to Peru; from hiking in the clouds at 15,000 feet of elevation to venturing in the jungles at the headwaters of the Amazon, I got plenty of variety (**FIGURE 14.4**). Just about any green space or park, however, has potential as a source.

Never underestimate the value of generating your own image archive, so whether it's sunny, rainy, or snowing in your main background shot, you'll always be ready to hunt down just the right textures and appropriate image palette needed. Never stop gathering! (You will see just how valuable this motto is in Bonus Chapter 16.)

As usual, I next gathered the group folders and organized them into the layer order of my composite document (**FIGURE 14.5**). Notice that effects are once again on top and that the parts that need to be painted and composited over are towards the bottom. Although you might be tempted to skip this step and create folders on the fly, I find it worth a few minutes of extra time to set up my folders like scaffolding, so I can more easily build from there. Later, you can always work on different levels and jump back and forth as needed—much simpler than finding yourself painted in a corner without the right ladder.

Step 3: Sharpen and Reduce Noise

I needed to clean up my base image a little before I could match all the other layers to its look and feel. Like preparing the bed of a real garden to avoid veggie planting hell, I decided to apply the Smart Sharpen and Noise Reduction filters to the base image into which I planned to plant the scene elements. To keep the process nondestructive, I first converted the layer to a Smart Object by choosing Filter > Convert for Smart Filters so that I could apply the filters as Smart Filters (**FIGURE 14.6**). (Alternately, you can right-click the layer's name in the Layers panel and choose Convert to Smart Object from the context menu.) The power behind Smart Filters is that I can mask, edit, or remove them later or even just turn off their visibility temporarily.

FIGURE 14.5 These group folders set the framework of depth for the rest of the composite.

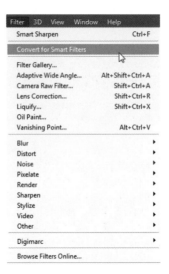

FIGURE 14.6 Convert the layer to a Smart Object to apply nondestructive Smart Filters.

NOTE Although it's possible to choose possible to convert to a Smart Object for a layer that already is one, don't do it, don't do it. Re-converting a Smart Object layer will more or less flatten the layer's previous smart edits. Likewise, don't do any masking work before converting to a Smart Object. During the conversion Photoshop applies the mask, which simply deletes the masked image content.

The Smart Sharpen filter (Filter > Sharpen > Smart Sharpen) was revamped in Photoshop CC, adding a Reduce Noise slider to the usual Amount and Radius controls. I tend to sharpen right up to the point before I get a small hint of halos creeping in from both the Radius and Amount levels. As you can see in **FIGURE 14.7**, setting Amount to 300%, Radius to 2px, and Reduce Noise to 38% worked well for the background shot. (If you're using Photoshop CS6 or older, keeping Amount at 100% and Radius under 3 does the trick just fine, although with a touch more noise.)

Noise Reduction

Noise—that visual static in an image, like bits of sand thrown onto the picture—has met its match in Photoshop CC. Not only does its Reduce Noise filter clear up this noise better than in earlier versions, it also works especially well on *color* noise, in which colors are randomized and exaggerated (**FIGURE 14.8**).

> **TIP** When you shoot in RAW, use the noise reduction features within the RAW Editor before bringing the image into your composite. The RAW noise reduction sliders are more powerful and refined with the various ways you can tackle noise in all its forms.

I typically use the Reduce Noise filter (concentrating mostly on color) after Smart Sharpen, so that I have a better idea of how much to apply. When you enhance and sharpen, you also sharpen all the noise bits and pieces as well. If you apply Reduce Noise first, you may end up making the image a little soft with small islands of high-contrast noise left over. Choosing Filter > Noise > Reduce Noise, I applied the Reduce Noise filter and reduced color noise by 100% (**FIGURE 14.9**).

FIGURE 14.7 Smart Sharpen does as its name implies—and does it *very* well in Photoshop CC.

FIGURE 14.8 Noise, especially the color noise shown here, can detract from your digital images to sabotage your compositing efforts—like when combining noisy shots with already noise-free shots.

However much noise remains in the end, the various images must be matched up as close as possible when compositing (including any noise), so I try to get everything at a fairly low noise level when starting out (and always getting rid of color noise). On occasion though, a layer being added must have a slight bit of noise *increased* for a better fit if the image it is being matched to cannot be fixed any further. This is rare in my own workflow, but it does come up. In these situations you can *add* noise by going to Filter > Noise > Add Noise, but make sure that monochromatic is checked so no color noise is brought in, only contrasting noise!

TIP Avoid noise altogether by using the lowest ISO possible combined with a proper exposure, or at least not one that was severely under-exposed! (See Chapter 5 for more advice on reducing in-camera noise.)

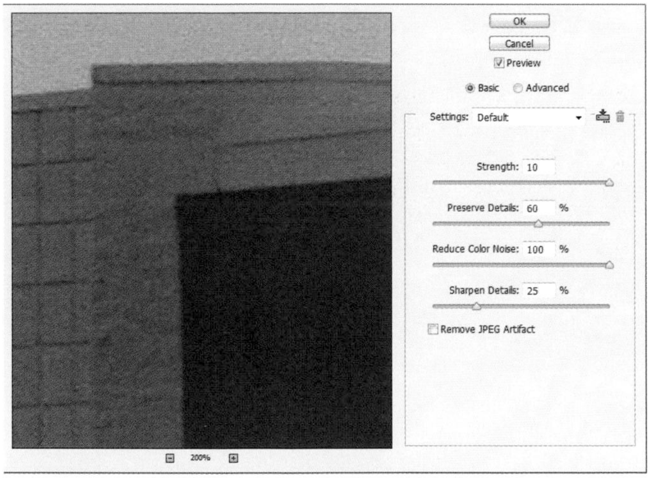

Step 4: Plant a Foreground, Grow Depth

Creating a sense of depth is vital for a more immersive feel, having a foreground and deep background will take you a long way. For this project, I was lucky to have one image in my archive that provided both: the tree with clouds behind shown in **FIGURE 14.10**.

Taken in Machu Picchu on a similarly cloudy and wet day as my background shot, it provided not only a foreground and background in a single photograph, but also matched the project's mood and lighting while simultaneously creating more visual interest. When you find a gift like this, take it! Why labor to force your photographs together, when you can let them work for you with their own continuity? Overlaying the two images worked easily; because of their framing, they both left room in all the right spots for the other to contribute to the narrative.

FIGURE 14.9 Reduce Noise filter is great at knocking out noise left over from sharpening, especially with versions of Photoshop CS6 and older.

FIGURE 14.10 This one shot serves as both an interesting foreground and background image for the composite.

Slice an Image in Two

For the Machu Picchu image to work as both foreground and background, I needed to split it in two, then place the foreground portion (the tree) in the Tree folder above the Box Store folder (which held the base image) and the background portion (the mountains and clouds) in the Background folder below in the layer stack. Basically, I had to split the Machu Picchu shot into two slices of bread for a store sandwich.

After bringing the tree shot into the document, I copied and placed it (Ctrl/Cmd+J) into the two folders. Jumping up to the Tree folder copy, I selected the tree trunk pieces with the Quick Selection tool, being sure to deselect (by Alt/Opt-clicking) some spots where the viewer would need to see through larger gaps in the leaves. Making the right de-selections is important, because the Refine Edge tool is good at adding to the selection, but not subtracting. So in your own projects, make sure to not only make the right selection, but the right de-selections, as you will see why in a moment (**FIGURE 14.11**).

NOTE Using the Quick Selection tool may be the best choice in situations where there are edges to seek out, but it still has trouble where the selection area and background are extremely similar in value and color. Going over areas repeatedly and in detail does help improve your results.

FIGURE 14.11 Make selections using the Quick Selection tool, but be sure to subtract from the selection for such areas as large gaps between leaves and branches.

Because the top part of this layer would be repeated as the background, I focused on the bottom trunk and leaves. Clicking the Refine Edge icon in the options bar to open the Refine Edge dialog box, I then chose the Refine Radius tool 🖌 to paint the selection edges. I changed my brush size so I could capture the edges without Photoshop biting too deep into the bark or leaves for its edge analysis. Because it will occasionally take away parts that need to stay, be safe and only paint areas that need it.

> **TIP** If you go too far with your Refine Radius brushing, you can switch to its alter ego, the Erase Refinements tool, which functions just like an eraser for the areas where you applied Refine Radius.

When I was satisfied with my painting with the Refine Radius tool and its slider adjustments, I clicked OK to return to the main image to see the new selections that took place (**FIGURE 14.12**). All was in order, so I clicked the Add Mask icon 🔲 in the Layers panel to create the mask.

Step 5: Mask the Big Box

To remove the boring blah-gray sky to make room for mist and mountains, I again started with the Quick Selection tool (W). I first selected the sky, because it was more uniform and easier for the tool to pick up, then pressed Ctrl/Cmd+Shift+I to inverse the selection (**FIGURE 14.13**).

To fine-tune the selection, I again turned to the Refine Edge dialog box and its sliders. Specifically, I used the Smooth slider to even out the selection (**FIGURE 14.14**), because the Quick Selection tool had trouble with the sloped straight edge on the first try. (Note that this is a larger problem with older versions of Photoshop.) As for the other sliders, I always like to add a slight 1px feathering to soften those sharp collage-like borders, and bite

FIGURE 14.12 Paint around the leaves with the Refine Radius tool inside the Refine Edge dialog box.

FIGURE 14.13 To make the selections just a fraction more efficient, select the piece with the most uniformity like the sky, then inverse the selection with Ctrl/Cmd+Shift+I.

into the selection with about a −40 Shift Edge setting to be rid of remaining halos left over from slight bits of sky.

Selections may look nice from far away, but in reality may need some fine-tuning—like looking more closely in your mirror in the morning to discover, yes, you do need to comb that bed-head before facing the world. In the world of selections visible halos and other unwanted pieces are the equivalent of bed-head. To better see the remaining bits that need fixing, I like to use Quick Mask mode (press Q or click the Quick Mask icon 🔲 at the bottom of the toolbar), which displays everything that is not selected in a semi-transparent red.

Whenever you use the Smooth slider within Refine Edge, for example, it will inevitably iron out some details you want to keep. In this case, part of the light post was a bit over ironed and got a little burnt in the process. Besides helping with visibility, Quick Mask mode enables you to paint with black to subtract from a selection and paint with white to add to the selection, just like painting on a mask (**FIGURE 14.15**). To get the lighting pole brought back into the main selection, I needed to draw in straight lines with white, then refine them with black lines to remove any halo.

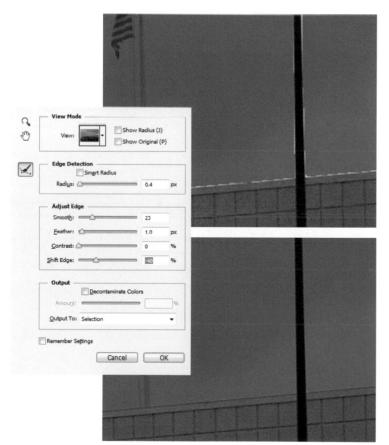

FIGURE 14.14 The Smooth slider does a nice job ironing out the wrinkles of rugged selections for elements that should be simple and straight.

FIGURE 14.15 Quick Mask mode can be a great way to visualize a selection before committing into mask.

Bringing the pole and light back into the selection, I painted straight lines by clicking once at the bottom right edge of the pole using the small and soft brush set to 15px, then Shift-clicked the top right edge of the pole.

Photoshop translated this into drawing a straight line from point A to B. I did this around the entire light post until everything was looking better. A few corners and the security cameras also needed some custom brushing for the selection. When I was satisfied, I clicked the Add Mask icon. **FIGURE 14.16** shows how all that sandwich preparation paid off.

Step 6: Sink in the Scenery

With my foreground and background features planted, I turned to painting in greenery from my Peruvian photo palette. When painting your own vegetation, having options is always helpful—and I do mean painting. Unlike other elements that I *selected* with good edges and then masked, these organic bits were quickly cut and pasted in. Then I applied a mask and used brush strokes directly on the mask to refine the shape—no selections needed (**FIGURE 14.17**).

FIGURE 14.16 With the mask on the tree and building applied, you can see how the building is sandwiched between the two separated foreground and background pieces.

FIGURE 14.17 Apply a mask directly to pieces of greenery and simply paint in the desired shapes and forms.

Swallowing a Truck

As you can see in **FIGURE 14.18**, the truck is being swallowed by six painted-in greenery layers that constitute the first bite of green development. Grabbing pieces of the photo palette using the Marquee tool, I copied (Ctrl/Cmd+C) and pasted (Ctrl/Cmd+V) each one into the composite, immediately clicking the Add Mask icon ⬚ in the Layers panel to give it a mask upon arrival. Painting on the masks, as with the previous example, helps constrain their unruly nature to just the areas intended to be covering the truck.

When choosing pieces from your palette, you're aiming for elements that might fit and not look too "off" once in place, or at least have potential to be blended seamlessly. My strategies for searching and collecting are:

- Look at an object's form from all angles, and consider the form you need. Starting with the big chunk taking over the truck, I had to turn my head sideways to see the potential as it matched the angle and form I needed (**FIGURE 14.19**).

- Match lighting as closely to perfect as possible. For overcast days you are given a start with generally soft lighting, and can then paint in the lighting you want afterwards. For sunny direct light, you are more or less stuck with the high contrast shadows from those sunbeams, so make sure the chosen pieces have continuity with the rest of the composite.

- Find details that can provide a potential edge for the element you're painting in. Working *with* the material as a guide whenever possible significantly assists in blending the piece in seamlessly. Try to match a path of natural variation; brushing in any shape just because you can may work against you, producing a forced, cut-out look.

FIGURE 14.18 I used six pieces from the greenery photo palette and added new masks for each when brought into the composite.

FIGURE 14.19 I choose the first major piece by looking at its shape and form and matching it with the scenario in the composite.

Vegetation Painting Lessons

With my pieces roughly positioned over the truck and masked out (using Ctrl/Cmd+I to invert each selected mask one by one), I began painting back into view the portions of their shapes that I wanted. Painting vegetation sounds, at worst, environmentally unfriendly, and at best messy, but it's actually quite simple. For each piece, I followed the same basic procedure:

1. Using the advice in the "Brush Tips" sidebar, I found an organic looking speckled brush (Dry Brush #1), toggled Transfer, then changed the brush's Control setting to Pen Pressure `Control: Pen Pressure ⇕` for tablet use (**FIGURE 14.20**).

2. I clicked on the vegetation's mask and inverted it (Ctrl/Cmd+I) to turn the white mask to black and temporarily erase the vegetation.

3. Painting with white, I started with the general intended shape outline, then worked towards the outer edges of the final shape. The best strategy is to follow the natural formations and direction of material, whether it is clumps of grass, leaves, a mound of dirt, or anything else that has an identifiable mass or good cohesion. To see what material you can incorporate into the form, try painting a little too far beyond the edges you want.

FIGURE 14.20 Dry Brush #1 and others like it have a workable organic speckled shape that's versatile for simulating foliage edges and perfect for painting onto a mask.

4. As necessary, I subtracted from the image by painting with black on the mask (press X to flip between the black and white defaults). If you paint too far beyond workable areas of vegetation (say you accidentally paint in a rock as well), pressing X to flip back to black lets you mask things back out of the picture. Not only are you tossing the rock aside, but you can do so knowing exactly where to leave an edge or shape. In this case, I knew the point right before where the rock was hanging out.

In this way I painted in each layer, fitting it into place before using black and white on the mask. The couple exceptions included some bits that already had a defined edge I wanted to use, such as the trees on top of the store; for these layers it was more efficient to make a selection before masking and refining the edge. But for all other custom work that doesn't have easy to find edges, any kind of selection is most likely going to be fairly pointless.

TIP Add variety to the edges of the form. Even if you find areas that work as straight edges, bring some variation whenever possible.

BRUSH TIPS

You need a good brush when painting in bits of organic material, or any other masked element. To create some interesting brush combinations all within the Brush panel, try these tips:

- Use scattering. This can help when you need those moments of randomized strokes that break up the obviousness of something being brushed in. It also can be good for adding in texture as the connected smear-like stroke portion is replaced with more of a brush dabbing simulation.

- Toggle the Dual brush option for subtracting or limiting a brush choice shape. Depending on the shape you choose for the second brush, it will take away certain outside areas of the stroke, again adding to a more organic feel. Disguising that things were painted is crucial for keeping a photorealistic effect.

- Use the simply brilliant Transfer setting if you have a tablet. With Transfer specified, choose Pen Pressure from the Control drop-down in the options bar to give every stroke greater control over opacity and gain the ability to create even more variety in the look and feel. The more you can simulate real mediums of painting, the better the control and look generally.

- Bring your brush's Flow down to 50% or less in the options bar (or press Shift+5) to articulate greater control and subtle variation without a palette.

- Use the Flow setting when you want to soften the effects and edges of a brush while still keeping the desired shape of the brush. Flow lets you paint in repetitive movements, building up opacity with each return gesture to an area—all with a single click (only movements are needed, not single-click strokes).

- Don't over-complicate the brush. You need not use a complex brush to achieve a good effect. Just be sure the brush has some kind of controlled variation to it.

Step 7: Enter Grunge, Exit the X

In new development and construction zones, nature attempts to go about its business as usual for as long as it can, and in this role reversal project, so too does the intrepid Big Box store (tired of being anonymous it petitioned for a new identity from witness protection), which is still determined to serve consumers despite some grunge and its X becoming a snack for an over-achiever of a tree.

To create the grungy discoloring texture, I used the same rusty metal source image with which I added texture to buildings in Chapter 9 (**FIGURE 14.21**). Once you find a good texture, you will find a million and one uses for it over time, so always be on the lookout. I added the texture layer directly above the building's layer and its mask, then Alt/Opt-clicked between the two layers to clip the texture layer to the visible parts of the building layer below. As in Chapter 9, I next changed the texture layer's blending mode to Overlay, which allowed for both discoloration and darkening in parts that had much darker patches of rust. A custom mask on this layer enabled me to paint exactly where and how much rust I wanted (**FIGURE 14.22**). Overlay also let me stay lighter and kept the texture from getting too harsh or dark as Multiply or Color Burn mode would have done in this situation. With a few variations of this layer (including scaling and rotation) and heavily controlled masking, the results came out quite grungy, yet refined.

FIGURE 14.21 With a couple layers of rusty metal set to an Overlay mode, this building is grunged up quite nicely.

FIGURE 14.22 Overlay blending mode combined with a controlling mask lets you choose exactly where to add grunge and where to keep clean.

FIGURE 14.23 The O and the X were part of the demolition narrative and important to create a bit of humor as well as draw some attention to the subject.

Rebrand Techniques

While grafting a new identity on the store, I found the logo an especially fun challenge. I painted in the letters, gave them shading (both highlights and shadows) for a little added depth, then rearranged a couple letters in compromised positions. In order for the name to still be understood as a stand in representing all big-box stores, I kept a copy of the letter shapes that were used to darken where they supposedly were keeping the original paint rich.

The O felt like it needed to just hang out like an excavated boulder in the process of being moved, but I felt the X needed to bring in a hint of mystery, narrative, and humor at the same time, so I tossed it up into the tree (**FIGURE 14.23**). Once I got the X shape fleshed out and slightly shaded for depth, I added the mask ▣ and moved the layer to the top of the Top Green stack in the Layers panel.

To make the letter look like it was being held by the tree, I moved and rotated the X. Specifically, I chose the Move tool (V), toggled on Show Transform Controls in the options bar, and rotated the X clockwise. Next, I flipped it horizontally by right-clicking the image then choosing Flip Horizontal from the context menu. Painting a little black on the mask where some leaves would be over the X completed the look (**FIGURE 14.24**).

FIGURE 14.24 Paint onto the mask where some leaves would be on top of the X and it sinks right in.

Step 8: Turn On the Fog Machine

Clouds, mist, and fog are hard to create and control in Photoshop. *Any* water is for that matter. So the trick is a combination attack using real pictures of clouds and a specialized brush, just like when working with the greenery. The more you can co-opt the credibility of the actual photograph, the better the end result in most cases. It just needs the right touch and brush to complement it! Here are some tips for creating a mist wrapped building:

- Find a cloud picture that matches the feel of the other clouds and mist. For *Forest Construction*, I used the atmosphere from another shot of a misty mountain in the background of Machu Picchu (**FIGURE 14.25**). The main thing to look for is variety of dissipating edges and a little definition in the body of the cloud as well.

- Completely paint out the edges with solid black before anything else once you have a mask on the layer. Again, because you're not selecting before masking, be careful to leave no digital grease in your wake. Brush out anything that could be seen as a hard edge; zoom in close for this do be sure!

- Paint the water vapors using some advanced brush parameters; the next section discusses these in detail.

FIGURE 14.25 Find a cloud with some variety and dissipating edges that you can use for blending.

Create a Cloud Brush

You may be thinking about turning a cloud into a brush, which is easy enough, but that gives you only a single stamp-like use out of the cloud brush—pretty limiting! Because I wanted full flexibility and customization for my brush, I used an existing cloud image (much like the vegetation) and designed a brush that simulated floating water vapors that I applied to the cloud's mask. Combining the actual cloud image's characteristics with a specially designed brush, I could paint on the mask going back and forth with black and white (X) until just the right pieces and shapes were remaining of the initial cloud—the perfect balance of real and simulated water vapors! Here are the parameters that I used for a pretty killer brush to simulate cloud and mist:

- The Spatter 39 brush ▓ set up a nice base with decent variety.

- I checked Shape Dynamics on, made sure that Control was set to Off, and adjusted the Angle Jitter slider to 50% to enable a randomized variation of the spattering that would avoid making unwanted patterns as I painted.

- I checked Scatter on and increased the Scatter slider to 210%. I made sure to toggle on the Both Axes check box (**FIGURE 14.26**) to produce a thicker concentration of mist towards the center of the scatter.

- I toggled Transfer on and selected Pen Pressure from the Control drop-down (for tablet users this is a must); this is but one more parameter of control you can add to the painting and is incredibly helpful for more natural-gestured strokes and repeated movements with a light touch. When working on something like mist and clouds, changing the density in just the right way (adding an organic randomized effect) is the only thing that makes the technique effective.

- I lowered the Flow setting to 20% so that the back and forth gesturing over an area would thicken and simultaneously soften the brush's spatter. At 100% Flow, the spatter shape is too pronounced and strong to be an authentic water vapor (even when I lowered opacity). Flow forces the brush to have many more spatters before it adds up to something with density, very much like the small water vapors accumulating themselves (**FIGURE 14.27**).

FIGURE 14.27 With a combination of custom brushing and use of an existing cloud photograph, the mist nicely wraps around the store.

FIGURE 14.26 Adjust the Brush panel's parameters for the best effect; here I increased the Scatter slider and checked the Both Axes check box.

Step 9: Adjust the Final Touches

Finally, I added a bit more atmospheric perspective to soften the darks of the greenery above the store to blend them within the composite more convincingly, and then I made some global lighting adjustments to balance the entire scene.

To create a little more atmosphere, I added a blank new layer within the Top Green group folder, enabling me to paint on top of both the store *and* greenery, while staying underneath the foreground tree and truck being swallowed up. Using an extremely low opacity (6%) white and a soft, large, round brush (no texturing this time), I gently brushed in greater atmosphere and set the feeling of depth back a bit more, matching the mist that's wrapping around the side of the building (**FIGURE 14.28**). One last Curves adjustment layer brought up the brightness on just about everything except the bottom of the composite where I still wanted it to look a bit dark and not draw attention (**FIGURE 14.29**).

FIGURE 14.28 Brush white with a soft, low-opacity, round brush very gently for creating greater depth with added atmosphere.

FIGURE 14.29 Add one last Curves adjustment layer to make the image pop and draw attention to the parts of the scene you intend.

Conclusion

Much of a project such as this comes down to control. It is about figuring out ways to control each layer, its mask, noise, sharpness, shape, color, and overall lighting. This is all part of the craft of working in Photoshop, and a project like *Forest Construction* allows for a balanced practice with a variety of small challenges. Much like levels to a game, each step has its own lessons and victories! The other component to creating scenes like *Forest Construction* is generating an idea that you can work with and implement your techniques on, an idea that's fun and has meaning all in one. When you have an idea and try to visualize it, it becomes a matter of applying craft to concept—and in my case, releasing hungry vegetation on symbols of consumerism.

ERIK JOHANSSON

erikjohanssonphoto.com

Erik Johansson is a full-time photographer and retoucher from Sweden, who is based in Berlin, Germany. He works on both personal and commissioned projects, as well as sometimes creates street illusions. Erik describes his work by saying, "I don't capture moments, I capture ideas. To me, photography is just a way to collect material to realize the ideas in my mind. I get inspired by things around me in my daily life and all kinds of things I see. Although one photo can consist of hundreds of layers, I always want it to look like it could have been captured. Every new project is a new challenge and my goal is to realize it as realistically as possible."

How would you describe your use and control of lighting in a shoot and editing?

Light and perspective are super important in creating a realistic montage, which is why I always shoot everything myself and avoid stock photography. I want to be in full control. I often shoot in natural light but keep the direction of light in mind. If I use lighting I just use it to make it look like the sun or cloudy sky. I don't want the studio look.

Do you have any suggestions for getting colors to look right for the final composite? Do you begin with a specific color palette in mind?

I usually give all my images some final adjustment in terms of color and tone, but I begin with a quite natural look. It's a lot easier to change that afterwards instead of in the beginning. I do like a quite high contrast look with desaturated colors, but I try to experiment.

Any good tips for staying organized from start to finish?

Try to keep everything layered and work in a nondestructive way. Try to put names on the layers as well and use folders for the layers. Sometimes it's a mess, but I try to stick with these rules.

What is your favorite aspect or tool in Photoshop?

I love the simplicity of the Smudge tool; I use it all the time. I always start by masking out the parts I don't want to be visible in a photo with a rough mask. I then use the Smudge tool to push and pull the borders of the mask to make it perfect and blend it together with the rest of the picture.

Go Your Own Road, 2011

How do you go about shooting your photographs for an idea you are realizing?

It always starts with planning, trying to figure out where to find the location. When it comes to the photos, it's super important that all photos combined should have the same light and perspective. That is something I keep in mind for looking at locations as well.

Do you have ideas that just never quite work out as planned? If so, how do you overcome this obstacle?

Yes, it's not so often, but it does happen that I work with something for a long time, almost finish it, and then think that it isn't good enough or that I don't like the composition. I just move on to the next idea, no reason to cry over that. Just move on, move forward.

Any general advice for people wanting to go into the industry?

Learning by trying is just great! It takes time, but it's the best way to figure out how the tools work! It's also a lot about quantity, at least in the beginning; you have to do mistakes and learn by them. Just do as many photos as you can, and you will learn something from every time you do something. Don't just sit and wait for inspiration; go out there, and inspiration will come to you!

What has been your most favorite work to date? Why?

It's always the next one I'm about to create. Always moving forward! ∎

ROADWORK COFFEE BREAK, 2011

◀ CUT FOLD, 2009

CHAPTER 15

Epic Fantasy Landscapes

COVERED IN THIS CHAPTER

- Matching scale and perspective for subjects and landscapes
- Matching flow and physics of water
- Using masks as mortar for stone work
- Custom thatching from a single texture
- Construction with texture, duplication, and painted shading
- Adding wildlife and sun-rays for detail

Creating fantasy landscapes is one part imagination, two parts persistence and as usual, *completely* fun—or at least that's about how it goes for me. In the midst of a study on over-fantasized nature and its use in graphics for advertising (such as greenwash), I decided to try my hand at some seductive and fun eye candy while I was at it. The result was *Rainbow's End* (**FIGURE 15.1**), which represents a collision of most techniques and lessons presented in this book's earlier projects.

As usual, the project began with a typical previsualization and being inspired by the natural beauty I found hiking, adventuring, and constantly photographing. Memory is cheap, so there's really no excuse to not grab something that might have potential, and this project ended up containing hundreds of images from years of digital hording. It also contains some fresh lessons on blending waterfalls and various natural elements—both liquid and green—into a landscape, as well as how to construct a cottage texture-on-texture from multiple selections and assemble an entire waterwheel from two planks of wood.

Step 1: Lay the Groundwork

After much summer hiking in lush upstate New York and taking pictures of just about every waterfall within a 100 mile radius of Syracuse, I came up with some ideas and just enough reference material to create an epic nature scene. Keeping these shots, as well as those in my photo archive, in mind, I made a preliminary sketch—the first step on the road

▸ **FIGURE 15.1** Made of more than 200 layers, *Rainbow's End* contains a bit of Yosemite National Park, upstate New York, Peru, Spain, and elsewhere.

FIGURE 15.2 A sketch is always a good way to initiate the creative process; this one provided a good starting point to dive into the greenery.

to *Rainbow's End* (**FIGURE 15.2**). Then, with the sketch in mind, I began assembling my photo palette of raw material for the composite.

Here are some strategies I learned from this project for fleshing out an idea before getting too deep into the groove of one track:

- Start on paper. For my process I find it useful to begin on a pad while looking though my image archive and source material on the screen.

- Block out the key features you want the composite to have. For me it was a waterwheel of some kind, a waterfall or two, a cottage, a lake, garden, and mountains in the background. Including the key features in some form can get you looking for the right pieces, just know that depending on the images you have, placement may deviate from your sketch dramatically—this is totally okay!

- Scan or photograph your sketch, then make some digital revisions and additions. This revision process will also be informed by the source material you can or cannot find. For example, I couldn't find a workable spiral stairwell, so out of the sketch it went.

TIP Always shoot a huge variety of different points of view so you have options when you sit down to piece them all together. A work like Rainbow's End was possible only because I gave myself the flexibility of many perspectives.

Chapter 6 and others previously covered the mechanics of creating and managing a photo palette, but a project the size of *Rainbow's End* presents additional challenges. Some strategies I use when gathering potential source images for a complex project are:

- Look at the sketch and start searching for images that match both the perspective and visual elements required, such as point of view (POV). For a cliff, look for one at the right angle and consistency. (Is it straight on, angled, higher or lower than the viewer?). For trees, try to match the proposed vantage, foliage, and size. Lakes and water need to be spot-on matches with the intended perspective and have good obedience to gravity; any angles where water isn't flowing as it should for the composite's POV will look so very wrong.

- Gather by category: waterfalls, cliffs, trees, mountains, thatch. Grouping potential images by category makes searching easier when you begin compositing. You can use Adobe Bridge if creating a photo palette is not your workflow or if your computer doesn't have the memory to handle multiple, heavily layered documents open at once. At least bring the pieces within reach so that after you take a break you easily can reopen all the elements you need.

- Find images that you like, and see if they can play a role in the project. For me this was **FIGURE 15.3**: a photo of sunflowers from a nearby ranch. The lighting was right, it seemed to fit with the idea, and the flowers added a new dimension to my original concept.

> **TIP** You can use Adobe Bridge not just to browse regular folders, but to browse collections. The Collections feature enables you add similarly themed pictures (such as waterfalls) and place them into a virtual folder—and it doesn't actually move the file to a new location. This virtual folder can be composed of files from many locations including multiple hard drives. Add selected files to a new collection by clicking the Collections icon within the Collection panel in Adobe Bridge, then you can drag future files into this folder at any time.

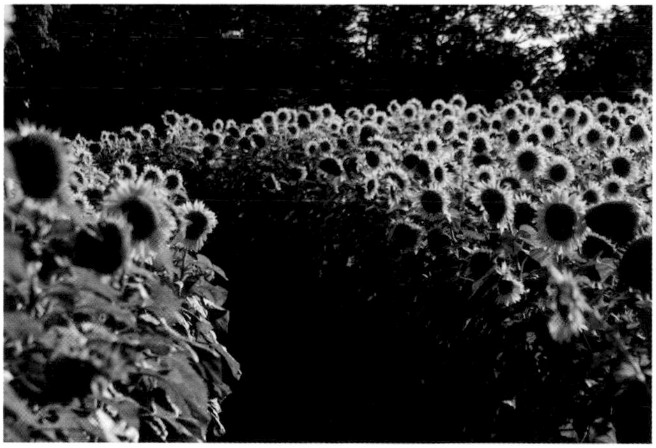

FIGURE 15.3 Find an image or concept that you like (for me it was these sunflowers) and see if you can work it into the project.

Step 2: Work on Scale and Perspective

After looking at the photo options and generating a photo palette, the next stage is to develop a more solid plan in regards to perspective and scale, which will evolve as you go. For me, once I get the project plan fleshed out, I start throwing images in the composite to see where key pieces may need to change to better fit with the new contents of my photo palette. When I found the great waterfall shown in **FIGURE 15.4**, I altered my overall plan a bit to accommodate its wonderfully long cascading shape. A lot of working on a composite of this nature is a give and take: Try to conform the images you find to your idea, but also let them guide where the composite needs to go so things stay looking right. Shifting plans to help make an image more believable can make quite the difference in the end.

Part of getting the perspective right is planning the sense of depth within the image. Finding matching imagery early on helps dramatically. With it, try to rough out the three major components to the landscape: the foreground, middle ground, and background. Doing this really does help establish everything else in between, so pay close attention to getting it right. **FIGURE 15.5** shows a first draft of my depth planning: sunflowers in the foreground, some mountains behind the cottage, and even more mountains beyond. Seeing the elements in relation to each other literally helped me lay the groundwork for all the other pieces and details to come.

I wanted the sunflowers large and close to help generate an immersive feeling, as if the viewer is peering through them, looking at the scene from a bridge or ledge. The flower image worked as a perfect foreground base to root the point of view. The back mountains I added mostly in one layer. Setting these two extremes (foreground

FIGURE 15.4 If you find an especially interesting image that has potential, it's a good idea to alter your original plans to make it work.

and background) laid the foundation for all other blocks to build on and scale to match. Sketching on top of them helped me envision the rest, such as the cottage placement.

TIP Our eyes stop seeing a scene objectively, so it's good to flip the image frequently along the horizontal axis (Image > Image Rotation > Horizontal). This makes the image look completely new to your brain, refreshing your critical eye and helping to ensure things are looking right and not just increasingly normalized. If it looks very wrong when flipped, it's typically because it is still very wrong—so keep working it!.

Step 3: Fill in the Scene

Having fleshed out my sketch with the main depth components and a clearer POV, I was ready to tackle the epic jigsaw puzzle that is the essence of a large composite. Although not as simple as it sounds, all I needed to do was find the right source elements and position them where they belonged in the scene. **FIGURE 15.6** illustrates the elements beginning to take shape—stage by stage, piece by piece.

FIGURE 15.5 Rough in, scale, and mask some key images to help establish the depth and perspective for the project.

FIGURE 15.6 The process of filling in the pieces takes time, patience, and many lucky breaks, but with a continued critical eye you definitely can make progress.

Looking for elements that fit your composite is very much like assembling a gigantic jigsaw puzzle, only the box reference image is in your head and the pieces you're choosing belong to their own puzzles. In general, you look to see if the shape matches first, then compare the lights and darks, the size and scaling, and so on. As for any puzzle, some strategy helps, so here's a bit of my own:

- Use your imagination like a layer mask. For me, finding a piece means I have to look objectively at one small section of a larger image and use my mind's eye to "imagination mask" out everything but that one area that has potential (**FIGURE 15.7**).

- In Photoshop, turn those imagination masks into real ones by painting black with extreme detail and care on each layer's mask. Get in close and get it done right; fudging and roughing it will add up layer by layer, and every promise in the fantastical world won't help you

hunt down that digital grease left over in the end. You'll end up with less of a rainbow look and more of a mud-and-fuzz look.

- Combine multiple pieces to assemble a section for which you have no single image that works well. Your palette won't always contain an image that fleshes out an area as you may want. Combine two or more that have similar features, however, and you can get away with the perspective not exactly matching perfectly on any of them. For our brains to register something as "wrong," they require an unbroken area that doesn't fit entirely. Break your layer into multiple pieces, and it can blend in much better. In **FIGURE 15.8**, for example, I needed three pieces for the sunflowers to fit well.

- As usual, look for matching lighting. Harsh direct sunlight is a pain to match as it's not very flexible. If you happen to have a match, great! Otherwise, look for

THIS PART JUST MIGHT FIT ALONG THE RIVER'S EDGE...

FIGURE 15.7 During the process of searching out those workable pieces, just look in one area and not the whole picture; I call this imagination masking.

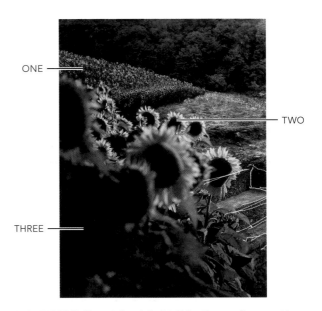

ONE

TWO

THREE

FIGURE 15.8 To get the right look for the sunflowers, three pieces worked much more effectively than a single, larger section of the source image.

those soft lighting shots and edit in your own lighting afterwards.

- Make clipped adjustments as you go. Each shot will have different issues with colors, lights and darks, noise, sharpness or blur, and so on, so your best practice is to create and clip adjustment layers to your image layer then apply Smart Filters as needed.

- Don't get discouraged! Most of the parts that you'll put together will match only somewhat in a physical sense and not at all aesthetically. For my own projects, I know that I can later add custom lighting with dodging and burning (nondestructively on an Overlay layer), bring in atmospheric perspective, and make a slew of adjustments that get refined as I work. So piece together with the confidence that mostly everything is workable to some extent; at this stage, you just want to match up shapes, perspective, and point of view.

Step 4: Go with the Flow: Convincing Water

Compositing water images adds a few new ripples of difficulty: working with gravity, flow, and reflections—all things our eyes can immediately pick up if they feel wrong. A waterfall, after all, should *fall*. So just make sure water flows and splashes in the right way, and you're good to go, right? Almost.

Waterfalls

Shaping and combining waterfalls is a challenge. A failure to obey the laws of gravity and flow is a tell-tale sign that can give the composite's illusion away. Here's a break-down of some watery advice that helped me when matching the pieces for the waterfall section of *Rainbow's End* (**FIGURE 15.9**):

FIGURE 15.9 Waterfalls must obey gravity, so make sure all pieces are flowing in the same downward direction.

FIGURE 15.10 Establish what the waterfalls will be placed over to ensure the forms match up.

FIGURE 15.11 Brush in the water that you want to flow, painting black directly on the layer's mask.

- Have an idea of the surface and form that will be underneath the waterfall: Would the water you plan to add actually flow over it naturally? From there you can begin to find the appropriate pieces to match the background. I mostly filled out the outer areas around the waterfalls in **FIGURE 15.10**, for example, before I added the water.

- Mask with a textured brush rather than selections. Painting with black on the mask gives you the control to break the technical conformity of selection tools, which in turn helps create a more believable look overall in massive jigsaw composites. When you make a selection before masking, it often includes areas that are similar or have easy-to-follow edges. When you need a more organic look that takes only small pieces from each waterfall layer in a very customized fashion, selections cause more interference and steps compared to manually finessing a brush directly on the mask. In the case of **FIGURE 15.11**, I used a textured speckle brush at a radius of 15px and painted along the edges of where I wanted water or pieces of rock.

- Use clipped adjustment layers as you go, always staying nondestructive and keeping the pieces matching as you work. Sometimes this is a Curves adjustment layer pushing the highlights for the whitewater, other times it's shifting a color to match those around it.

- Paint out all edges with black and be sure not to leave any digital grease, especially on hard edges of the copied pieces. I immediately paint with 100% opacity black with Mr. Round-and-Soft just to be sure I don't miss anything as I customize.

> **TIP** Visually check for digital grease by turning off the layer visibility and the mask visibility. Toggling the layer's Visibility icon 👁 while looking at areas that are supposed to be masked will faintly show a change if there is a little leftover grease. Similarly, disabling and enabling (Shift-clicking the mask thumbnail) will give a before and after of the mask.

- Paste in only the pieces that you can see fitting well with the rest of the waterfall. This would seem to go without saying, but it's easy to get this wrong. Grabbing the entire waterfall picture (such as with the Place feature in Adobe Bridge) in most cases doesn't help as much as you might think; it's more restraining and difficult to get looking right with other layers. Rock formations alter the way the water moves and falls, so taking smaller, more controlled pieces helps with creating a more seamless blend. Additionally, when you work with more than 200 layers as for *Rainbow's End*, using full images rather than pieces of images is way too cumbersome, even for super-machines and the 64-bit versions of Photoshop.

Rivers Run

Creating a river is much like the waterfall process, but has some added complexities, such as the water's color, depth, and flow direction, as well as rocks and, most importantly, POV. If these things don't line up with where the viewer is supposed to be looking from, the illusion is lost sooner than you can say running-river-rapids (**FIGURE 15.12**). Masking at the places of change, such as whitewater or a rock ledge, can help with the seamlessness. You can see in Figure 15.12 the green of the top water beneath the waterfall changed to the streaks of white as it turned into the bottom river and waterfall. This ledge drop going across the river is actually a seam between two river images.

FIGURE 15.12 To blend together pieces of water like flowing rivers, make sure they match in nearly every way, including flow direction and POV.

Lazy Lakes

At least lakes stay put. These placid entities are easier in some ways compared to rivers and waterfalls, but they do have one added element to keep you from relaxing too much: reflections. If you have the right shot and everything lines up perfectly, lucky you. Otherwise, it comes back to that give and take idea. You may have something else planned in that spot beyond the lake, but unless you have a shot that somewhat reflects what needs to be reflected, it can be difficult to get it in and still look okay. One compromise is to alter your original idea to better match the reflection. Alternately, you can paint in the reflections you need (which may have to happen a little in any case). For *Rainbow's End*, the bottom section of the lake began to give away the fact that the lake was not an exact match. I found a nice bushy tree to simply cover it up—another good option to keep in mind (**FIGURE 15.13**). Coloring the water with a layer set to Color blending mode can help a great deal for matching the rest of the scene and reflections. The original water reflection in this case was a nice sky blue.

FIGURE 15.13 You can see the added lake at least somewhat matched the reflections of the mountains and the gap between the ridges, but the close shore didn't match as well, so it got covered with greenery.

TIP Try to get the physics as close to real as possible, but when it's just not working, go with what works on an emotional and aesthetic level. Reflections may not be perfect, just keep them close enough plus working with the composition and overall feel.

Rainbows

Technically, rainbows aren't water but they do require water vapor. They also need direct sunlight, but this is a *fantasy* landscape so science can take a raft down the river at times. You can always stretch the impossible, as long as it is visually believable.

The key to the rainbow was finding one with a similar enough background; **FIGURE 15.14** was photographed in Yosemite National Park and already had a darker scene behind it. One more trick to getting rainbows to shine: Although they're water based, they work on the same principle as flames. Just as you did for the flames in the fiery creation in Chapter 8, change the rainbow's blending mode to Screen. This allows just the lighter elements to peak through—perfect for a rainbow situation! Beyond that, careful and softly brushed masking is always in order.

TIP You can create rainbows from scratch using the Gradient tool (G) and changing the gradient to a rainbow preset within the options bar. Make a wide marquee selection and apply the gradient across the short end. From there, mask and warp to the desired shape.

FIGURE 15.14 For rainbows with a darker background you can change the blending mode to Screen to give the colors prominence while most of the background drops out.

Step 5: Plant the Tree

Finding the right tree, bush, or stone sometimes can be quite a pain in the quaking aspen—and finding the right perspective and angle can be even harder. So getting out and doing some location scouting and searching for those pieces that fit just the right way can be substantially more fruitful than *forcing* something to fit out of pure stubbornness (and this goes for any of the puzzle pieces mentioned so far).

Besides, there's more than one benefit to getting outside! Your eyes actually become accustomed to an image you've been working on for hours on hours without a break, and they simply stop being objective evaluators. Ever notice when you work on something all night and you feel like you're just nailing it to perfection, then you come back the next day and wonder what blindfolded baboon made the mess you're looking at? So do yourself, your eyes, and your project a favor: Get out and shoot some matching material rather than forcing an existing image too much.

For me, this meant finding a particular tree, a perfect tree with the perfectly matching POV. I found it in a park where I was able to shoot from a higher vantage using a gentle hill (**FIGURE 15.15**). The lighting also matched wonderfully once I flipped the image horizontally with the Move tool.

FIGURE 15.15 Go outside and shoot the right tree with the usable angle and perspective. You'll save yourself quite a lot of frustration in the end.

FIGURE 15.16 Hue blending mode clipped to a layer can help shift green leaves to pink flower-ish colors in a snap.

Alter Color with the Hue Blending Mode

Where did I find a pink tree? I didn't; I cheated! While working in the composition, I realized that although my tree *was* perfect in its shape, POV, and lighting, it still wasn't the right color. I needed it to stand out and bring further attention to the center of the image; green blended just a little too much. The remedy? A quick color shift using a new clipped layer and changing the blending mode to Hue (**FIGURE 15.16**). Like salting the stew, from there it was just a matter of painting in the desired color to taste.

Step 6: Build a Cottage, Rock by Rock

Okay, I'm not going to lie to you, the cottage (**FIGURE 15.17**) took a considerable amount of patience, masking muscle, and close-up detail work—but at least my back doesn't hurt from lifting all those stones in person (though that might have been faster). The process began with a fleshed-out sketch and a search through my source photos for the right stones to build with—a digital quarry, if you will. Having shot many different angles of various terrace stone-walls while in Peru, I had plenty of material (**FIGURE 15.18**).

▶ **FIGURE 15.17** Building the cottage was a long process in itself, but was quite rewarding in the end.

Unfortunately, the lighting was not quite what I needed in the shots that would form the main pieces of the cottage. The Peruvian stone walls that were in the shade (optimal) had the most potential and flexibility; however, they also had intense under lighting from the sunny dry grass at the base. That meant if I wanted the lighting to be from above, the original walls needed to be turned upside down. So that's what I did (**FIGURE 15.19**).

With the main walls in place, I finished the rest much like its real-life counterpart: I found and placed stone upon stone that matched. Careful masking along rock edges allowed for easy lines to follow, and duplicating an especially fruitful wall worked well for adding bits of variety with just one or two stones showing from the original wall (and the rest masked out).

The corners in particular needed to feel like edges and took some extra care in getting them masked and arranged just the right way (**FIGURE 15.20**). Honestly though, this is no different than any time you may have spent working with Legos: Find the right pieces, plug them in, and just have fun! Here are a few takeaway tips for stonework that I gleaned from this experience:

- Angle is everything. Finding the correct angle (or being able to rotate to match the correct angle) is the key to having the building not look flat or too much like a cheap Hollywood set.

- Use masking like mortar. Having the right space and shadows between stones makes it feel like a believable and cohesive wall, even if it was pieced together from five walls. Finish masking around one stone, keeping the shadow and any highlights before adding in a different piece around the first.

FIGURE 15.18 Incan ruins were the perfect stone walls to build with as they provided variety and many angles to choose from.

FIGURE 15.19 If lighting needs to be brighter from above, but the source is under lit, you can flip the orientation to match what you need, not what you see.

FIGURE 15.20 Finding more Incan ruin pictures with edges of stonework was perfect for the corners of the sketched cottage.

- Take it slow. Like any good masonry, a thorough job yields the best results and quick and sloppy work looks—well, quick and sloppy! If this kind of work drags too much, go play in another part of the scene and come back with renewed patience.

I filled in other details around the house piece by custom piece, such as the various windows (imported from Spain), the entrance (more Incan stonework), and even gardens (thanks to the Syracuse rose garden). Some of the images matched well, but others had to be fudged and masked dramatically for the best fit. Even so, while not perfect up close, the pieces added up to a fairly adequate and convincing cottage.

Step 7: Brush in Thatch from Scratch

Sometimes you just don't have the shots you need nor can you really go out to shoot them either. Creating the thatch was a challenge for me: I didn't have much source material to work from or any thatch nearby to photograph. In these cases, you need to be a little more creative. For *Rainbow's End*, I made the most of my few usable shots, then created a custom brush for the rest of the thatching (**FIGURE 15.21**). To create your own custom brush—thatch or otherwise—from scratch, try these steps:

1. Select a fairly generic area from your thatch (or other) source image that doesn't contain too many unique features. If something repeats an obvious mark, it will give it a cookie-cutter look when you paint with the brush. I was fortunate to have at least one clean shot of thatch to use as a brush-able section.

FIGURE 15.21 Thatch is iconic for a nature-oriented cottage. With only a little in my archive, I improvised by creating a custom brush to paint in the rest.

2. Copy the selection (Ctrl/Cmd+C), then make a new document matching that size (the default after copying in most cases). Paste the copied content into a new document (Ctrl/Cmd+V). Note that this can be done within the main document on a layer, but I prefer separating it out in case I want to do additional adjustments or cleanup with the healing tools.

3. Create a mask using the Add Mask icon ◼ at the bottom of the Layers panel, and mask out all hard edges, leaving only the thatch inside (**FIGURE 15.22**).

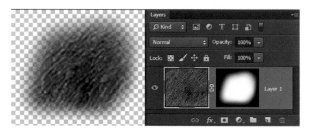

FIGURE 15.22 When defining a new brush preset, be sure to mask out all hard edges.

4. From the Edit menu, select Define Brush Preset. This will turn your active layer selection into a usable brush for repeated uses as a grayscale image. Be sure to name it something meaningful when prompted. Like other brushes, areas with content will paint the color you have selected, so grab a thatch-like yellow.

> **TIP** I typically paint with black and white once I make a brush in order to get the right lights and darks. I then add color through a new Color blending mode layer. On this layer I can paint the appropriate color that I've directly chosen with the Eyedropper tool from some other dark part of dry grass or thatch.

For the remainder of the thatch, I both painted with the custom brush and duplicated some sections, much like for the stonework. I used the brush only with quick clicks, as strokes blur the texture too much, but it worked quite well as a foundation to then add variety to afterwards.

Step 8: Build a Two-Board Waterwheel

When photos are limited, there's always the option of complete fabrication, even for complex objects like a waterwheel. That's right, I created the wheel in **FIGURE 15.23** entirely from a couple wood textures that were then arranged and painted over to create a believable dimension. The process I followed was surprisingly simple:

1. I started with a basic wood texture. This is equivalent to finding that first board in a construction project—and it was that first board in this construction process (**FIGURE 15.24**).

2. From there I copied (holding down Alt/Opt and dragging using the Move tool) and arranged the wood texture to follow a sketched out shape of the structural rings (**FIGURE 15.25**). As this part of the project would be fairly small, I wasn't too worried about it looking too similar and cookie-cutter like. Plus, I knew that painting in the shadows would add enough variation to compensate for any similarity.

FIGURE 15.23 The waterwheel was constructed from a couple wood textures and shading over the entire thing.

FIGURE 15.24 Start with a wood texture that is fairly lacking in dimension and shading.

FIGURE 15.25 Just like real woodworking projects, get the structural parts lined up and working before anything else.

3. After getting the first circle in place, I made an exact copy so that the wheel would have a second ring and more dimension. With the first wheel placed within a group folder, I selected the folder and Alt/Opt-dragged to place that folder directly below the original folder. This made a duplicate of all the layers within while also placing them behind the first wheel.

4. With the Move tool and the new group folder still active, I moved the second wheel group to an offset position for the 3D effect by dragging the layers to the left and upwards (FIGURE 15.26).

5. To create the paddles and spokes for the waterwheel, I again took a wood texture and angled it in a new orientation each time as needed (FIGURE 15.27). The best strategy for paddles, which are different each time, is keeping an eye on the perspective lines and also using the Move tool to free transform one corner at a time (Ctrl/Cmd-drag).

6. Shadows and highlights transform mere textures and shapes into three-dimensional forms, so I added a couple layers that brought out the highlights and added some shadows consistent with the scene's general lighting (FIGURE 15.28). I used two layers for this. On one I controlled the highlights, as well as most of the shadows and edge definition, with a layer set to Overlay blending mode. Painting with black on this layer darkened the natural attributes of the wood, while painting with white brightened them (imagine painting with the beam of a flashlight). On the second layer, I finished the effect by adding deeper shadows with less definition; this included a new Normal blending mode layer placed above the Overlay layer. Just the underside of the paddles and some other underside areas needed a little bit more darkening.

FIGURE 15.26 Rather than repeating a lot of time-consuming work matching individual plank for plank, duplicate the layers.

FIGURE 15.27 It wouldn't be a very functional waterwheel without some paddle action; these were customized using the Move tool's transform capabilities.

FIGURE 15.28 Shadows and highlights transform a textured shape into a believable object.

Step 9: Cue the Birds

The landscape projects that I find most enjoyable always contain an interplay between a vast expanse and the small details hidden within the scene. Something that takes us aback, yet draws us further in. Adding detail work is equally, if not *more*, important to a scene as the landscape itself. In *Rainbow's End* those hidden details came to life when I added birds—a variety of birds. Birds are the face and voice of a forest, and placing some variety in a scene indicates a specific tone and vitality. Advertisers and greenwashers have mastered the use of wildlife, so as a part of my study, this scene definitely needed a bird or two, including:

FIGURE 15.29 Create a quick reflection simulation by copying the layer, flipping it vertically, and lowering its opacity.

- **Ducks.** These fellows hanging out in the lake were brought in obviously, but didn't have workable reflections. To create some, I quickly made a copy of the ducks, flipped them upside down with the Move tools transform controls, and lowered the layer's opacity to 44% (**FIGURE 15.29**). With such a small detail, it didn't need to be perfect, simply suggestive of true reflections.

- **Flying geese.** These noisy buggers were quite easy to bring in as they were photographed on top of a blown out sky (all white with no detail). This meant that I could use Darken blending mode. Made just for these white-background situations, Darken lets only the darks show while the lights fall away. (Yes, it's the counterpart to Lighten mode used on the hands in Chapter 8.) Switching the blending mode to Darken knocked out the sky and left me with a flying V that I could place anywhere without a single mask (**FIGURE 15.30**).

FIGURE 15.30 For objects on a white background, often changing the blending mode to Darken will do a solid job of knocking out the background to leave just the dark bit visible, as the geese are here.

- **Swan.** This image of the swan was a lucky find, dating all the way back to darkroom photos I took in high school. And honestly, what super-green, fantasy cottage would be complete without its resident swan? As far as technical, swan-crafting techniques, the process was fairly straightforward. It already had a low profile reflection and needed only some masking and a layer for a slight bit of color. I created this using a blank new layer sitting above the swan with the blending mode switched to Color and a touch of yellow orange on the bill (**FIGURE 15.31**).

Step 10: Polish the Effects

In addition to darkening and lightening subtly with a large brush on an Overlay blending mode layer (as I do in each composite), I also used the sun-ray effects covered at the end of Chapter 9 along with some general atmospheric perspective for added depth and softening (covered in Chapter 9 and others as well). While earlier chapters contain more detail, here's a quick recap.

Sun-Rays

Create sun-rays by first painting white on a new layer with a large Spatter brush (setting Size to about 300px does the trick). With a single click, you get one instance of the brush pattern. Apply a fairly dramatic motion blur on the layer, then use the Move tool (V) to stretch the layer until it gets a nice effect of sun-rays through a faint mist. Rotate and transform to taste (**FIGURE 15.32**).

> **TIP** Ctrl/Cmd-drag one of the corner control points to customize the perspective. Sometimes rays flange outward as you look towards the source of light, so dragging the two bottom corners wider apart works well for this.

FIGURE 15.31 As the swan was a black-and-white image originally, the bill needed a little color with a new layer set to a Color blending mode.

FIGURE 15.32 Sun-rays through mist are a nice fantasy touch and are easy enough to make with some motion blurring.

Atmospheric Perspective

In addition to the rays, adding some general condensation in the air helps make an outdoor scene more believable. As shown in Chapter 9 and others, the technique is pretty straightforward: The more distant the object, the more atmosphere you pile on top of it. I do this by simply painting a pale yellow with a soft, round, low-opacity brush (or feel free to try out the mist brush shown in Chapter 14 for a moment like this). Painting faintly (under 10% opacity) reduces the contrast and clarity of distant objects, which is what actually happens in the real world when we look at distant peaks and far-away cities. If your world was looking pretty fake and flat up to this point, go wild with atmospherics and prepare to be amazed (**FIGURE 15.33**)!

Conclusion

As a compilation of nearly all the techniques covered in some form or another in this book, *Rainbow's End* illustrates the ways you can get inspired and apply a photographic archive in tandem with craft and technique. Creating fantasy landscapes forces us to pull out all the stops and reach for things that should be impossible—yet are still derived from the real. For me these scenes are a journey of sorts as well as a satisfying destination. Along the way of this particular journey I discovered that the best Photoshop projects are the ones that don't just leave you stuck in a room with a computer; they take you to another place, sometimes literally. I'm glad to say that *Rainbow's End* was just the beginning, one view along an adventurous path.

FIGURE 15.33 Adding atmosphere to distant objects creates a full sense of depth, continuity, and a more life-like look to the scene.

ANDRÉE WALLIN

andreewallin.com

Andrée Wallin is a concept artist and producer who works mainly with commercials and films. His projects range from concept and pre-visualization art to high-end promotional art, such as movie posters, magazine covers, and billboards. His clients include Universal, Warner Brothers, Disney, Digital Domain, MPC, Blur, and Legendary Pictures.

RAIN, 2012

How would you describe your own work and process?
That's a tough question. To be honest, I never really feel like an artist. I still get the feeling that I have no idea what I'm doing when I start out with a blank canvas. The same feeling I got the first time I opened the program, and it's a good thing. It forces your brain to be creative. Once you start going through the motions as an artist I think you're screwed. My process is usually just blocking out a very, very rough composition, and then try to build up momentum by throwing some photos or textures in there to build off of. You don't want it to look like a sloppy photo bash, but I love it when I'm able to keep a gritty, textured feel and still make it look like a painting.

When were you first drawn into using Photoshop?
It was back in 2001. I was 18 and stumbled across a tutorial made by Dhabih Eng, an artist that works at Valve. He made some Photoshop tutorial, and it just looked like so much fun I had to try it myself. It was love at first sight. I painted using a mouse for the first four or five years before finally getting a Wacom tablet.

What is your favorite capability of the application?
It's certainly not exclusive to Photoshop, but the way you can experiment with colors and brightness and contrast levels. When I was a kid I always liked to draw and scribble, but I rarely used colors. I was too lazy; I just

LA 2146, 2012

Postapocalyptic City, 2009

wanted to get an idea out as fast as I could before I lost interest. It's the same way now, but thanks to programs like Photoshop I have the ability to quickly try different color schemes and more.

What suggestions do you have for getting a composite looking "right?"

If you go to art school someone would most likely teach you what makes a good composition, how it all works from a theoretical point of view. I never studied art, I only learned the very basics of the rule of thirds, and that's about it. I honestly only go by what looks good in my eyes. I'll paint a rough composition, flip the image after a while, work on it some more, flip it back, and keep doing that for an hour or so. Then I usually save and close the program, do something else for a while to refresh my eyes, and then open it up after a couple of hours. If it still looks good, I'll start to flesh it out with details. If it doesn't feel right, I'll go back and try to figure out what's throwing me off.

DRAGON VS. SOLDIERS, 2009

How do you plan and prepare for one of your creations?

I don't like to plan or prepare. For my personal art, there's nothing more I love than just coming up with an idea on the spot and then paint it in a day. If I can finish a painting within a few hours I'm then able to go back the next day and look at it almost as if it was someone else's. I really like that, because it makes me look at my art much more objectively and I can enjoy it way more than if I'd spent a week on it.

Of course, if we're talking about client work then it's a whole different story. You have to collect reference material and study up on the subject matter—a process I'm not a big fan of.

Any general advice on going into the industry and living off of your artwork?

If you're going to work as a freelancer, prepare for a life of ups and downs. You've got to love what you do and you better be prepared to do it *a lot*. You're never going to succeed as a freelancing artist unless you're willing to make some sacrifices and really give it your best. This won't be a problem if art is your passion, then this will all come naturally. It's always easier said than done, but if you tough it out during the first few years and build up a network with clients and other artists you'll have an awesome life, there's no doubt about that.

What has been your most favorite piece of work to date? Why?

That's another tough one. If I had to pick one, I think it's a piece called *Dragons vs. Soldiers*, just because I feel like that was the piece where I really found my cinematic tone and style. It was also one of those paintings where the process went smoothly, it wasn't a big struggle to make it work and that's always fun. ∎

MOUNTAIN SERENITY, 2010

Index

A

ACR (Adobe Camera RAW) Editor
    editing images in, 83–84, 227
    filter adjustments within, 71
    icons for features, 88
    illustrated, 84
    reducing noise in images, 293
    saving adjustment presets for, 88
    slider adjustments for, 85–88
    workflow tips for, 88–89
actions, 102, 103–104
Adaptive Wide Angle filter, 162–165
adjustment layers, 58–65. *See also*
  B&W adjustment layers; Curves
  adjustment layers
    applying with mask, 44–45
    Black & White, 62–63
    clipping other layer to, 48
    Color Balance, 64, 123–124
    editing Smart Objects on, 204–206
    filters vs., 65
    fine-tuning lighting with, 129–132
    group folder clipped to, 124–126
    Hue/Saturation, 64–65, 126, 210
    modifying color with, 60
    pairing Curves with Hue/
      Saturation, 125
    used in *Rainbow's End*, 319, 320
    using, 58–59
Adobe Bridge
    access in ACR window from, 83
    actions vs. loading files with, 102
    loading files from, 100, 102–104,
      116

preparing composite document
    in, 110
    rating and sorting images with,
      107–110, 225–226
    working with collections in, 106,
      315
Adobe Camera Raw Editor. *See* ACR
  Editor
Adobe Photoshop. *See also* workflow;
  workspace
    alternatives to Adaptive Wide
      Angle filter in, 162
    clipping layer to group folder in,
      125
    creating documents in, 102, 110
    loading photos as separate tabs,
      100, 102–104, 116
    master artists' favorite tools, 219,
      245, 286, 308, 334, 336
    mastering, xii
    Smart Objects in versions of, 203
    Smart Sharpen filter features in,
      258
    updating Camera RAW for, 84
    workflow in Andres's work, 269–270
aerial photography, 279–281
Andres, Holly, 268–271
animals, 93
aperture, 79–80, 81–82
artists. *See* master artists
atmosphere. *See also* clouds
    adding in *Nature Rules*, 188
    condensation in air of *Rainbow's
      End*, 333

creating in *Forest Construction*,
    306
haze, 265
including rainbows in composite,
    322–323

B

B&W adjustment layers
    adjusting image look with, 175
    controlling grayscale images with,
      62–63
    fine-tuning lighting with, 131
    Slider Modifier icon for, 63
backgrounds
    creating for composite images, 228
    placing behind hair selections,
      28–29
    removing with blending modes,
      138–139
    selecting object by its, 232
    suggested for model, 256
    unlocking layers for, 251
    viewing selections against, 27
    working with composite, 114–116
    Zev Hoover on, 245
batch processing, 88, 227
birds, 331–332
blending modes, 49–54, 134–159
    adding to smoke and hand layers,
      149–150
    adjusting rainbows with, 323
    altering color with Hue, 324
    changing for multiple layers, 280